THE PHOTOGRAPH

THE PHOTOGRAPH

Joe Porcelli

Wyrick & Company

Published by
Wyrick & Company
1-A Pinckney Street
Charleston, S.C. 29401

Library of Congress Cataloging-in-Publication Data

Porcelli, Joe.
    The photograph / by Joe Porcelli.
        p.   cm.
    ISBN 0-941711-30-7
    1. Korean Americans--South Carolina--Charleston--Fiction.
2. Vietnamese Conflict, 1961-1975--Fiction. 3. Korean War,
1950-1953--Fiction. 4. Orphans--Korea--Fiction. I. Title.
PS35662.O62889P48   1995
813'.54--dc20   95-21153

Author's Note

This book is a work of fiction. Characters and
incidents are fictional archetypes created from personal
experience. They do not exist beyond these pages.

DEDICATION

This book is dedicated with love to my wife, Christine and my children, Travis, Troy, Pax and Charlaina. You are the quiet streams I have walked through so many forests to reach.

To Captain Charles V. Porcelli who plucked me from the rubble of war and gave me new life in America.

To Jerry and Marie Tuckner and the Tuckner children: Kathy, Christine, Nancy, Mary, Peter, Barb, Jack, Janet, Jean and Paul. I am proud to be a part of this family.

To Tom and Gloria Longbehn...for always being there.

To Douglas (Mat) Matheson...KIA Ashau Valley, Vietnam, May, 1969 (11:15 a.m.), and to the rest of my team for their supreme sacrifice.

To Yvette...with love.

THE PHOTOGRAPH

PROLOGUE

It was the boy he saw first. And not the boy so much as his eyes—two black, unflinching eyes that pierced him, glaring up at him from a dusty face streaked with dried tears, eyes that pulled him forward, drawing him toward the boy and the shattered body of a young woman that had been the child's mother. A baby lay in the crook of the dead woman's arm, cooing softly at the boy of perhaps six years of age who knelt next to them on the ground—a silent, determined little sentry. He didn't move as the young American captain and his team of Green Berets cautiously examined the smoldering remains of a Viet Cong hamlet. Only when the captain saw the body did he realize his enemies had included a woman and her two children.

There was no emotion in the boy's face as the captain knelt and looked closely into the eyes of the guardian. While the rest of his team moved nervously through the destroyed village, the captain found himself drawn into the eyes of the boy, like a wanderer being called into the deep, black pools of his own past. There was no fear any longer, no pain, no joy in these eyes. Only a burning, deadly hatred that had already etched itself into the boy's soul. Where there had once been childhood, there was now glaring, angry loss. And through the choking pall of explosives and dust, the captain suddenly recognized in this child, the boy he himself had been.

Against his will, he felt himself losing a tenuous grip on his surroundings, felt himself sliding inward to his most vicious memories. No longer a soldier in Vietnam, he saw the five-year-old boy he had once been, thousands of miles away in another lifetime, in another world called Korea. And yet the death was the same, the hatred was the same in a war he had survived as a refugee—not as a soldier.

His tortured mind was dragged back to the present and to the boy in front of him, when he heard the moans a few feet away. A Viet Cong that had somehow escaped death in the shelling lay slowly dying from a severe stomach wound. He rolled his head from side to side, oblivious to anything except the pain. Life oozed away from him in rivulets of blood that soaked the earth beneath him as he mumbled incoherently and stared through eyes that were rapidly becoming opaque and sightless. The captain watched for only a moment. He had seen it so many times before, had dwelled with the constant shadow of death from his earliest days. And he had once been this child in front of him now, full of pain and vengeance. The hatred in those eyes was his own.

Silently he took the unresisting boy's hand, guiding him to the wounded Viet Cong. Lifting the weapon that lay beside the dying man, he gently placed the AK–47 under the boy's right arm. He held the weapon firmly along with the boy, carefully directing the child's finger to the trigger. And in a short, resounding burst of fire, they both vented their hate, a hate so freshly born in the child, the same hate that had fermented for a lifetime in the captain.

The sound of the angry weapon died away and they remained wrapped in the deafening silence, side by side, the now quiet weapon hanging between them—two children from two different wars, sharing a brief moment in the same violent heritage.

KOREA

I

"I see fire," the old woman rasped, her face creasing into masses of deep wrinkles as she stared at the boy. Her eyes were bright with an unnatural light, a flickering gleam dancing on the fringes of madness. "I see fire and death...I see in your life the good fortune of the swallow, little one...But I see the fire and dark wings of war—I see you in the swallow's tears..."

The Sooth-Sayer of Sok-Cho
Spring 1950

"It's getting away from me!" she laughed, bracing herself in the ebbing wave. "Help me, lazy man, I can't hold it much longer!"

"Hang on to this end," the father told the boys, "and don't let go." While the school of grunion thickened the shallow water and packed themselves into the seine, he splashed toward her, laughing at her struggle with her end of the bulging net. Salt spray dampened his face as he ran, the muscles of his arms and back rippling in the late afternoon sun. She threw her head back and squealed as the sand shifted and sucked beneath her feet, the net tugging against the pole in her hands. Black tracings of long wet hair escaped from the clasp at her neck, painting her face with spidery fingers. "Hurry!" she called, her dark eyes sparkling, "Hurry!"

Both boys gripped their father's end of the net on the shore, giggling at the shimmering, squirming mass of fish. Their clothes were plastered to their bodies like an extra layer of wrinkled skin as they kicked at each other playfully, each trying to dislodge the other from his position on the net. The older boy made contact, causing the young one's feet to slip from beneath him, tumbling him onto his back in the wet sand. With an angry howl and murderous gleam in his five-year-old eyes, he jumped to his feet, tackled his six-year-old brother and propelled both of them kicking and squealing into the lapping edge of the surf.

The heavy orange sun slowly dropped behind the mountains that sat like giants with their feet in the Sea of Japan. Blue shadows covered the village while a young Korean family gathered the last of the day's catch that lay drying on pallets along the beach. Spring had finally made up her fickle mind to stay, lingering along the eastern shoreline. The air quickly turned cool when the sun disappeared, and the father called to his sons, gathering them away from the water's edge and into his arms.

"Come," Chang said. "Enough play. It's going to be dark soon and we need to finish helping your mother with the baskets. Up, up!" And he hoisted the giggling boys to his shoulders, running up the beach as the boys bobbed up and down, hanging onto his hair to keep from falling off. The sound of his laughter rolled out across the water and churned happily with the breaking waves.

The closing days of May, 1950 were the last good days the village of Sok-Cho would see for many years. In the trembling calm before a raging storm, the village prospered even as the sinister rumblings of a distant war began to reach the ears of the village elders. Bits and pieces of news from a far-away battle front drifted into the village. With the day's fishing done, the young mayor of Sok-Cho lay awake for a long time, listening to the heavy spring rain on the roof and thinking of his children—of all the children of Sok-Cho. The children listened to the fragments of news of the war with wide, wondering eyes, while the old ones listened with the sad eyes of wisdom. The old ones understand, he thought, as he stared at the ceiling from his sleeping mat. They understand, and they are afraid.

The children watched with envy as the young men of the village—fifteen and sixteen-year-old boys—were called to fight with the South Korean Army. He recalled the sight of children running along beside the young men as they left the village, marching with their would-be heroes until the old ones drew them back. To the children, it is a great and glorious thing, this war that makes men from boys. To the old ones, it is a continual howling in the distance, an evil wind that will eventually sweep them all away.

Chang closed his eyes and breathed deeply, trying to dispel the hard knot of anxiety forming in his stomach. He listened to the sounds inside his warm, one-room house, feeling his wife's quiet rhythmic breathing as she slept. Behind his closed eyes he pictured his sleeping family—the two boys on mats in the warmest corner, their faces peaceful and innocent in the dim light from a moon peering timidly through the rain clouds. His mind scanned the interior of the house—neat rows of pots and pans on wooden shelves along the walls, the low table where they all sat to eat, the rice-paper doors lit with the fluorescence of feeble moonlight. The gentle aromas of cooking spices and wood smoke still permeated the room. A dying fire burned in the cooking oven in the storage room, wafting drowsy waves of heat through vents dug beneath the dirt floor.

His mind drifted in slow spirals from the mud walls of his home, on beyond to the market of Sok-Cho, with its stalls and vendors, all quiet now and waiting for dawn. He could hear the gentle rumbling of the ocean just a moment away. He saw the stone jetties stretching into the bay, saw the small fishing boats rocking peacefully in their moorings with rain-slicked decks. He saw the surrounding hills and mountains that nudged against the village. His mind wandered to the busy main road that dissected the village, and he saw deep ruts made by ox carts during spring rains. He heard the high-pitched voices of the women as they hurried up and down the road, lifting their heavy muslin skirts to step over deeper ruts, carrying huge, skillfully balanced baskets on their heads. And the children—always he saw the children as they played next to the seashore, fled between houses in games of chase, scuttled along the road beside their mothers like fluttering leaves around the base of a tree. He heard the bickering in the market stalls and on the docks as daily catches of fish were bargained for. He smelled the wild rock roses of summer and the winter-chilled cooking fires of December. And he heard the laughter.

It was a home he had come to love. Chang saw himself as the caretaker of a society, a guardian of a way of life that was being threatened by an evil he could neither explain nor fight. Forces from both the North and the South were voraciously interested in Sok-Cho with her quiet harbors that would handle any size vessel, and her peaceful mountains commanding an advantageous view of surrounding territories. And the only people who had a right to this tiny portion of the world were the very people that would suffer the most in future days. His only hope, the only hope for his people, was with the forces of the South, with American military aid. By aligning himself and his people with the South, he felt he was dealing with the lesser of two greedy, carnivorous devils. So the meetings continued with the unpleasant liaison from Pusan, who treated the mayor as though he were doing him a great favor by even talking to him. But with luck, the mayor hoped to see a South Korean Army base established just below the village. He prayed it would happen before the Communists decided to make their move.

He turned to his side, feeling his wife stir next to him, moaning softly in her sleep. He had done all he could. The plans were in motion and now all he could do was to wait— and pray. He closed his eyes again and drifted out to sea where he slept and dreamt of two small boys who bobbed up and down on his shoulders as he ran into the sunset—a sunset darkened with the black wings of screaming birds. Or were they war planes...?

"Look at the swallows!" the young one said, pointing excitedly to the tight clusters of birds that formed on the wires and on rooftops. The morning had dawned misty and cool as the birds chattered and ruffled their feathers, drying themselves in the rising sun. And when one would fly away, it would make no difference at all—there were so many it was as if none had ever left.

The hard, marble-sized rain had pummeled the earth into renewal. The dusty streets of the village were smooth and wet when the two boys emerged from the house, and the feel of the cool mud between their toes felt wonderfully different from the sand on the beach. Sitting on the wooden step outside their rice-paper door, the boys wiggled their toes in the ooze and stared up at the single power line stretching into the village, a line furry and thick with throngs of swallows.

"That means much good fortune," their mother said as she knelt in the doorway behind them, smiling up at the birds. "A swallow resting somewhere nearby brings good luck. And so many swallows—oh my! Such good fortune must be waiting for us!" Won Mee smiled down at the two dark heads in front of her as they listened to the old legend. "Clean your feet and come inside," she said. "I have a present for you both."

They quickly wiped their feet and sat on the floor, waiting. She handed each of them what looked like a small piece of paper.

"Remember the photograph we had taken almost a month ago when your father was away? Well, the photographer came back through the village yesterday with the finished pictures. I have only two—one for each of you."

The boys stared intently at the pictures, smiling as they recognized themselves. She had worn her best gown for the occasion, a silk gown of three colors that didn't show in the black-and-white photo. Her long black hair was drawn back and bound at her neck in a heavy roll. The two boys were dressed in their best clothes, standing stiff and serious next to their mother. None of them smiled—that would have been undignified.

"These are for you to keep always," she said softly. "Don't lose them because they are the only ones I have. They are to remind you of what a good spring this has been. Look how tall you've both grown!"

A silence fell over the three, a near-reverence as they all stared at the photos. It hadn't been intended, but she found herself smiling with mild amusement at the solemnity of the moment as the boys carefully tucked the pictures into the deepest pocket of their white muslin pants. It was the first time either boy had seen a picture of himself. She shook off the lingering wisps of an emotion that toyed with the fringes of her heart, telling her that the reverence was much more than the mere novelty of seeing themselves in a photo.

"Now come with me," she said, turning towards the door. "I have some errands to run in the village before your father comes home to eat. Hurry, hurry! The sun is already up!"

Dodging puddles in the roadway, the boys scampered ahead of her along the ruts. She pulled her skirt into a tight, crumpled wad in one hand, drawing it up snugly around her small hips, showing delicate bare legs as she smoothly maneuvered around the worst of the mud holes. Bracing a large empty basket against her hip, her face set in a deliberate calm, she watched the boys up ahead and thought of the future. She had felt her husband's restlessness all through the night, knowing he was lying awake and worrying. It was a large responsibility for a man so young to have the weight of so many on his shoulders. Even the oldest ones of the village who at first tried to ignore her husband's authority, were now turning to him for strength and advice. They would come hurrying to the mayor's house to ask him if the rumors were true. Was there really going to be a military base in Sok-Cho? Were the Americans really coming here? Were the Communists actually murdering innocent people in other villages? Should we stay? Should we leave? What do we do?

Though she hadn't discussed it with her husband, she could tell he was aware of her forced smiles, the almost too-cheerful attitude, aware that she knew something was terribly wrong with the world. She knew of his meetings with the government envoy from Pusan. Though he never discussed the meetings with her, she knew well enough of Sok-Cho's strategic location near the 38th parallel. She knew her husband's meetings with the thin, sour-looking government man meant the beginnings of a vicious tug-of-war for the village and its coveted harbor. Knowing the war would find them eventually, there were often times when she would weep silently for her family. Deep worry lines in her husband's forehead and around his eyes told her he was afraid, too. So she smiled and chattered and tried hard not to look him too closely in the eye.

The voices of her children rose to a crescendo as they began to argue about something, and she picked up her stride, shaking off the worries and fears. Enough of this. *My husband has no need of a woman who frets and wrings her hands. What will be will surely be, and all we can do is trust in the gods. Perhaps the gods will look kindly on Sok-Cho and soon this horrible war somewhere beyond the mountains will cease.*

"Your ear is hidden under your cap," Bok Chang Kim was insisting loudly. His shorter legs were working rapidly to keep up with his taller brother. "You can't even see your bad ear in this picture. You can't even tell."

Yoon Chang Kim was scowling, trying to hurry ahead of his brother. "It's your fault," he groused, staring down at the photo as he walked. "You caught me with that fish hook on purpose; I know you did! You ruined my ear! I'll always have to wear a hat when I have my picture taken."

"I did not! I did not!" But the older boy was determined to make his brother feel guilty one more time for the loss of his ear lobe, and he strode on ahead, ignoring the protests from behind him. It was one of those freak childhood accidents that was much less serious than it appeared at the time—the young one wielding a fishing pole misjudged his back swing and caught his older brother neatly in the left earlobe with the hook, jerked with all his strength and tore the flesh through. The remaining skin, hanging like discarded beef tallow, had been neatly removed with scissors at home. Yoon's left earlobe was completely gone.

There had been much sympathy for the older boy and much embarrassment for Bok, and there were times like this when the older boy couldn't resist an opportunity to take one more poke at a sensitive nerve. In reality, however, they were each other's best friend, even when they squabbled.

"Shhh!" Yoon hissed suddenly, "don't talk so loud—the old witch is sitting in front of her house and she might turn you into a toad if she hears you."

Bok immediately silenced his protests and drew closer to his brother as they passed the ram-shackle hut by the road. The old woman sat on a wooden crate, basking in the early-morning sunshine. Her eyes were closed, her mouth open, the tattered scarf tied around her head seeming to hold her jaw in place and keeping it from dropping onto her chest. She was a study in wrinkles and folds, her eyes disappearing completely into a mass of creases when she closed them. Her aging body seemed shapeless under the long tatters of rags she wore, her gnarled hands protruding from frayed sleeves. She was a source of mystery and delight to the children of the village, surrounded by an aura of darkness. She was a sooth-sayer, a fortune teller, a healer of diseases and caster of spells. She had the bright, penetrating eyes of a small animal and the wheezing laughter of the aged. She had foretold just enough significant events to seal her reputation in the village, and sometimes even the adults walked a wide circle around her. She was at once fearful and magical. Lately, with so many unexplained mysteries in the world beyond their village, a few of the villagers could be seen casually strolling by the old woman's hut, then furtively hurrying in. When logic fails, the old woman knew, people will turn to the illogical for answers.

Yoon grasped his brother's hand, keeping a wary eye on the sleeping witch, tiptoeing in the mud past her house, hoping not to waken her. Their mother smiled indulgently as she walked a short distance behind. As soon as the boys were a few steps beyond the shack, they broke into a run.

"They need not run from me," the old woman croaked, and the mother jumped slightly with the sound, staring at the heap of rags on the crate. The old eyes were still closed, the scarfed head still lolled back as in sleep.

"Your children run from me, but they need not," she repeated without opening her eyes. Almost against her will, Won Mee found herself slowing to a stop in front of the hut. "What did you say, old one?" she asked softly.

"You—" the woman bleated, "you have need to be swift. You have not much time to dwell in this life. Just as your

12

children run far ahead of you now, they will be left to run without you soon."

The old woman's eyes never opened, she never looked to see who she was speaking to. After a moment her mouth dropped slowly open again. The young woman took the opportunity to hurry away from the house and try to catch up with her children, feeling an odd, nervous buzzing in her head.

She hurried on toward the comforting chaos of the market, pushing her way into the gradually expanding early-morning crowd.

The market was an unending delight for the children, and they quickly disappeared into the haggling, bartering, arguing, laughing throngs of people jostling each other for first pick of the morning's fresh catch. Lined with stalls and vendor's carts, the street was already churned into a heavy soup of mud from the night's rain. Discarded pieces of fish, bunches of loose feathers and bits of rotting vegetables were strewn in filthy chains around the perimeters of the stalls.

Bok pushed his way toward the noodle vendor, staring up at the different stalls and carefully maneuvering away from trampling feet. His senses were flooded with the wonderful, musky stench of the place: a strange, enticingly foul odor of animal waste from the chickens, pigs and ducks that were waiting to be sold; from rotting food and cooked food; of wet earth and human bodies. It was a smell unlike any other, and the boy sniffed deeply as he moved along. He stopped only briefly at the stalls selling radishes and cabbages, all bounty from an early harvest. He toyed with hanging bunches of bright red and yellow peppers that blazed against the drab brown stalls.

His brother caught up with him at the noodle vendor's stall, and together they plunged eager hands into their pockets for the two small coins it took to buy a bowl full of the delicious, hot noodles and broth that everyone could smell, even above the odor of the pigs. The boys squatted to the side, out of the way of hurrying feet and began devouring the food, their chopsticks working rapidly from bowl to mouth, staring at the activity around them.

Their mother was a skillful haggler, knowing what she needed and how much she was willing to give for it. She moved from stall to cart, her expression serious and concentrated, unlike her usually light air. With gestures and a few clucks of indignation mixed with brief, artificially heated arguments that were more for saving face than establishing a price, she slowly filled the basket, ignoring the commotion around her. With her last purchase, she began looking for her boys, motioning them to come along. Won Mee was suddenly anxious to get home. She was having a hard time concentrating, her mind constantly tiptoeing back to the witch's words.

On their return, she saw the old woman had gone inside and she breathed a sigh of relief, feeling foolish for her earlier anxiety. But as she drew nearer the house, the words became louder and louder inside her head. She walked slower, the boys glancing up at her questionably. She stared at the hut for long moments, the voice in her mind sounding like a thousand voices. Suddenly dropping the heavy basket, Won Mee took the two boys by the hand and pushed through the entrance. For a reason she couldn't explain, she was determined to have her fortune told.

The two stunned boys followed her into the hut, their eyes wide with fear. Bok tugged at his mother's hand, not wanting to be thought a coward, but not wanting to venture into the witch's lair.

The hut was almost dark, only one small candle lighting the windowless interior. With the door open, a ribbon of sunlight danced on a curtain of incense smoke, glinting off traveling specks of dust that passed in and out of a narrow column of light. When the door closed, the flame from the candle cast an eerie glow over the dusty room, highlighting strange objects neither boy had ever seen before. They gazed around them with apprehension from behind their mother's long skirt.

There were herbs and bells and wooden bowls with pestles. There were bottles hidden in dusty alcoves containing long-unused herbal potions concocted from superstition and prepared with belief—the makings of spells cast and spells broken. Things that made men strong and women beautiful and bad boys into toads. Bok curled his fists deeper into the folds of his mother's skirt, looking nervously around for the old woman.

"I knew you'd return," she rasped, and he jumped with the sudden sound. "You had to know the truth." She stepped into the pale light of the candle, her smile creating an odd gash in her wrinkled face. She examined the three of them with her bright, ferret-like eyes, finally looking closely at the younger boy, her expression softening as she gazed at the frightened face peering from behind the skirt.

"My!" she croaked, "What a handsome young man you are becoming!"

She created a soft, muted bulk in the smoky room and the boy wasn't certain where the room ended and the old woman began. All he could see clearly were her eyes—the bright, piercing eyes of an inward examiner. She finally lifted the wrinkled expanse of her face and gazed with concentration at the mother who swallowed hard and tried to appear calm. There was a tremulous vibration in the atmosphere, a tangible riffling of air against skin, and the young woman shivered under the fortune-teller's gaze.

"In you, I see fire," the old one began, her eyes fixed on a point beyond the mother's face. "I see fire, black wings slashing the night and snakes slithering in the pits. I see the swallow with tears in its eyes." With some difficulty, the old woman began to focus her eyes again, and she reached up a hand of twisted fingers, gently touching the young woman's cheek. "I see all these things in your face, young lady, for I see only the truth. Only the truth."

There was silence in the room, both boys gazing up at the rigid form of their mother. The two women faced each other wordlessly, until the mother's hand began to tremble. Then the old woman's solemn expression changed and she lowered her shapeless form to look at the youngest boy. Her eyes sparkled and the gash reappeared in her face as she spoke again.

"My dear, dear little one," she whispered, and Bok shrank back a step. "I see you. Oh yes, I see you." And again her gaze was fixed on an illusive point somewhere beyond the confines of the little room, somewhere deep inside the child. "I see you all alone. So alone. I see you across a far-away river, clutching a woman to you. She is different, her hair is like the silk of corn. You have grown much and I see wealth in your youth. And I see..." she hesitated, her forehead creasing into deep furrows of confusion. "I see...fire. And much death. I see you in the tears of the swallow."

Bok buried his face in the fabric of the skirt, allowing only his eyes to stare out at the woman. He didn't understand what she was saying, but her tone—and the vibrations in the room—frightened him. The old woman sighed, as if she were burdened under the weight of something too heavy to carry. She understood the fear in the boy's eyes and felt it best to stop, though she hadn't even begun to tell him all she had seen flash through the reaches of her mind. She rose awkwardly to her feet and stepped back, becoming undefined again, melting into the smoke. The older brother straightened his back, trying his best not to let his fear show, bracing himself for what the old woman would say. But the old one never met his gaze, never said a word to him, as though she had used up a lifetime of allotted forecasts on his younger brother. When he realized he was to be spared the fortune-teller's scrutiny, his shoulders relaxed and he breathed a sigh of relief.

Out in the late morning sunlight, the tiny, clouded world inside the hut seemed like something from a dream. The crisp aroma of drying earth and the familiar, friendly objects all around them were highlighted by a platinum sun, making them feel slightly foolish for ever having been afraid.

Won Mee scooped up her discarded basket and hurried toward home. The boys scurried along behind her, saying nothing, trying to keep up. She was agitated by what the old woman had said, but more irritated with herself for ever having gone inside to begin with.

"I should never have stopped to see that old fool," she mumbled, shaking her skirt to loosen some flecks of mud on the hem. "She's ruined my whole day. And to think—I paid that old hag! What foolishness!"

She busied herself for the rest of the day in the house, cleaning and cooking, doing anything she could to throw off the feelings of foreboding the old woman left her with. She mumbled and clucked to herself, her movements swift and fluttering like bird wings.

By evening, after the family had eaten, she was finally able to joke with her husband about the images the old witch had conjured up.

"Snakes, black wings, swallow's tears—how stupid!" she laughed. But her husband noticed that the laughter was a pitch too high.

Later, when the house was quiet and she lay still in her husband's arms, she tried to put the old lady out of her mind.

But when she slept, she made small cries in the night as images of death and fire flickered at the edges of her dreams.

II

His lungs ached from running, and when he moved his bare feet he could feel the ragged cuts and bruises. His legs hurt and he felt a powerful urge to relieve himself. Lying on his stomach, trying to press himself flatter to make himself more invisible, Bok could feel the pre-dawn dampness seeping through the front of his dirty shirt. Vaguely, he realized his nose was running. He lifted his head to wipe his face with the back of his arm and glanced at his older brother lying on the ground next to him. Yoon was staring at him with wide, confused eyes.

"You're covered with soot," was all he said, but Bok wasn't listening. He was staring down at his home, at the smashed door, at the terrified villagers standing in the morning chill near the well, guarded by a platoon of Communist soldiers. His throat constricted as he tried to swallow a dry film of grit and his body shuddered with an effort to remain still. He ducked his head when he saw one of the soldiers casually scan the hillside where the two boys were hiding.

From his vantage point, Bok could see the extent of destruction that had descended on the village—slaughtered animals lay scattered in the road, doors were smashed, and in the distance some of the houses were burning. On the breeze that wafted up from the horror below, he could hear the weeping women and children as they stood near the mayor's home, forced to stand and wait. He blinked his eyes and reached his hand beneath him, squeezing himself tightly to keep from urinating on himself again. Every time he thought of the sound of soldiers crashing through his front door, remembering his terror from his hiding place in the oven, his heart would begin to pound with renewed strength and he would come close to losing control again.

It had all happened so fast—he remembered only fragments of the morning, seen in flashes of red in his mind. He had awakened to find his father's hand cupped over his mouth, hearing his father's whispered order to be quiet and go with his brother. He could remember wriggling into the small space of the cooking oven and asking his brother why they were hiding. "Soldiers are coming," he said. He remembered gunshots that startled him and caused him to nearly gag on the heavy soot. He remembered biting his fist to keep from crying out or coughing. And when he heard the door burst open, he remembered urinating on himself out of fear. His brother, hiding in the woodpile next to the oven, had heard a muffled cry and reached carefully into the oven to grab his brother's arm in a gesture of frail comfort.

The mayor of Sok-Cho stood and faced the intruders with a vast calm the Communist commander instantly resented. The two men examined each other in a brief moment of inventory. The solid, stocky commander drew himself up to his full height, unable to equal the tall, muscled stature of the mayor. He threw his heavy chest forward in a gesture of assumed authority, while the mayor stood with the quiet dignity of someone who didn't have to assume anything. A half dozen soldiers with weapons had crowded into the room, and the commander felt an obvious satisfaction that, regardless of the mayor's stature or position, his own power could not be questioned.

"There is an American priest somewhere in the village," he said, speaking in the rough dialect of a peasant. "Where is he?" The mayor shook his head and shrugged. Unruffled, the commander smiled with a surliness that extended to his eyes. "Very well. We'll find him eventually anyway. You might have spared him some discomfort by telling me where he is now, but so be it." He turned to one of his men. "Find the priest," he snapped. "And when you find him, kill him."

For the first time Chang spoke, his voice level and soft. "We are not Christians and do not know where he is," he said. "But the priest has been among us for many years and is harmless. He knows nothing."

The commander smiled, feeling he had already gained a small victory over the self-assured mayor.

"Find the priest," he repeated. "And bring him to me."

The commander turned his back on the mayor and casually examined the room. "You have information concerning American Army build-up in this area." It wasn't a question, and the mayor said nothing. His wife stood next to him, her shoulders straight, trying to mask her fear with a look of indignation. The commander looked at her, deliberately allowing his gaze to wander the length of her body. She lifted her chin and met his scrutiny, though it made her cheeks burn with disgust.

The commander stepped closer to the mayor, his eyes reflecting the mindless brutality of a man who has broken an eagle's wing to prevent it from flying. The sun-darkened skin on his moon-shaped face began to separate into a slow, confident smile.

"Before we leave, Chang," he said between clenched teeth, "we will have the information we want. Your people out there," he gestured toward the doorway where some of the villagers stared into the house, "your people who revere you so much now, good mayor, will see how easy it is to turn a hero into a babbling coward."

Bok could only hear muffled words from the next room, and as they were spoken some of his fear began to dissipate. Maybe these aren't bad soldiers, he thought, maybe they'll go away and leave us alone. But with the first startling "whack" of flesh meeting flesh in a violent blow, he felt his whole body cringe in fear. He heard the commander's angry voice asking more questions. There was the sound of scuffling feet, a pan clattering to the floor. And then the brutal, systematic beating began with alternating sounds of flesh being struck, of air being forced from a man's body by a powerful blow to the stomach, the sound of retching, more scuffling, more intense questions from the commander. For several minutes, the beating continued, and the grip on the boy's arm tightened and trembled. The villagers outside were beginning to wail and plead, but with the blast of a sudden gunshot, the pleading subsided. The heavy soot in the oven nearly suffocated him, but Bok was too frightened to remove the fist from his mouth. He could taste the blood seeping from the teeth marks.

"You will talk!" the commander screamed. "You're going to tell me everything by the time I'm through with you!"

The cold wave of terror the boy had been battling finally washed over him when he heard the commander's orders and his father's helpless moan in reply. He burst from the oven and ran toward the back door in a frenzied clattering of pans, firewood and cooking utensils, with his brother close on his heels.

"Stop them!" the commander yelled, and one of his men aimed his weapon at the fleeing boys. Their mother screamed and lunged for the weapon, pushing the barrel upward, sending the bullet harmlessly through the roof. The soldier jerked the gun from her grasp and viciously jabbed the stock into her stomach, knocking her to the floor. When he took aim again, it was too late. The boys had vanished.

The sun seemed to rise slowly, tentatively out of the ocean as though ashamed to shine on a scene so disgusting as the one in the village. The boys began to shiver with the onset of a released shock and from the crisp air of a late spring morning. Their thin clothing was soaked from the dew and their teeth began to chatter. The first feeble rays of light crept through the village, casting a gold shaft against the roof of the mayor's house. The boys raised their heads to hear the faint voices from inside. For an agonizing hour they listened to the commotion inside their home—voices at first intensely angry, shouting, demanding. Then there was silence. And the laughter began. Strange, hollow laughter, unlike any the boys had heard before. Mingled with the rise and fall of sea-bird cries along the shore, the laughter drifted up to them on thin wisps of air.

"What are they doing?" Bok whispered. "What are they laughing at?" His brother shook his head and motioned him to be silent. Bok knew only one thing—the laughter coming from the house didn't include his father's. He lowered his head to his smudged hands and waited.

The crowd of weeping women, old men and children suddenly stiffened and retreated into themselves as the commander appeared in the mayor's doorway. Adjusting the buttons on his coat in a slow deliberate movement, he stared with disdain at the cowering villagers, shifting his weight slowly back and forth from one solid leg to the other. Clasping his hands behind him and throwing his chest out, the image of a sturdy little grouse crossed the boy's mind as he stared with wide-eyed anticipation from the hillside.

"It appears that the forces of the Imperialistic South have done their job well," he began, curling the corner of his upper lip into a sneer. Looking down his nose as he would peer down the sights of a weapon, he scanned the frightened faces and smiled in self-satisfaction. "Not a fit man remains in the village to serve the new masters of the North. They have left you only the weak and the old—even your mayor is of no use to you." He stepped to the side, and the young couple was pushed roughly through the door, stumbling into the street.

The boys on the hillside gasped in disbelief when they saw their parents. Bok opened his mouth to cry out, but was silenced by his brother's hand over his mouth.

The mayor stood as straight as his cracked ribs and wobbling legs would allow, staring at the terrified crowd through two ugly, swollen slits that were his eyes, his jaw hanging slack and bloodied at an odd angle. Blood was caked on two split lips, a grotesque underline to the bruise-blackened face. The torn muslin shirt was soaked with blood, and a vicious gash on his right thigh was oozing a stream of red. With a left arm limp and useless at his side, two smashed and pulpy hands, he was an image from a nightmare. But even through the blood and pain, there was a quiet nobility to his bearing that his awkward stance couldn't hide. He still held his head up, not avoiding anyone's gaze.

22

With his right arm across his wife's shoulders, Chang made a weak gesture of helping her to hide her own battered nakedness from the eyes of the crowd, looking down at her in concern. She turned her bruised face into his chest while he pushed her long, tangled hair beyond her shoulders. Won Mee looked up at him, and he attempted a smile. Through her pain and humiliation she tried to smile back, slowly pulling herself erect, drawing a damaged emotional strength from him. She turned to face the crowd. Her clothes had been torn from her, and what little remained hung loosely over one small breast. Her torso and legs were blotched with bruises and streaked with blood from a dozen small cuts. Her legs trembled with the effort to stand, but she didn't look away. The commander faced the couple, his look of disdain gradually changing to one of discomfort, finally turning petulant.

"Your mayor is a stupid man," he finally yelled, his voice shrill, his eyes riveted to Chang. "He risks all your lives by keeping silent, because he cares nothing for you. He isn't worthy of your trust. He would see you all die before cooperating with me—he risked the lives of his children and sacrificed his wife for his selfish ambitions. He isn't worthy to be your leader!"

The commander whirled to face the crowd. "You'll all learn what it means to defy me!" he screamed, his face turning red, veins bulging on his squat neck. "On this day, you will see how stubbornness and selfishness are dealt with, and you will all remember!" He spun back around to face the mayor. "Your stupidity will see you buried, do you understand? DO YOU UNDERSTAND?"

Chang never spoke, his swollen eyes never wavered. The man's calm was infuriating and the commander began to vibrate with rage. "I WILL SEE YOU DIE!" he screamed, shaking his finger in the mayor's face. There was no reply, and he barked a furious order to his men. "Bring me the priest!"

From within the crowd, a soldier pushed forward, dragging a tall, red-haired man by the arm. Dressed in the cassock of a Catholic priest, his pale blue eyes mirroring the confusion and hurt that a man of God feels when faced with mindless violence. His thin, freckled face bore the markings of a recent interrogation—a split lip and bruised cheeks. A small trickle of blood slithered from a wound somewhere on his head. His thatch of fiery red hair was disheveled, his clothes were dusty and he tripped over the awkward cassock when he was shoved by the soldier, falling face down in the dirt at the commander's boots. Dragged to his feet, he faced the commander with quiet bewilderment.

"I am told by my sergeant," the commander began, his voice derisive, "that you know nothing, that you are here only to serve these people and teach them of God." The priest said nothing, wiping the blood from his lip. "Well, you now have an opportunity to make yourself useful to these people." Another order was barked and a shovel was thrust into the priest's hands. "Dig, you bastard priest!"

The soft blue eyes, seen in striking contrast to the shining black eyes of the people around him, began to fill with tears as Father Scully realized what he was supposed to do, and he opened his mouth to protest. Before his first word could be uttered, the commander doubled his fist and struck him in the face, snapping the priest's head violently backward. "I said DIG!" he yelled, gesturing to the ground in front of the battered couple.

The boys watched the priest as he laboriously dug a long ditch, tossing each shovelful of dirt into a pile near the hole. They had seen him before, moving among the villagers with a congenial smile on his face, always stopping to talk to somebody, patting the children on the head as they scampered past him, snickering at his funny dress. He communicated with them in their own language, telling them stories of a kind and loving god who looked after everyone and protected the weak. Bok stared at him as the hole got deeper, wondering why this god hadn't saved the priest from the soldiers.

The sun was beginning to warm the boys' backs and their teeth finally stopped chattering when they heard the commander tell the priest to stand aside. They saw the priest turn and say something to the commander, his hands in a gesture of pleading. The commander shook his head and pushed the priest roughly aside, but he was back again, pleading, begging. The boys strained forward to hear, but the words drifted away on a rising wind. Two soldiers stepped forward and forced the priest away at gunpoint, pushing him back to the villagers. Bok stifled a cough as he saw six of the soldiers line up a few paces in front of his parents. Rubbing his nose again and sniffing, he watched as his parents were pushed to the edge of the hole. His brother nudged him with his elbow to silence the sniffing and pointed to the commander.

"This is your last chance to save yourself. Tell me! Tell me what I already know!" Though the morning was cool, beads of sweat were forming on his forehead and his movements were the short, edgy movements of a man on the verge of losing an important contest of will. He sensed the end, and was unwilling to accept it. The mayor stood immobile with a serenity that said he had already known the outcome and had accepted it. He pulled his wife close and waited.

In the boy's mind, the next moments moved forward in slow, painfully stark outline, forever highlighted and colored by the shock. Though it took only seconds, the vision swirled in a mist of slow, agonized precision. The commander stepped away and issued a terse order. The line of soldiers raised their weapons and took aim. And at the moment the boy gasped in understanding, the volley of shots echoed from the hillsides and mountains, the sound rushing out to sea and back a thousand horrible times. There were several quick splashes of blood against his parents' torsos, then their bodies dropped forward, falling through time and space, through eons of pain and loss, down, down through the echoing blasts, into the priest's shallow ditch.

And then there was silence. No sound in the world—no sea-birds, no weeping villagers, no echoes. Silence. His first conscious sensation after those moments was the rustle of the wind through his hair. It was the wind that made Bok blink his eyes and swallow the scream that ached in his throat. The scene below was a frozen tableau that burned itself into the canvas of his mind—the stunned gathering of villagers around the well near his home—the stiff, silent soldiers looking awkward and uncertain now the deed was done—the commander standing erect, but looking strangely diminished, deflated—and a few feet away, the grave with the bodies of his parents exposed. He saw it all as a frozen painting with no sound. The only movement was the distant billowing of smoke from burning homes, and the gentle ruffling of the priest's cassock in the breeze.

Clearing his throat and glancing around him, the commander finally issued a clipped order. His men, relieved to be able to move, to act, to do anything but stand in the eerie silence, told the villagers to go home and began nudging the stunned people to get them moving. One by one, the people turned away and walked slowly back to their shattered homes. Like tattered wraiths, their clothing fluttering in the wind, they disappeared down the road, leaving the priest beside the open grave.

When the last handful of dirt was pushed over the bodies, the priest stood to wipe his hands and was met with the cold, petulant stare of the commander.

"So," he said, "You've found some use for yourself at last." Father Scully met his derision with a look of sadness and pity that made the commander begin to fidget. The priest stared at the orderly group of men behind the commander, their field packs in place, their weapons shouldered, obviously ready to move out. The commander noticed his questioning stare. "I'll be leaving a small detachment behind to—" he cleared his throat, "to maintain order." He turned quickly away to avoid the priest's calm scrutiny, signaled his men to move forward, and the platoon filed down the road to the south.

The boys on the hillside watched the soldiers leave, and a small surge of hope began to rise between them. Though their parents were no longer visible, the urge to be near them again was overwhelming and with the departure of the soldiers, Bok finally dared to stand and relieve himself.

"Let's go," he whispered to Yoon, who shook his head and hissed at him to get down.

"There might still be some soldiers left. Maybe we should wait." When he finished, Bok dropped back to the ground and watched. "It's just the priest now," he urged. "Let's go see."

But Yoon's caution finally won, and they waited on the hillside, watching the priest as he knelt by the grave, wondering why he didn't leave. "What's he waiting for?" the young one asked, and the older boy shrugged. Neither boy had noticed the priest's casual scanning of the hillside, or the patient smile. The priest knelt and prayed. The boys waited.

The sun vanished behind the mountains, the village huddled in a frightened blue shadow and kerosene lanterns began to flicker here and there in some of the windows. Bok pushed himself to his feet.

"I'm going," he said firmly. "There's no one there but the priest." Beginning to feel the evening chill through his thin nightshirt, Yoon stood and followed his brother back down the hillside, stumbling over rocks and thistle bushes.

The priest looked up over his folded hands when he heard the boys approaching, and his heart lurched with a mixed spasm of relief and sorrow. He silently thanked God that the boys were safe, and felt the hot stab of grief when he saw their sooty faces.

"I knew you'd come," Father Scully told them as they stared at the mound of earth. "I've been waiting for you."

Ignoring the priest, the boys squatted next to the grave and stared, their eyes wide and dry. The priest straightened his stiffened back, feeling the raw, grating pain from his interrogation, and he waited for them to weep, to feel the pain and begin to deal with it.

As minutes passed, the boys crossed their legs and sat, staring toward the village. The priest watched in mild bewilderment, until he realized what was happening. He approached quietly and knelt between them.

"You can't stay here," he said softly. "Your mother and father aren't coming back." The boys looked at him, an unasked question in their eyes. The blood on the priest's lip had dried, his cheeks and eyes were swollen and bluish in the fading light, but his eyes were bright and soft as he tried to make them understand. "In some future day when the suffering of this world is finished, you'll perhaps be with your parents in God's care. But for now, and for a long time to come, your parents won't be with you. They're dead, little ones, and now you belong to me—and to God."

Father Scully continued to talk quietly, his voice falling like soothing rain on the hot, dry places in their hearts. He spoke of things they didn't understand, but they felt his caring, and they huddled closer to him as he spoke. In a world suddenly turned mad, the three of them sat together trying to make sense of something senseless, trying to gain a direction in a sea of confusion. The priest talked, the boys listened, polarizing themselves and their emotions in order to begin moving forward again. When he was finished, the priest reached up and touched the dirty cheeks that bore no signs of tears.

"You know," he said, smiling and taking their unresisting hands, "it's all right to cry if you want to. Sometimes tears are a good thing—they make you feel better when you're afraid." But as they walked slowly away toward the mission there was no weeping, no sound of sorrow. Their eyes remained dry and expressionless.

He sighed deeply and began to talk again, the sound of his gentle voice floating into the darkness, away into the distant reaches of a world where nothing was the same anymore, a world that left two orphaned boys and a misplaced priest at the mercy of capricious gods. The three figures disappeared into the darkness, leaving the grave behind them in the night.

III

Father Jerry Scully folded his arms across his chest, wincing from the pain in his ribs. Shifting his weight from one lanky leg to the other, he stood in front of his mission building on the northwest slope of the village, trying to focus his concentration on the moon rising from the ocean. The expression on his face was that of a man who kept losing track of his central thoughts, the bewildered, innocent look of one who knew there was something he had to remember, but couldn't focus his ideas. He mumbled softly to himself, feeling disjointed and scattered. His body ached, his head throbbed, the mission was in shambles after being ransacked by the soldiers; small pillars of smoke still coiled slowly from smoldering ruins of homes in the village; nothing made sense anymore. There was a fresh grave in the darkness below, there were two orphaned boys thrust into his care, and within the space from yesterday's sunset to this, his entire life had been altered.

The giant silver disk suspended over a plate-glass mirror of ocean cast a muted gleam in the wake of its rising. Several boats moored at the docks sat motionless, unconcerned, darkly graceful silhouettes resting on the mirror of water. He swallowed hard and rubbed his boney hand across burning eyes. Stroking his bruised chin, he became vaguely aware of the pale stubble of a day's growth of beard, and wondered why he had forgotten to shave. He shaved every morning; why had he not? Ah yes. The soldiers. He smiled to himself, feeling a tiny moment of satisfaction at having recalled something, anything of what had been perplexing him. Yes, the soldiers, yes....

He sat on the grass, tucking his long legs under his cassock, resting his chin on his knees as he decided to start at the beginning in order to find the end. He mumbled softly, scratching his unshaven neck.

Nothing in his life had prepared him for this. His quiet, stilted upbringing in a rigid Catholic home in Duluth, Minnesota, had prepared him for nothing more than a silent desire to be away, to find more, to do something of importance. Images of his family swam into reflection on the still water: his pinched, dour-faced mother with her "bend your knee to the Lord, repent of your slothfulness"; the perpetual look of defeat on his father's face as they all bent to family prayer on frozen mornings before leaving for work in the shipyards of Duluth's massive harbor. In all the recalled voices of his home there was one screaming silence that drove him ever outward: the frozen glare of no affection, the emptiness of never being touched with love. He felt that he probably loved his parents, yet felt his emotion for them was closer to reverence, a glacial type of honor; but oh God! he thought helplessly, dear God, the loneliness! His inherently gentle nature and instinctive urge to serve, to be accepted, all the giant mixing of emotions in his youth drew him to the seminary and the priesthood where he submerged himself in the warm folds of the gospel, taking refuge in an unfailing atmosphere of total acceptance, finding comfort and position in a world where a family life was not expected of him. His only task was to reach out to the extended "family of man," to give them his hand, to teach them his faith. He retreated into the confines of the Church where he found solace and a lack of scrutiny—his own of himself. He was safe. And he was no longer lonely.

Jerry Scully's orderly progression through his memory, through his days beside another moonlit harbor worlds away, finally brought him back to his outpost on the hills above Sok-Cho, and he had to smile with the irony of it. In his desperate urge to be away from the cold and emptiness of his upbringing, he had come full circle: Sok-Cho was as cold as any place he had ever lived in winter, and his solitude was deep and absolute. These people, he thought, musing fondly of his choice in mission callings, these people are what keep me here. The beauty of their clear, non-hypocritical natures, their open, innocent acceptance of me even though they don't accept the Church. Odd, he thought as he tilted his head to one side as if listening to a voice somewhere in the middle distance. How odd that my existence leaves me alone in a family that only recognizes my love for them without understanding my need for them.

And now this. How do I deal with this, oh Lord? What is it I'm supposed to understand of all this? There's no sin here worthy of this horror. There've been no acts of evil aggression committed by these people that would justify this brutality. I have no parameters with which to gauge this madness. There's an orphan boy sitting a few yards away down the slope, staring at a home that's no longer his, hungering for parents that are no longer alive, and I have no answers for him. He sits and he watches, and I have no answers for questions he will not ask. What is my purpose in his life and the life of his older brother? What can I give him that he can use now? Dear God, tell me what to do!

Father Scully's back was aching and he realized he'd been straining forward with intense searching. He slowly stretched his legs. He stood, staring at the back of the boy's small body on the grass. He finally sighed, resigning himself to finding nothing of value to give, and turned slowly back to the mission, toying with an odd, growing suspicion that perhaps this child, in his innocence, had already found some of the answers.

Bok knew the priest was behind him somewhere on the hillside, knew he had been watching him. But he had no concept of the priest or what role he was supposed to play in his life. The man was simply—there. Like the trees or the sea. The boy ignored the searching glances and concentrated on his home—a small dark box in the valley below that had once been alive with warmth. It haunted him now as he sat cross-legged and serious. "What happened in there?" he kept asking himself. "What does it look like now?"

In the furious whirl of emotions and memories that pulsed through his mind, a quiet, solid core began to form, and instinctively his heart went after it. He understood that something immensely important had been taken from him, but he had no system by which to judge the exact value of what he had lost. He had few reference points in his past to use as guides for his rampant emotions. In those first raw hours of darkness on the hillside as he stared at the empty shell of his home, all of his free-floating, splintered feelings gathered themselves together as one powerful, consuming need. With the pure, unfettered reckoning of a child, the boy had no way of knowing that this newly-born center of his being was the cold, clean fire of revenge.

Somewhere on the road below, Bok could hear faint voices approaching. Something about the rough laughter and shouting made him jerk his head in the direction of the noise. A group of people were shuffling up the road, illuminated by the light of two lanterns carried with them. The laughter was punctuated with the sounds of female protests—frantic, pleading cries in the dark. The boy leaned forward, a questioning frown crossing his forehead. The lanterns cast pale yellow patches of light on the men's clothing, and he froze. Soldiers! Six or seven of them with bottles in their hands, laughing, swearing, and dragging two of the young girls from the village along with them. The girls were screaming, trying to free themselves. One girl's long hair had come undone and was flying wildly about as she struggled to get away. No one stepped from the houses to try and help. No one dared challenge the men who still carried their weapons loosely slung over their shoulders.

The group moved up the road toward the village well, stopping at the darkened mayor's home. They hesitated only a moment, the men weaving drunkenly as they stared at the empty house, the girls pleading to be set free. Then they pushed their way into the house and the lanterns filled the windows with fragile light.

Bok stood and watched the house, knowing that the men inside were responsible for taking his parents from him, and knowing he wanted to make them suffer. There was no hesitation, no wavering of purpose. Without looking behind him to see if he was being watched, he set out for his home.

Moving with the skill of a child acquainted with every rock and bush in his world, he slipped away from the mission, down the slope toward the edge of the village. A moon riding high in the sky shed a fluorescence on the small figure clad in cast-off muslin clothing. Slinking around the perimeter of the town like a nimble, baggy little ghost, he dodged in and out of the shadows until he reached the stick fence around his backyard. Finding the familiar crack he knew he could squeeze through, he slipped behind one of the huge earthen crocks his mother used to store her summer vegetables and waited to hear what was going on in the house.

By now the screams from the girls had subsided into sobs and intermittent piercing cries of pain, while the men continued to laugh and curse and grunt. As he listened and waited, the force of his determination pushed him into a cold placidness within. His age, his size, his vast helplessness in the situation were swept away in the consuming calm.

The moon rose higher, changing the shape of shadows cast from objects in the backyard as Bok sat with his legs tucked to his chest. The sound of laughing and groaning gradually diminished, replaced with an occasional loud snore. It was time to move. He hurried across the yard and slipped silently in the back entrance, having no idea what he would do once inside, knowing only that something would be done.

The storage room was dark, but in the reflection of kerosene light from the next room, he could barely make out the scattered wood and utensils from his escape that morning lying in untouched disarray. The moment he crept into the main room, his steel-like calm burned away under the rise of anger when he saw the sprawled, half-naked bodies of drunk, sleeping soldiers lying all over the room. Bottles and clothing were strewn everywhere, the stench of liquor and passed gas looming like a dirty cloud in the air.

33

There was movement from a shadowed corner, and he thought for a moment one of the soldiers was awake and had seen him. What he saw stunned him into immobility. The two village girls were huddled together against the cold mud wall, their faces red and swollen from weeping, their eyes wide and frightened. They were naked, and the pale skin of their bodies glowed softly in the dim light. The boy stared at them, wondering why they hadn't sneaked away from the sleeping soldiers.

The girls stared back at him, startled by his sudden entrance. They had been frozen by fear after their brutal usage by the soldiers, and even when it was safe to leave, they dared not move. The abrupt appearance of another intruder had served as a cold slap of awareness, the one impetus they needed to move again. Bok fixed his rigid gaze on them as they slowly stood, edging their way to the door. They were struck by the strangeness of his eyes—a look of deadly calm and hatred. They reached the door and bolted through, disappearing into the darkness.

Turning his attention back to the roomful of soldiers, he wondered vaguely how best to go about killing them. His limited understanding of death and dying left room for only undefined meanings of the act of killing, but he had seen animals die and he knew there was a finality to it, a finality that his sense of revenge cried for. He quickly surveyed the room for any possible weapons, seeing first their bayonets (he'd be able to stab only one or two before being stopped), then their guns (they were too heavy—he couldn't lift them).

Then he saw the grenades.

Attached to each man's belt were one or two long-handled grenades, some with their protective caps missing, exposing the pull-strings. Memories of fishing expeditions with his father came rushing back, memories of his father using the same type of grenades to stun large schools of tuna or mullet. He had never been allowed to toss one, but he had been allowed to pull the cord, and he knew it was only seconds before the thing exploded. He had his answer.

Moving swiftly from one drunken man to the next, he

pulled the strings on four of the grenades before an earth-splitting blast smashed his body through the mud wall and into the street. Several spontaneous blasts followed, demolishing the house in a huge eruption of dirt, wood and debris. The walls flew apart and the home crumbled into a smoldering ruin.

At first, he felt nothing. Lying as if dead in the road beside the smoking wreckage, his senses came back to him in slow, bewildered stages, beginning with the deafening roar in his head.

Feeling spread gradually to his chest and arms and he began to gasp for air. He pushed himself up with trembling arms and his stomach came to painful life, threatening a violent upheaval. He rolled to his side, gagged and spat blood into the dirt, still struggling for air and wondering why he couldn't keep his balance. Moisture trickled from his ears, down his cheeks and he watched without comprehending as drops of blood fell into the dust beneath his face. When he could finally turn his head without becoming dizzy, he wiped the grit from his eyes and stared at the pile of rubble that had been his home. With the growing pain in his head Bok remembered the soldiers that would be buried beneath the heap. Dead. There was a surge of an emotion he would later come to know as satisfaction; the hollow, lukewarm envelope of justice served.

Little by little the world began to expand in his vision from the circle of destruction where he sat; and with his awareness of his surroundings, he realized he was in the midst of a crowd of excited villagers. Carrying torches and lanterns, they had all rushed to the scene and stood gaping in astonishment first at the boy, then at the demolished house. A wave of whispers rippled through the crowd, swelling to soft exclamations, then excited chatter. Bok wiped the blood from under his nose, smearing it across his face as he stood on wobbly legs. No one reached out to help him to his feet, no one touched him, as though he were at once charmed and damned.

From within the smoking rubble the villagers could hear

the sounds of coughing and moaning. The crowd fell silent. Three of the soldiers painfully rose from the ruins, stumbling blindly and groaning for help. Their faces were bloody masks of horror, their uniforms shredded, exposing burned and blackened skin covering their torsos. The group of villagers stared in stricken silence; but then a change began to take place. The full impact of the pain and terror of the day finally crashed into their hearts, and the villagers, with one spirit, were swept forward on a red, pounding wave of vengeance. With a savagery inspired by atrocity, they used torches, rocks, sticks, anything they could lay their hands on, and without speaking a word between them they converged on the three men, beating, gouging, hacking them until there was no more movement from the mutilated bodies.

Standing on shaky legs, trying to keep his damaged equilibrium in the wake of his broken eardrums, Bok watched the people of his childhood disintegrate into an animalistic brutality that stunned him. These same people whom he knew to be kind, gentle neighbors, who never even raised a hand to reprimand their own children, were now a transformed mass, a frightening horde of executioners whose capacity for violence shocked him to the center of his soul.

When the act was finished and the people stood back, there was a giant, cold feeling of relief among them, an unquestioned justification. They gathered tightly together, drawing strength from each other to try and ease their wretched spirits. It was finished. The soldiers were dead, and for one small moment, the villagers were avenged. But the stoop of their shoulders said that they knew this was only a horrible beginning. The destruction had come full circle in the tiny village, but the horror of the years of war ahead, a terror reflected now in all their eyes, had only just begun.

Unnoticed, his ears still bleeding in slow, black trickles in the dark, Bok turned away from the silent crowd and limped back into the night towards the mission.

IV

In his dreams, none of it ever happened. In his dreams, his mother and father were still alive, laughing, standing in the surf and beckoning the children to come into the water. The water shimmered and twinkled with an exaggerated light and was a deep, unnatural blue. His brother was still with him, running by his side into the surf to join their parents. Sea birds poised above the gentle swells with frozen wings, buoyed up by a warm, salty breeze. The air sparkled with tiny diamonds of salt spray dancing in yellow-gold sunlight as the boys ran for their parents, who seemed to keep retreating further into the waves, calling soundlessly to the boys, beckoning with their arms. In his dreams, the boy realized with some surprise that there was no sound: no sea bird calls, no voices, no rushing of the sea. The boys call to their parents, but there is no voice, only moving lips and legs that are getting heavier in the deeper water, as their parents retreat. When he can barely see his parents' heads above the water, his father turns and he is laughing—and the boy hears it: the joyous rumbling laughter of a day so long ago....

He awakened slowly, feeling someone stroking his hair and talking softly. A man's voice. A man's hand. His stomach ached with the continual spasms of hunger and his head hurt. His mouth was dry and tasted badly, and he had difficulty focusing on his surroundings. Then he remembered where he was.

The camp. He was still in the concentration camp.

He sat up slowly, his body aching from hunger, and

realized he was still holding the photo in his hand. A quiet
sense of discouragement settled over him as he recalled the
last group of prisoners to be ushered through the gates that
day; how he had once again jumped hopefully to his feet and
approached each one as they entered the compound, showing
them the photo and asking them: "Have you seen him? Have
you seen him?" And once again the answers had all been the
same: "No."

He had dropped dejectedly to his mound of dirt next to
the hole he was using as a home. The daily rations of rice had
dwindled to a spare handful per day, and he slept as much as he
could to save his energy, especially in the freezing weather.
Drowsiness overcame his feelings of futility, and for a few
moments, he had dozed off. He was fully awake now, with
Father Scully sitting beside him, offering his small bits of
consolation, knowing that the boy had been making the rounds
with his photo again, and that he had been disappointed. It
was becoming a melancholy tradition, this routine of hurting
and comforting.

"Don't grieve, son," he was saying softly, almost absently,
while he tangled his long fingers in and out of the boy's hair.
"God will protect him, and if it is God's will, you'll find him
someday. Be comforted. God is with us."

Father Scully's voice continued to soothe him, crooning
his scriptures and his doctrines, the sound of his voice
becoming a soft monotone in the boy's head, most of the
words not making any sense. Bok put the photo back in his
pocket, wondering about this god, this power, this huge
"thing" the priest kept telling him of. He gazed around him at
the harshness, cruelty and starvation of the camp. He thought
of his brother, Yoon, out there somewhere alone—what was
the mystery he couldn't unravel about this god? He trusted the
priest, tried to believe him when he spoke of this great
benevolent spirit, and he wondered what it was he was missing
that kept him from understanding why a kind and loving god
would allow his life to be the way it was. He wondered if this
god loved only certain people. He wondered what he had done
to make this god angry with him, but the only thing he could

think of was the time so long ago when he had killed a swallow with his slingshot. Perhaps he was being punished for killing such a special omen of good luck.

From the time he and his brother had been sent away from the mission along the road south, the two boys had drawn their courage together, gathering up all the bravery they could find inside, knowing they would be completely alone. They had no concept of their insignificance as they joined the ranks of over eighteen million other homeless refugees. They were important only to each other, neither asking for or receiving from anyone—not even Father Scully's god.

The boy would return to the deep, raw crevices of his memory over and over during the long hungry days and nights in the camp, always coming back to the day they had left the mission, spinning backward, backward to the snow-covered hills and Father Scully on his knees in front of them....

"I have no choice," the priest was saying as he looked into the eyes of each boy, thinking they were like shining stones in a bundle of rags. He rubbed his thin hands briskly together to try to coax some warmth into the blue, freckled skin.

The late months of autumn had passed frigidly into the early months of winter. The children had been easy companions—they asked for nothing and accepted whatever was given without complaint. Though they seldom smiled and never laughed, the boys had made the dark days after the first Communist probe seem more bearable. The priest bowed his head, his mass of red hair tousled by a freezing wind. Bok watched him attentively, thinking that the man's neck was so thin it appeared to have given up trying to support the large head. The priest looked older since the blistering days of summer—the skin on his face was slack and sallow and he had faint blue circles under his eyes. A face the boy had come to know as red and robust was now creased with worry and unhappiness.

"I have no choice," Father Scully repeated, though he knew they believed him. "Most of the villagers have already gone, and soon there will be only enemy soldiers here in Sok-

Cho. I must stay to attend to those who cannot leave. But you must go."

It's their eyes, the priest decided as he forced himself to meet their unflinching gaze. The trust, the complete acceptance in their eyes; that's what's making this so hard, he realized. There was no trace of sadness, fear, mistrust or anger, any one of which would have made his job easier, would have given him some tangible thing to justify, to combat. Instead, he was left in the anchorless sea of their understanding, and he felt an irrational frustration. He wanted to explain to them, let them know that he loved them and wanted to keep them, but they all knew that and accepted it. Instead of the solace of rationalizing the situation, he was left with the aimless fidgeting of someone who has the answers, but isn't approached with the questions. Fumbling nonsensically with the tatters of fabric wrapped around their thin bodies, the priest performed a useless show of trying to make them warmer. Even this, he knew, was a waste of time. All too soon it would be so cold that the few shreds of clothes would do little to prevent them from freezing to death.

"Travel with the other refugees when you can," he said, trying to smile, the effort disappearing like his breath on the frozen air, "but if you must travel alone, try to travel at night. Don't get separated. Follow the main road. It'll take you to Kangnung. From there, try to find your way to Seoul, where there are orphanages and people who will take care of you."

With his mention of the orphanages, Father Scully realized just how many new words these two had learned in the last weeks and months—words like "death" and "enemy" and "refugee" and "orphan." The vocabulary of war.

"Don't lose the bag of rice," he instructed, tugging on the small pouches hanging from their cloth belts. "And take care of the cooking utensils. Try to make the dried fish last as long as you can."

His hands were becoming numb and he knew he would have to stop his fussing, but he lingered, satisfying his own need to bestow a few last vestiges of caring before letting them go.

Finally straightening his tall frame, he breathed deeply, blinking his eyes against the blinding white glare of the snow, using the burning light in his eyes as ample excuse for the tears to begin forming. He turned the boys around and gently pushed them to begin their journey. The tears spilled unchecked down his cheeks as he watched the two awkward heaps of rags trundle away into a world blanketed with white.

"God be with you," he whispered hoarsely, and the sound of his words froze like heavy crystals, falling into the snow at his feet.

Like two misplaced little blotches on a painting done in white, Bok and Yoon moved southward away from Sok-Cho. Rolling hills, gentle flat-lands that blended into beaches, steep, rugged mountains—the whole world was covered with a deep, soft snow. The simple enormity of the winter-locked world insulated them, pulling them closer to each other in a shared vacuum of isolation. A world compelling in its beauty, vast in its cruelty.

By the end of their first week on the road the small bundles of rice and fish were gone, and one more new sensation began to overtake them—the first tremblings of hunger. They foraged where they could, feeling fortunate when they came upon abandoned homes or shacks, thinking there would surely be food left behind. But after days of surviving on the one small bag of old potatoes that they scrounged from a bombed-out barn, they began to realize that no one left food behind—not intentionally.

The farther south they moved, the more evidence they saw of a war that had only been a whisper before, a brief rumor on the wind. Now the countryside was littered with the remains of people who had been forced from their homes. The snow-covered ground was pock-marked with craters from bombing raids, leaving the landscape blistered with the ugly sores of battle.

Into the third week Yoon began to conquer his revulsion of the frozen bodies left lying in the snow. He foraged through the clothing of the dead, hoping for something, anything to eat, taking what few meager scraps of clothing they could.

When he brought those days back to mind, Bok could recall above all else a sense of trust in his older brother, a calm understanding that he would always be there. He remembered no threat of death, knowing that the grinding spasms of hunger were only temporary and that somehow they would be all right. The moments of deepest futility were lost in the continual belief in survival. And after weeks of scrounging and foraging and finally finding nothing for days, when the insides of their legs were raw, chafed and bleeding from the constant diarrhea, when they didn't have the energy any longer to wipe the continual stream of mucus from their noses, even when Bok felt he could go no further—even then there was no hopelessness. Because his brother was still there, still scolding him, still urging him on.

"Get up," Yoon said, as he tugged at his brother's arm. "We have to keep walking." The boy heard the voice through a muted, frosty cloud in his mind, crystal drops of sound in a sleepy world. He was too weak to stand and he crumbled to a heap in the snow.

"I want to sleep for a little while," Bok moaned. "Just a little while."

"Not now," his brother said firmly, "we have to find something to eat. We have to find a place to stay. Get up. GET UP!"

The voice was fading, disappearing into the spongy mass of numbness overtaking the small child's mind and body. The snow looked so soft—he was so sleepy—just a few minutes....

"If you don't get up, I'm leaving you!"

Bok never saw his brother get to his feet and trudge angrily away, hoping to frighten him into moving. He never saw him turn and look over his shoulder at the pitiful heap of rags lying in a small, shapeless huddle in the giant emptiness of snow. He never saw Yoon turn and run back down the slope, never felt the desperate grasp of affection as his brother held him close and rocked him back and forth, tears in his face, a helpless resolution in his eyes.

"You have to wake up," Yoon mumbled, sniffing and wiping his nose with his arm. "You have to wake up. You have to wake up." It became an incantation he knew the boy couldn't hear. Looking around him as he rocked back and forth, he realized the sun was going down and they would soon be left in the dark with no shelter. Though they had suffered through many such nights in the past weeks, he knew instinctively that his little brother wouldn't make it through the night if they didn't find a place to stay. A growing sense of urgency pushed him to his feet and Yoon stood, examining his brother, then gazing up to the top of the slope they would have to climb to get out of the valley they were in. He pulled and tugged, pushed and grunted, trying to find a way to move the boy up the slope with him. Nothing was working; Bok was too heavy and he was losing strength. In desperation, Yoon finally dropped to his knees, reached behind him and grabbed the boy's arms, pulling one across each shoulder, gripping the skinny wrists as tightly as he could. In a series of lunges and jerks he got to his feet, dragging his helpless brother behind him like a rag doll.

For the next hour Yoon struggled up the hill with the lifeless weight on his back, his brother's feet scraping trails in the snow. Every few yards he would fall forward to his knees, gasping for air, gathering strength for the next few yards. Twice he lost his grip on the boy's wrists and went sliding into the snow behind him. There were a few moments of near-consciousness when Bok realized he was supposed to move his feet; he would stagger a few steps, then his head would roll back, his eyes would close and the pull would begin again.

The sun had gone down, the hillside was in shadow, but the older boy felt no cold. Groaning and straining, he neared the top of the hill, and just below the summit he collapsed to his knees. The top of the hill, so near, yet looked so far away and he breathed in big gasps of air trying to catch his breath. "I have to make it," he mumbled, "I can't stop." Going down the other side, he knew he could manage, if he could just make it to the top. He turned around, faced his sleeping brother, and, still sitting, he grabbed the boy's wrists, braced his feet as best he could in the snow, then pushed himself backward up the slope, dragging the boy along. Again he dug in and pushed, and again, and again, stopping for deep gulps of air between tugs. When he thought he could pull no more, when his strength was completely gone, he thought of the many people he had seen frozen to death in the past weeks, how they stiffened up and turned a sick gray color with their eyes frosted over. Renewing his grip on the tiny wrists he pushed back one more time, turned around to see where he was going, and found himself sitting at the top. He let himself drop back into the snow, throwing his arms wide. He coughed and wheezed, feeling the ache of fatigue all over his body, wondering where they would go from here. For the moment he didn't know and didn't care. He had made it to the top!

Bok's moans finally brought Yoon back to reality and he knew it was time to move on. He sat wearily, feeling the heavy cold of dusk begin to settle in, and he looked around in the direction he would have to go. His mouth flew open in shock and a huge surge of hope pulsed through him. He could see the dim light from a kerosene lamp at a window in the valley below, and a thin curl of smoke coming from the chimney. Cooking! Someone was cooking!

He labored to his knees, pulling his brother's arms across his shoulders again, feeling the boy's head resting against his back. He started clumsily down the slope, slipping, sliding, losing his balance several times, but never losing a grip on the boy. The child flopped along behind him, his tattered rags coming apart in the snow, as they dragged from his feet and legs like a ball of unraveling yarn.

Whether the people in the house were friend or foe never occurred to Yoon when the smells from the cooking fire reached him. It would have made no difference. He saw only the chance for survival where there had been none before.

He reached the bottom of the slope and began the short journey across the flat land to the house. Though it was not far, this final stretch seemed to be the expanse of all the world. His breath wheezed in his chest, his hold on his brother's wrists kept slipping, but he trudged forward, his head up, his eyes, his mind, his whole body concentrated on the front door of the house. He saw the door as an end in itself, a grand goal, the final challenge. In his hunger and fatigue-fogged mind, there was no house beyond the door—only the door, framed in an odd, unnatural light. Even the thought of food had vanished in his burning determination to reach the door. Falling to his knees again, he let out a cry of protest, feeling that he would never be able to rise again. The door was just out of reach. With one final push, he lunged to his feet and bolted forward, banging his head and arms against the rough wood, sliding downward until he collapsed on his knees, still holding his brother's wrists.

Yoon wasn't sure how long he'd been there when the door flew open with a rush. He lifted his face with effort and found himself looking at an old woman holding a large stick in her hand. Her eyes were wide, wild, but not frightened. Her hair was gray, flying in disarranged wisps. One weathered, blue-veined hand gripped a heavy woolen shawl around her shoulders, and her muslin skirt moved in the sudden gust of air through the open door. She stared down at the two bundles on her doorstep and suddenly caught her breath. Dropping the stick of wood, she bent down and began shaking a knurled finger in his face.

"Where have you two been?" she screeched, her voice old and graveled. "I've been waiting for you for hours! Have you been playing on the road again, bad boy? I told you never to play on the road! Now just look at you, all dirty and cold."

As unexplained and sudden as her outburst, the boy was more surprised by the instant switch of moods that overtook her next. The look on her face softened like a lake when the wind died, and she gathered the boys in her arms, comforting them, crooning to them, "My babies, my babies!" she wailed. "My boys are home!"

She scooped them up in her arms and brought them into the house, chattering to herself while she wrapped them in warm blankets and lay them on a mat next to the earthen oven that warmed the tidy, one-room house. "Sleep now," she ordered, "and when you wake up mama will have something for you to eat."

She fussed and fluttered around the room, preparing

utensils and reaching into bags, mumbling as she moved, her motions quick and nervous. Yoon pulled Bok closer to him while he watched the wild-eyed woman. He was determined to keep an eye on her to see what she would do next; but the warmth of the oven and his exhaustion finally conquered him, and he drifted into the first sound sleep he had known in weeks.

She was an early casualty of a war that was now forever removed from her mind. Existence had been reduced to a small, closely-guarded sphere where tragedy no longer had a place. Three smooth mounds of snow under a willow tree not far from the house marked the graves of her husband and sons, but they had never left her. They moved with her around the house, accompanied her on her chores outside. She scolded them, instructed them, loved them. At meal times, they seemed always to be somewhere else, busy doing something she couldn't see, and she would make the pilgrimage to the graves and tell them to come home soon, supper was ready. Her mind had created a quiet, safe place for her to live out the rest of her days, insuring that she would never be alone. The fragile veil between fantasy and reality had been stripped away, revealing a world in which the only sanity was madness. She was hopelessly, harmlessly insane.

Over the next weeks and months the boys recovered their strength and grew accustomed to the old woman's companionship and care, ignoring her frequent trips to the graves, shrugging with indifference at the knowledge that she believed them to be her own sons. They allowed her to dwell in her world, playing their own parts and trying not to get in the way. She asked little more of them than the gathering of firewood, and only once did either of them protest her treatment of them when, on the first night at her house, she had attempted to breast-feed the younger boy. Driven deeper into her fantasy by the actual presence of her two "sons", she had gathered the little one in her arms as soon as he awakened, opened her dress and produced a sagging, elongated breast.

"Mama has plenty of milk," she cooed, grinning down at the boy and squeezing her scabby, misshapen nipple, trying to force it into the boy's protesting mouth. "He doesn't need that anymore," Yoon said, staring at the thin strings of flesh hanging from her chest like grotesque tumors. After brutally kneading her fruitless breasts, she finally gave up, her eyes glassing over as she stood, leaving the two boys to stare at each other in bewilderment.

They shared the long harsh days of winter, each taking a quiet comfort from the other—she from her "sons" and they from her gentle madness. The fear and loneliness of their journey to Kangnung was relegated to safer corners of their minds and they contented themselves to wait for spring in the tranquil cocoon created by a crazy woman.

But her serene insanity was often punctuated by moments of unnerving disquiet, of swift, unnatural movements, of sudden stares that held no recognition of anything or anyone, and as the winter moved by in frozen solitude, the boys became more and more jittery when she was around. Her sudden whirling, eyes wide and questioning when she had spoken to them only a second before, made their senses tingle with apprehension. She was unpredictable. She would go on for days and behave as if the boys had lived with her all her life, and then in the flash of an instant she didn't recognize them anymore. Their gratitude for her unwittingly saving their lives was short-lived in their innocent, childhood selfishness, and from the beginning there was a mutually instinctive understanding between the two boys; when the time was right, when spring arrived and the opportunity presented itself, they would continue their journey southward.

Spring pushed itself slowly into the little valley, wafting sensuously up the hillsides of green that are only seen during those first breathless days of warmth. The stream winding behind the house was coaxed into trickling, then flowing, then rushing freely, nudging at its banks. Everything stretched, reached, bulged, expanded, anxious for new life. But when the first swallows began making nests under the eaves of the hut, Bok felt a persistent nervousness he couldn't explain. And carried in on the wind that bore the swallows was the sound of distant shelling that was becoming closer and more frequent as the days warmed.

From a vantage point atop the knoll from which they had first entered the valley, the two children lay on their stomachs and watched a long line of trucks roll by beneath them. The dust churned up by the convoy could be seen for miles. Though they said nothing, each felt the nervousness, the rising urge to go south. A torrential rain had left the air clean and smelling of warm earth, filling their minds with fresh hope. The boys lay in their familiar outpost, listening to the monotonous grinding of vehicles on the road below.

Their chins resting on their hands, they watched a truck struggle and dig at the muddy road. The opportunity was presenting itself, and Yoon frowned with anxiety, knowing what Bok was thinking.

"It's an enemy truck," Yoon said, almost reproachfully. Bok nodded. "I know. But it's going south, and maybe if we sneak on now we can jump off again when they stop, before anyone sees us."

"What about the old woman?" Yoon gestured with his head to the valley behind them. "She's not our mother," Bok said with finality, "and she scares me. You know we don't belong here, so let's go—now!"

There was a look of near-pleading in the younger boy's eyes as he tried to convince his brother to leave, and finally Yoon nodded. Taking a deep breath and focusing on the stalled truck below, he pushed himself quickly to his feet and began running down the hill. Bok followed, but paused for a moment to turn and gaze at the valley. It was a soothing pocket of green swept over by a sky stretched taut and blue in a canopy over the old woman's domain. The sun dappled her movements around the front of the hut as she worked over a cauldron of steaming laundry, talking to herself, shaking her head and gesturing with her hands. The scene brought back a tug of familiarity, Bok's first feelings of genuine gratitude toward her sounding on his heart. He would never know where she had found the huge amounts of food that stocked her woodshed all winter, never know for certain just how old she was or what had happened to the three people that filled the graves under her willow tree. She was a dream, a crafty bit of whimsy placed in his path to save his life, and Bok had no idea why. It was only a brief moment, a fractured warp in which he felt that if he closed his eyes and opened them again, she would be gone and the valley would be empty except for the fat, chuckling stream and the languid willow tree.

He turned and ran down the hill after his brother, leaving the woman behind in her valley protected by nothing more than her illusions and an open, smiling sky.

V

When the two boys had scrambled aboard the floundering military truck, they could never have imagined that such places as "indoctrination camps" existed. Had they known where their journey was taking them they would have remained in the valley with the crazy woman—at least for a while longer.

It was a place carefully contrived to inspire, foster and bring forth the fruits of oppressive societies all over the world. Had they been older, the boys would have understood that such hells as these were the perfect settings for the forcible molding of an emerging personality; where obedience is rewarded by withdrawing punishment; a place where disobedience became a disease to be trampled, eradicated by the children themselves out of fear of being cast again into the retribution of physical pain and emotional starvation. They would see the scales of human life thrown off balance, creating the lop-sided personalities and twisted priorities found in "the mentality of the masses."

But all these things they discovered only after enduring the nightmare of the journey itself, when they realized they were not alone in the back of the truck. Though the odor had been a vaguely familiar one, it wasn't until they slipped under a canvas tarp toward the cab of the truck that they remembered what the horrible smell was. They found themselves lying next to the decomposing bodies of several dead soldiers.

Though the specter of death had become an all-too-familiar companion to the boys over the course of the long winter, the sudden proximity of such putrid death made their stomachs rise in uncontrollable waves of nausea, and for the next hour they wretched and vomited until there was nothing left to vomit. The stench of vomit mixed with the stench of decaying bodies only perpetuated the nausea, and in a dizzying round of sickness, exhaustion and more sickness, they lay in the back of the empty medical transport not knowing, not caring where they were going. The metal stretchers lining the sides rattled and clanked in the jostling vehicle, some of the loose ones banging against the sides with maddening regularity. Their heads pounded with pain until they finally dozed off, leaning against each other as far from the bodies as they could get.

When the truck finally growled to a halt, the boys were too sick to abide by their original plan to escape before being seen, and the next few hours were a blur of pain and confusion as they were kicked and pushed from the truck by soldiers disgusted at finding the stinking stowaways. Yoon was kicked and shoved, losing his balance and falling into one of the dangling stretchers where an exposed piece of metal pierced the soft underside of his upper left arm, tearing an ugly, jagged gash from his elbow to his armpit. The wound began pouring blood.

In flashes of stern faces, harshly-barked orders, vague blurs of barely-remembered events, the boys were cleaned up, the wound was bandaged and they were each given a thin blanket and led to what someone called a "holding area."

They stood and stared at the roomful of boys, all different ages, and knew by the expressions on their faces this was a place full of fear. The two boys knew they were no longer free, and knew with equal certainty they would do everything they could to get away.

Their intended journey south had taken a northwesterly turn sometime while they slept in the truck. They had no idea how many hours they had been traveling, had no idea where they were, and now that nightfall had settled in they had no choice but to take their assigned places on the hard-packed dirt floor and try to get some sleep. That first night spent at the camp was a night filled with doubts and suppressed fears while in their dreams they saw the bright red Communist star of the soldiers' uniforms emblazoned on everything.

There was no hunger here, no struggle for survival—not physically. But in this peaceful, springtime setting on a large, well-cared-for farm, the struggle for possession of human minds was being waged and usually won by a predatory doctrine. Father Scully's admonition to travel with groups or travel at night finally became frighteningly clear as groups of young male orphans were shuttled into the camp with regularity. Children who had been ejected by the war into the same bottomless world were easy prey for the North Koreans. The Communists found soft targets in the defeated and terrorized minds of the orphaned boys, and though the children of the camps had no choice, most of them found safety in cooperation, found a tiny glimmer of acceptance in what had been a pitiless, forbidding world. Most of them clung to obedience in the camps the way a damaged ship finds solace in an enemy harbor: simply grateful to be saved from sinking.

At one time the farm itself had been some landowner's dream of prosperity. The main house was large and warm with rooms that once ushered in sunlight, rooms that had bustled with the daily activities of a family that understood the land. Now the rooms were filled with groups of boys sitting in rigid attention as uniformed, unsmiling instructors presented them with their first lessons in the "beauty of obedience." Rooms that had echoed with the laughter of a farmer's children on summer evenings now resounded with the sharp, frequent "whack" of the instructor's baton across the backs of children who offered wrong answers to his questions. Several other buildings near the main house were converted into classrooms and sleeping quarters; the entire complex of what had been a family's existence now nurtured the vulnerable children who had lost everything—except their desire to live. The house commanded a restful view of three expansive rice fields that shimmered bright and green in the spring sunlight. Fanned out below the house, the fields were now training grounds for children being taught the paralytic concept of working for the good of all before working for one's self. Every morning after a few hours of classroom instruction, the fields would see the orderly migration of boys dressed in white muslin clothing moving in to work the rice crop. Each boy had an assigned task and each boy learned early that his job would be done properly or he would suffer; and suffering, they knew, always meant pain. Their reward for obedience was an occasional extra ration, or a terse compliment in front of the other boys. They were taught to be ever-alert and watchful of any activity among their group that was out of keeping with their instructions, and spies and informers were rewarded better than anyone. It was a dual-edged lesson in how to achieve the most—and in never trusting anybody.

Young rice plants were systematically appearing in the fields, the hillsides around the farm were turning a gradually-deepening shade of green. The blue of the sky shone in brilliant contrast to the hues of emerald below. The green of the fields was speckled with the white of muslin and tiny circles of black that were the boys' heads, bent to their work. It was a scene of falsehood, of pseudo-serenity, finally exposed as a fraud by the frequent arrival and departure of military trucks off-loading supplies at a large thatch-covered shack at the edge of the fields. Bags of rice would be unloaded by one convoy coming from the North, and reloaded by another convoy heading south. Supplies of all kinds found their way to this northern farm that served as a clearing house for materials supporting the Communists in the south, and as an embarking station for groups of boys who had completed their "education" and were headed into the deepest reaches of North Korea and further on—into mainland China to live out the rest of their lives.

In the beginning, the prospect of being held captive was less terrifying than the possibility of being separated from one another. But almost immediately their fears were realized and they were placed in separate fields to work. Twice in the course of the first day, Yoon felt the sharp lash of the overseer's willow whip when he was caught anxiously staring into the far fields, looking for his brother. During the hours from sunrise to evening, their world was a sudden vacuum of anxiety, eased only at night by the sight of each other's faces as they lay next to each other, avoiding sleep.

"We have to escape," Yoon whispered the first night, his voice tight and determined. "We can't let them separate us anymore." He lay awake for a long time, realizing that if he were caught being disobedient one more time, it would be Bok who would be punished. He closed his eyes, imagining the young one on his knees, his thin bare back exposed to the angry snap of the whip while Yoon was forced to stand and watch. He couldn't bear it. It was this fear—the fear of being used against each other, as well as the fear of being split up—that drove deeper the understanding that they would have to escape.

For the next two days the boys worked and watched, noting activities around the fields, watching the movements of trucks, keeping track of the number of soldiers. At night they lay awake and whispered to each other, trying to devise a plan.

"We should wait till your arm gets better," the young one said, pointing to the ugly gash on Yoon's arm, still in the first stages of healing. "We can't wait," Yoon replied firmly. "We have to leave as soon as we can, before they separate us for good. If they do that, we'll never see each other again."

Bok had decided that his was not an unpleasant job. In fact, there were times when he would only dimly realize where he was as he sat peacefully by his assigned floodgate, waiting for the order to pull it open or lower it again. The deep pools behind the gates had been stocked with fish for easy harvest and he would sit for hours, entranced by the moving light reflected from their shiny surfaces under the water. But on the fourth day, he sat by the floodgate, ignoring the fish in the pool and concentrating on his brother who was planting rice a short distance away, working his way closer and closer to Bok's field.

The over-seer, an unarmed soldier who kept a vigilant eye on the progress of the field, was on the far side giving instructions to a few of the older boys. His attention was temporarily diverted from the edge of the field closest to the road. He never noticed the slow-moving convoy that had picked up supplies from the station and was preparing to move south. Bok riveted his attention on his brother, waiting for the signal.

As the vehicles crawled by, the boy waved to the drivers who waved back in casual unconcern. The driver of the last truck stared forward, his concentration absorbed by the dust filling his windshield, making it difficult for him to see the road ahead. He never saw the two children dash onto the road behind his truck, their small legs pumping to keep up with the steadily-increasing speed of the vehicle.

Bok caught up with the truck and grabbed the chain on the tailgate, hanging on while his feet dragged the hard-packed road. Yoon clung to the bumper while trying to push the young one up over the tailgate. The deep cut in his arm made his grip on the bumper almost unbearable, ribbons of pain reaching into his hand. Bracing his shoulder under his brother's buttocks, the older boy lunged forward and finally boosted the boy over the edge. Bok quickly reached out over the tailgate to grab his brother's extended hand. The truck was picking up more speed and the older boy's legs worked furiously as he half-ran, half-dragged along behind, reaching up, trying to grasp the hand stretched out for him.

"Run!" Bok shouted. "Run faster! Give me your hand!"

He was screaming above the increasing whine of the engine as the driver shifted gears, and he leaned desperately forward, his body extended as far over the tailgate as he could get.

"Don't let go!" he screamed. "Keep running!"

Hot fingers of pain coursed from Yoon's freshly bleeding arm, making every nerve-ending in his body scream for relief. His left hand was weakening, slipping on the bumper until he was hanging on with raw finger-tips alone. Gathering all his strength, he jumped forward, trying to fling his good arm over the tailgate. The young one reached for him, felt the brush of his brother's fingers, but in a growing sense of desperation he felt the fingers slip from his grasp. Yoon lost his hold on the bumper as the truck lunged forward again, and he came slamming down face first on the road.

Picking himself up, he ran after the departing truck on skinned, bleeding legs, holding his injured arm and staring at the departing truck with wide, frightened eyes. In disbelief and terror, Bok watched the dust boil up in the road behind the truck, watched as it engulfed and finally swallowed his brother like an angry monster that had been stalking him, waiting for an opportunity to devour him. Bok never made a sound, but every fiber of his body screamed in protest, an agonized animal cry that rose from the center of his soul, rushing along his veins, battling for a voice. His eyes and mouth were filled with dust, his throat constricted and gagged, his whole body ached to stop the speeding truck. Squatting on his haunches, his knuckles turning white under the strain of an unreleased pain, he felt the howling emptiness deep inside, a vast crater suddenly blasted into his heart—and still, he could make no sound. The last tightly-held threads binding him to a lost family, a lost way of life, had simply vanished in a carnivorous cloud of dust and in those few tortured moments his life took a vicious new turn. For the first time he knew what it meant to be desperately lonely, and deeply afraid.

When Bok's legs began to tremble with the strain of his squatting position, when the fields of the camp were long minutes behind, he collapsed—never noticing the rough jostling as the truck bounced southward, never hearing the steady roar of the engine, his eyes seeing nothing but his brother's face before the dust covered him. Bok heard only the sound of his own voice yelling for him to run faster, don't let go, don't let go, DON'T LET GO! A coldness settled over him, a chill that began deep within, extending outward to his eyes. There were no tears, nothing to suggest the heat of pain inside—only a deep reflection of something ice-like and frozen. Closing the rest of the world off, his mind continued to work but now there was no frenzy, no desperation. Pushing his emotions forward through a tunnel of clear resolve, he formed the echoes of promise from deep inside, a promise kept alive with the pure, single-minded strength of a little boy who was no longer a child.

"I will find my brother," the promise whispered. "Someday, somewhere I will find him—I will find him!" The echo rang along the tunnel of resolve, reflecting back and forth across his mind, glinting in flecks of aching through his heart, each word sealing itself within the cold: "I...will...find...my...brother." With the disappearance of the only love he knew, the promise was chiseled into the emptiness that was left.

VI

Beyond the hunger of those first weeks after the loss of his brother, beyond the pounding loneliness, Bok Chang Kim discovered that of all the enemies to his survival, fear was the greatest. In the beginning it was the night he dreaded the most, with its hordes of moving shadows and choruses of sounds. The sounds and shadows had always been there, but never so big before, so loud, so threatening. With his brother to curl up next to, even on the coldest, darkest nights with no shelter, the fear was only a visitor, a guest he could let in or turn out at will. Now, fear crashed the gates of his bravery, and with no one there to face the intruder with him, he became small and powerless. The fear was the greatest challenge in his struggle to remain alive, and when he began to master the fear, he took the largest step along his road to survival.

Without the murkiness of imposed civility, with an innocent lack of understanding of social expectations, he reverted to a primal form of basic existence, with a cleverness born of instinct. He slept at night in hollowed-out trees, surrounding himself with a cushion of pine straw and leaves; he competed with squirrels for pine nuts on the ground, and devised ways of cheating bees out of their honey; with a heavy rock and a stick he stunned fish under small rocks in streams by slamming a larger rock on them so hard the little fish would be immobile from the concussion and float to the surface; and, using a method learned from his father, he broke off the tops of pine saplings, peeled back the tender bark to expose a moist layer of gelatinous pulp that satisfied his lack of fresh water. There were mulberry bushes covered with the cocoons of silk worms and he would gather them, remembering how the old women of Sok-Cho had done it—he would boil the cocoons, then carefully unravel the silk to expose the sweet, nut-like larvae inside, popping them into his mouth one after the other. In a hasty rush of remembering, the natural being emerged and survived within him. He never gave a moment's thought to the fact he was living like an animal. He knew only that he was living. It never occurred to him to hope things might get better, and the lack of yearning offered its own solace, leaving him oddly free to accept his life with a measure of peace.

He moved onward, always headed south, seldom seeing anyone. There were times when he stumbled across villages along the road and his heart would jump with the thought of a possible meal. But the villages were always deserted, and there was seldom enough food left behind to even encourage the rats to stay. He haunted the empty homes and streets in search of anything to eat, slipping in and out of vacant houses that always left him feeling like an intruder to someone else's private past. Though he was always hopeful and anxious when he came across a deserted village, he was always equally relieved to be gone.

Spring moved nervously into the warm months of summer. He sat quietly one bright morning on a hillside overlooking a tranquil hollow. He sat with his thin legs drawn up, his chin resting on his knees, his eyes bright with concentration on the few houses below. A slow, fragrant breeze heavy with the scent of the hills pushed through his dirty hair, creating the only motion around his immobile figure. He had watched the houses for over an hour, waiting for any movement, any sign of life. With the caution inspired by danger, knowing that enemy soldiers were in the area, he waited and watched.

The houses were battered remnants of a recent bombing raid, their roofs blown away, walls charred and blackened from fire; but in his continual search for food he never ignored anything, leaving no possible source unchecked. When he was convinced there was no one in the valley, he stood and quietly made his way down the hillside.

From the moment he pushed slowly into the first house, a keen sixth sense, a sense of human proximity, sent sparks of heat racing along his skin, causing the hair on his arms to stiffen. Without seeing anything or anyone, he knew he was being watched.

He froze like a deer, listening, feeling, smelling, posing himself for flight. Someone was in the room, and he slowly scanned the interior; the place was in shambles, piles of rubble pushed haphazardly against blackened walls, remnants of a family's lifestyle heaped in bits and pieces everywhere.

That was it; the rubble had been pushed aside, there were cooking utensils on the floor in a neat row. The house was being lived in. He was on the verge of darting back out when his eyes caught a movement from behind a mound of debris in the corner. Huddled so tightly together they were almost invisible, was a man, a woman, two children of about eight and ten, and a young baby that stared at him with wide, curious eyes. Bok let out his breath in a sigh of relief—refugees who were more frightened of being discovered than he had been. The look of relief on their faces reflected his own.

They gathered around him, the father talking rapidly with words that tumbled over themselves in relief. "We thought you were an enemy soldier," he said, his voice trembling. "I saw a group of them earlier up there on the hill. We were just going to find a place to hide when we heard you outside, and I didn't have time—I didn't dare leave my family..." He continued to rush through his explanation and when he had finished, the boy knew what he needed to do.

"You find a place to hide," Bok said. "I'll go check the path where you saw the soldiers."

He would never be certain why he felt instinctively like the self-appointed protector of these helpless strangers. Perhaps it was his instinctive need to be with people. Or perhaps, he thought as he ran toward the hills, it was the heart-wrenching look of fear they had in their eyes. He felt older than they, wiser, many steps ahead because it was the same fear he had been forced to conquer himself. He felt he had an advantage, like an older brother who doesn't mind exploring the dark because he isn't afraid of it anymore.

He reached the summit of the hills and instantly froze. Four Communist soldiers were approaching from the opposite direction, coming toward the valley. They didn't see him as he whirled around and ran back down the path, watching the man hurry his family away from the bombed-out house toward the latrine.

No! he thought desperately as he ran. He knew instantly that the latrine was the worst place to hide. It would be one of the first places the soldiers would look. But by the time he reached the bottom of the hill, the soldiers were coming over the top. It was too late. He knew they'd have to take their chances in the latrine.

There was a silent exchange between Bok and the father when they crowded into the foul-smelling latrine, the man's eyes saying, "I know, I know, but what else can I do?" The man looked around him frantically, trying to decide what options were left to them.

The latrine was fashioned of wooden poles lashed together around a deep hole spanned by two planks wide enough for good footing while the user squatted on his haunches. The hole was nearly full, ready to be emptied and used for fertilizer. It was a pitiful choice in hiding places.

In a wild hope that the soldiers wouldn't search the latrine, and if they did it would be for only a moment, the father made a crucial decision. Lowering the children into the mess, then helping his wife and the baby, he slipped in next and helped Bok slide in beside him. In whispers and gestures, the man orchestrated the dunking process, telling them they would have to put their heads under the filth and hold their breath if a soldier entered to search. As they all nodded in agreement, the man silently prayed that any search would be a brief one. He turned his head away from the desperation in their eyes, looking at the boy whom he knew would need no instructing—when the time came, he knew the boy would do what needed to be done. With his head straining upward, hanging onto the man's arm to keep his balance, Bok stared intently at the entrance to the latrine, listening to the sounds of the approaching soldiers.

Tremors of fear rippled through the family as the sound of footsteps came closer to the huts. Muted voices drifted across the hollow, punctuated by moments of casual laughter. Sounds outside became the embodiment of horror, every twig snap, every boot scrape and voice roared with a volume produced by naked terror. Bok sank lower in the sludge, pulling himself inward, trying to become invisible.

The baby had been still and curious, but as the tense moments went by the child began to squirm while the mother struggled silently to keep the baby immobile. Pushing and twisting, the baby finally began to whimper. The mother looked at the child and whispered softly into its ear, her eyes growing wide and frantic as she tried to soothe the child into silence. The whimpers grew louder, and the father took the baby in his arms, rocking it quietly. The whimpering continued and one of the crunching footsteps stopped abruptly nearby. The father looked at his wife in helpless frustration, the desperate look in his eyes telling her what he had to do, the agonized expression in her eyes answering that she understood.

When one last attempt to quiet the child failed, the father looked at his wife again, saying "I'm sorry" with his eyes. Then he clamped his hand over the baby's mouth and nose as he slowly lowered the struggling infant into the maggot-infested sludge.

Staring down at the spot where the baby disappeared beneath the surface, he held the child firmly, silent tears coursing down his cheeks. Even after the small movements stopped he kept his eyes on the surface without bringing the baby back up. In the father's mind, in those few moments there was no latrine, no terrified family, no soldiers just a whisper away. For those brief moments, there was nothing for him but the lifeless baby in his hands.

The soldiers had fanned out through the hollow, systematically searching the homes and shacks. The nearby footsteps came closer and the fear inside the nauseating pit was a thing alive of itself, feeding on the foul air. The soldier was only a footfall away from the entrance, and the family breathed deeply and prepared to submerge when they heard another soldier call from across the compound. The soldier casually turned and walked back toward the voice, and after several minutes of retreating conversations, there was silence.

Finally feeling the return of his senses, feeling the huge crush of living in the wake of the death of the child, the father hung his head in silence, and softly wept.

For two more hours the group waited in the latrine until they were absolutely certain the soldiers were gone. They emerged slowly from the filthy hole into the warm summer air that felt unnatural in its cleanliness, as if the entire world should be reeking with the stench of fear, the foulness of death. The father was the last to climb out, carrying the lifeless baby in his arms. They stood numbly staring at each other, the stinking waste beginning to cake in patches over their bodies. The father finally motioned them away with his hand, absently indicating a nearby stream. The grief-stricken mother guided her children to the water. Bok stayed back, watching the father who seemed to have lost track of where he was. Hurrying to one of the out-buildings, Bok quickly located a discarded spade and dragged it back to the man, who blinked down at him. He took the shovel from the boy and walked back into the latrine.

Nearly an hour later the man walked out, dropping the spade outside the latrine, his arms empty.

They cleaned up together at the stream, then sat in morose silence and ate part of what little food they had left. The sun warmed their backs, a friendly breeze tugged at their faces, and birds sang a background of music that seemed glaringly out of place, everything beautiful appearing as a badly-timed effort by a guilty world to apologize.

Shortly after the meal, the father handed Bok a few rags that belonged to one of his children, along with a bit of food wrapped in a cloth. "You'll have to leave," he said, placing his hands on the boy's thin shoulders. "I don't have enough food..."

There was no need to explain. Bok understood, never having expected to move on with these people. He looked into the man's face with eyes that didn't question, didn't condemn, knowing that neither would serve any purpose.

The images of the day had burned into his mind like separate brands of fire that became one searing understanding: man will do whatever it takes to survive, and there are times when the weak must die that the rest might live. Grasping the concept with the clarity of primal perception, Bok was introduced to an ancient law, lived and relived through the ages in its purest form when a man is forced to become an animal.

Bok got to his feet, thanking the family for the clean clothes and the food. Facing the father and looking into the sad, defeated eyes, he straightened his shoulders for a moment, then deeply, slowly bowed. A sound escaped the man's throat, something small and strangled and painful, and he turned quickly away from the boy's gesture of respect. He didn't see the boy as he pulled the bundle of rags close and walked quietly away.

VII

There were times when he tried to remember what it had been like before, tried to recall what it felt like to be just a child again. His small, round face would look puzzled, his forehead creasing in a question, his dark head cocked to one side as he concentrated on those days, trying to think—What games did I play? What kind of food did I like? What did I really do all day? At times, he couldn't begin to imagine that he had ever done anything different, had been anyone different than who he was now. When he thought of his brother, which he did continually, he thought of him as someone that had always been with him; there was no future until they were together again.

Though he had tried to heed Father Scully's warning about traveling only at night, the selfish beast of hunger that gnawed at him in the weeks after leaving the family at the latrine pushed him onto the road whenever he could manage the strength. He reached a point where he no longer cared where he was going, and no longer knew whether it was night or day.

By the time he was picked up by a passing patrol of Communist soldiers, and by the time he awakened in the back of a truck full of other captured refugees, he allowed himself to lose consciousness again, wondering distantly if they would feed him before they shot him.

In those first few hours of captivity, before the derangement of hunger had dissipated with a few small bowls of rice, he was only dimly aware that he was among familiar faces. He could hear Father Scully's voice but had difficulty focusing on his face. He could hear the old sooth-sayer and wondered if by some incredible chance he might be home in Sok-Cho. But with the returning of his lucidity came a clear grasp of where he was, along with the realization that many of the villagers of Sok-Cho had been rounded up and brought here also.

The camp was located on a bare, shrubless knoll that nestled between distant rising spears of mountains. Nothing grew on this windswept piece of ground that sat like an open, festering sore on the cool green face of the mountains fringing the knoll on three sides. To the south, the ground slipped away with steady erosion.

There were no shelters here, no latrines, just masses of humanity contained in an elaborate tangle of barbed wire. People huddled on the ground in groups, large and small. The trampled khaki surface of the compound was pock-marked with holes dug as shelters where people lived like animals with a piece of cardboard or scrap of tin for a roof. The place was crowded with old women, women with children and babies. The place smelled of death and dying more than it did of life, and the life it smelled of was rotten, covered with filth.

The only source of water was a small stream that ran through the center of the compound. The cooking and drinking water was drawn from a large hole dug at the upper end of the stream, with the remainder of the feeble trickle used to wash clothes and defecate in. Everyone had long since foregone any sense of modesty, and at any time of the day or night bare behinds could be seen squatting over the creek. But the stream was sluggish and much of the waste remained washed against the banks where it reeked of decay, adding to the dismal pall of captivity.

The old sooth-sayer had swept him up the first day after his arrival, insisting he share her dug-out home. There had been a gentle, well-intended squabble between her and the priest for the guardianship of the boy, with the priest finally smiling in good-natured acquiescence.

"The child needs a woman's hand," she croaked, defiantly

thrusting her chin upward as she stood toe-to-toe with the tall man.

"He has suffered a great deal, old woman," the priest said. "He needs the consolation offered by the gospel."

She sniffed and stamped her rag-bound foot. "Bah! Go peddle your foolish god to someone else, priest. The boy stays with me."

Father Scully smiled, a tiny flicker of his old joviality lighting his watery eyes. He grabbed the old woman by the shoulders and hugged her in mock roughness. "You are a delightful old fool and God loves you as much as I do!"

She pushed herself away from him pretending irritation. "Go away!" she said, trying not to smile. "The boy is hungry and your loving god is silent, as usual, about why we are all starving in this place. Go talk to him and don't come back until he talks to you!" She turned away in a pretended huff, trying to hide the blush of pleasure in her weathered old cheeks.

Of all the grinding discomforts he experienced at the camp, it was the wind Bok hated the most. Without the wind, even the sub-zero temperatures might have been tolerable. Rushing down from the mountains on three sides of the barren knoll, its shrill voice and bitter fingers tore at everyone's senses until they nearly went mad with the fear of freezing to death.

He stood in the food line in front of Father Scully, pulling a thin cotton rag tighter around his shoulders in a futile game of tug-of-war with the wind that he never won—he always kept the rag, but never kept warm. He shuffled slowly forward in the line of pitiful-looking prisoners, all of them sharing the battle with the gusting wind, all of them equally ill-equipped. They were all dressed like him in the uniform of the refugee—layer upon layer of rags wrapped from head to foot. It was a procession of disheveled mummies with only the dark, frightened eyes showing between slits in the torn cloth.

They held tin cups, wooden bowls, or merely held out their eager hands to the soldiers scooping out the scant cupful of raw rice. Over the winter, the handful had become increasingly smaller, and now during the last fierce blast of winter before spring, the rations of rice had been cut again, leaving everyone with next to nothing on which to survive. The war was going badly for the North: supplies were running low, and the first to suffer—as always—were those in concentration camps.

Father Scully nudged the boy, gently urging him forward. He reached the soldier and looked up into the man's irritated eyes, knowing there was a scowl of disgust under the heavy woolen scarf that covered the lower half of his face. The soldier hated the wind too, and was anxious to get back to his warm tent and hot rations. Bok held out his battered wooden bowl. The soldier dropped the tiny portion inside and jerked his head to get the child moving. Bok moved to the side and waited for Father Scully. When the priest stepped up and held out a small, dented cup, the soldier leered up at him and hesitated. There were no words exchanged, but the obvious loathing for the American priest was mirrored in the soldier's eyes, and when he reached forward with the scoop of rice, half of it fell into the cup and half of it on the ground. Ignoring the guard's scornful laughter, Father Scully dropped to his knees anxiously searching the frozen ground for as many grains as he could retrieve.

As if in open challenge to the shrinking rations, Father Scully routinely gave most of his own portion away to the others. He defied the grinding hunger he felt continually, and in a cruel mockery of his willingness to suffer, the guards derived a perverse pleasure in making him suffer even more.

Squatting next to the feeble cooking fire, Bok told the old fortune-teller about the incident with an unemotional matter-of-factness. It had happened so many times before that it hardly warranted mentioning, but the woman clucked in disgust as she stirred the pan of boiling rice.

"Fools," she muttered. "But who are the bigger fools—the guards for their stupid cruelty, or us for expecting any mercy?" She shook her head and clucked her tongue, thinking of the famished priest and his near-skeletal face with the strange blue eyes. She sighed and looked at the boy. "And you," she said accusingly, pointing the stirring stick at him. "You've been asking around about your brother again." He was silent, feeling the vacant sensation of hunger over his entire body as he stared at the pot of thin rice gruel. "No one has seen him and you're afraid he's dead." She plunged the stick back into the pot, tightening her grip on a tattered shawl around her head as the wind battled her for it. She eyed him closely as she absently stirred the bluish liquid. Finally, she dropped the stick, reached out and pulled the little ball of rags to her, snuggling him in close. They huddled together for a long time, watching the fire struggle for life in the wind, like everything else in the camp. She coughed, her thin shoulders heaving under the shawl. Staring into the fretful fire, her eyes gradually glazed over, creating two smooth opaque mirrors that reflected twin drops of flame.

"Your brother is alive," she said, her voice thin and far away. "I don't know where he is, but I see that he lives." A gust of wind pushed the fire completely into extinction, but the flame in her eyes never faltered, burning steady and clear.

"On the day he dies—you will know," she whispered.

In the innocent pragmatism of a child, Bok was never hasty to believe the old sooth-sayer's prattlings any quicker than he trusted Father Scully's invisible god. Of the two, the old woman had come closer to predicting the destruction of his world through black wings and fire and swallows' tears, but she had no more answers to the question "Why?" than did Father Scully, and to Bok, a result without a cause never took proper shape in his mind. Until the pieces were made to fit, there was a permanent bend in his logic. Instinctively, he avoided any concept that couldn't be handled by at least one of his five senses. Though he knew the chance that Yoon might still be alive was not nearly as great as the chance he might be dead, Bok rolled the words around in his mind, testing them, examining them, warming up to them. He decided that it felt good to hope, and he sighed deeply, recalling their last days together, and even those memories were easier to live with— now that there was hope.

After his raging bouts of hunger on the road, the daily

handful of rice seemed like an abundant feast to the boy, and he settled into the melancholy days and weeks without the one huge trial of trying to find food. But with the removal of the fear of starving, he felt the replacement emotion of an animal that is caged and fed. Of the two, he knew he would face the struggle to live, rather than fight the mushy, undefined, lonely spirit of a captive. He wanted desperately and continually to be free, even if it meant he would die of hunger.

He watched the meager activities in the camp with the pragmatism of someone who is no longer shocked by anything. He watched with casual understanding as parents of young girls bartered with the guards for extra rations in return for the sexual favors of their daughters. It was a constant daily occurrence, one that was so common as to be negligible, and the undeluded boy dismissed it with the rationale that these were people at least fortunate enough to have something with which to barter, when most others had nothing. He paid little attention to the ten- and twelve-year-old girls who knelt at the barbed wire and performed oral sex on the guards while the mother or father stood somewhere nearby, their backs turned, waiting for payment. Every day several of the girls would be taken out of camp to the tents beyond the enclosure where they would remain for several hours, sometimes for a couple of days. They would return looking old and weary, but always with more food and, on rare days, with cast-off clothing for their families. He watched as the parents tried to hide the humiliation, turning quickly away from their daughters after a terse thank you, or no thank you at all. The parents tried to cover the despair, avoiding their daughters' eyes, almost shunning them in order to escape the horrible guilt.

He watched other people in the camp, others with no daughters to offer, people who felt the hot grip of jealousy as they spurned the girls in obscure, hurtful ways. Frustrated and frightened, these were people who tried to rid themselves of some of the helplessness of their plight by forcing the girls to endure more guilt than they deserved. Bok knew from experience that these same people who pretended a self-righteous indignation, these same people who would turn their faces away and mutter "Tong kal bo" just loud enough for the girls to hear as they walked by, these same people who felt justified in calling a ten-year-old girl a "whore" were the very people who would be the first to offer one of their daughters if they had been fortunate enough to have one. He was never able to fully understand how one person could condemn another for merely wanting to survive.

Father Scully did what he could to try and stem the activity, tried to petition the guards over and over again when he saw another girl being taken to the tents, but he found an impenetrable wall of cruelty in one group, and furious desire to live in the other. Together, the two fueled each other, and the parents were his loudest and strongest adversaries in his futile fight to save the girls. Though he never stopped trying, he knew his protests were useless. The hunger was too great and the commodity of girlhood too valuable. This, too, was a price of war the Seminary never prepared him for, and the emotional strain of learning these things and coming to grips with them was exhausting.

During the endless freezing days of winter, Father Scully moved like a constant shadow among the people, offering what small comfort he could as people froze to death or starved in droves. He acted as a self-appointed arbitrator between refugees who squabbled over the clothing of a dead prisoner, stepping in resolutely and breaking up arguments that often turned violent. He worked endlessly with the sick, begging the guards for medicine and bandages he never received, staying by the afflicted until they finally died; rarely did the sick ones recover.

In all the stories from the Bible that the priest told the boy, the one that most reminded him of the priest was something about an "angel of mercy." The man was tireless, almost driven with a fanaticism that everyone admired, but few understood. His face continued to age, the skin clinging to the sharp bones like dry parchment, the circles under his eyes deepening, his fiery hair beginning to turn a sickly shade of yellow-gray. Father Scully was paying a price he felt he must surely owe, feeling that he had the least to offer a people who didn't even believe in God.

"Sit down and have the rice water, priest," the old woman barked at him one morning toward the end of winter. "You'll be the next to die if you don't eat and get some rest, foolish crane."

He folded his skeletal frame and sat heavily next to the boy, reaching his hands toward the fire. The priest seemed unusually agitated, even angry, and the old woman watched him closely as she handed him the warm rice water.

"So it finally catches up to you, does it priest?" He looked up at her hovering over him as she absently reached out and tightened the scarf around his scrawny neck. "Your god is still not speaking to you and you're upset with him, is that it?"

He smiled weakly, apparently having no strength for their usual verbal fencing match. "Do you know what tires me the most, old woman? It's the ones who give up. I discovered that they are the ones that take the most from me, because I try to fight their battle for them, and I can't."

The old woman grunted and sat next to him. "It's your own fault for trying to assume your god's responsibilities for him. You deserve to be exhausted and sick, you ridiculous old bird. What good will you be to your deaf-mute god if you die because you work too hard and you won't eat? Now sit still and drink the broth. Think of yourself for a change because no one else will."

He finally smiled, putting his arm across her shoulder and chucking her under her leathery chin. "Some day, my beauty, some day you will turn to God and tell him yourself you were only teasing when you criticized him, and you will beg him not to punish you for having such a wicked sense of humor. Some day, my sweet...!"

She pushed his arm away in a fit of indignation and grunted awkwardly to her feet, hurrying once again to hide the sudden flush to her face. "Old crane..." she mumbled as she waddled away.

The war grew steadily worse for the North Koreans, and with every diminished supply needed on the front lines, another ration would be removed from the prisoners in the camps. The wood-gathering details were allowed to leave the camp less and less often—they had to go too far to get what they needed—so wood was rationed now, too. The guards were growing increasingly edgy and short-tempered as spring approached. From somewhere far to the south, the sound of jet fighters rumbled like a far-off giant clearing his throat. Over and over again the rumbling reached the camp, but the guards paid no attention at first, behaving as though they heard nothing. With the first cold days of spring the planes began to get closer, finally visible just below the rain clouds rolling in from the south. The soldiers could no longer ignore them. There was a perceptible nervousness that increased with every new morning.

At night, Bok lay awake next to the old woman in their hole, wondering what the planes meant—would they come closer some day soon and bomb them, the way he had seen planes bomb hillsides and houses? Would they all be killed? Or perhaps set free? These were new, bitter-sweet thoughts to experiment with, rolling the ideas around in his mind. Up to now, there had been no question of being saved—they were simply there, with no moves forward or backward. He drifted off to sleep under the intoxicating elixir of "what if..."

Sometime in the night the rain came again. It wasn't the usual torrent that caused the stream to overflow, sending ribbons of decaying fecal matter into the dug-outs. Rather, it was an uncertain rain falling from a shy cloud that seemed embarrassed by the pitiful camp below, and hurried away, leaving the earth damp and cold. It was just enough to peck out a tentative greeting on the cardboard that covered the dug-out shared with a snoring old woman, barely enough to rouse the boy from a deep sleep. He lay in the half-world between wakefulness and oblivion, hearing sounds he distantly recognized. Above the gentle tattoo of rain he could hear men talking, sounds of scraping, sounds of heavy metal on metal...He floated back into a fitful sleep, a small, insistent curiosity jumping up and down excitedly at the back of his mind, trying to get his attention.

When he awakened just before dawn the boy could smell

the odor of a wet camp—damp earth, wet ashes from doused fires, a faint scent of the mountains in the distance, and the prevailing odor of the stream. He pushed the cardboard aside, rubbing his eyes to adjust them in the heavy blue light before sunrise. When his eyes focused, he gazed around at the slowly awakening camp and listened to the sound of coughing, harsh and full of phlegm; distant sounds of soft weeping which meant someone had died in the night; groans from people stretching to unstiffen their bodies; the distinct splash of men urinating in the stream. All sounds of familiarity, comforting and disheartening all at once.

The timid rain had moistened the earth just enough to allow a thick, blue mist to begin rising, and the world was shrouded in a heavy veil of moisture that chilled him to the bone. His clothing was damp, his nose was running, his teeth chattered as his vision extended on beyond the compound, beyond the barbed wire fence outlined in the weak light. Suddenly, his teeth stopped clacking and he involuntarily gasped and sniffed at the same time, putting a halt to his runny nose. His eyes widened in concentration as he tried to convince himself he wasn't imagining what he saw just beyond the wire.

The mist was a mobile thing, moving upward and outward, swirling gently around anything that stirred it, drifting languidly between the cold, menacing strands of wire. Standing motionless in the mist, appearing and disappearing in the fog, the boy could make out the figures of the guards. They stood silently, their weapons held casually in their hands. They were all there, all twenty-five of them, lined up outside the enclosure, staring in at the refugees. Behind them through the intermittent fog, he could see several trucks, their canvas tops pulled tight and secured. The tents were gone. Everything had been loaded onto the trucks during the night, and with a glimmer of recollection he realized what the noises in the night had been. The soldiers had struck camp and were prepared to move out.

He climbed from the hole and stood watching the guards, waiting for them to speak, to move, anything. They simply stood there in the mist, a long line of undefined yet startlingly real images. Little by little, the refugees began to notice the guards. In groups of twos and threes the refugees got slowly to their feet, crawled from under the heaps of rags, lifted pieces of tin or cardboard and emerged from beneath like bewildered grubs. It's because of the planes, the boy thought, his breathing becoming quicker with excitement. They're moving because they're afraid of the planes, and they're letting us go. They can't move us, there are too many—they're going to let us go! He looked around quickly at the others. They were all feeling the same timid hope. No one seemed able to comprehend the idea of being set free, not even enough to whisper their hopes to each other. No one spoke.

Father Scully stood a short distance away, rubbing his thin blue hands briskly together, the same look of bewilderment on his face. He cupped his hands and blew into them, trying to urge warmth into them. His pale, aging eyes kept a close watch on the guards from above his fingertips.

Turning back to the hole, Bok pushed the cardboard aside and began shaking the old woman. "Wake up!" he whispered loudly, his voice tight with enthusiasm. "They're going to let us go—wake up!" She awakened with the sluggishness of the aged, coming to awareness in slow stages. "What?" she mumbled. "What did you say?" His eyes were bright with animation, his smudged face was lit with the glow that went beyond hope—this was belief. They were being set free, he knew it! "I said, they're letting us—"

They all heard the order at the same moment, heard it reverberate across the camp and onward into the hills. One word that made eyes and mouths fly open, made hearts stop in mid-beat, one word that screamed through their minds, through their souls— "FIRE!"

The guards never moved, but the weapons in their hands came to thunderous life all at once, blasts of fire exploding from the barrels. Bok stood when the shooting began, staring in total disbelief at the fence, at the unreal spits of fire erupting in the fog, looking as if they were coming from nowhere, produced by no one. For the briefest moment, he believed he was the only one who saw the guards, the only one who could see the flashes from the weapons. He believed for an instant he had contrived this whole scene in his nightmares and perhaps no one had any part in it.

The screams of the refugees slapped him back to reality, back to the camp where the crowd of people had burst apart like a dandelion gone to seed. Scattering in all directions, screaming, crying, clawing to escape the hailstorm of bullets, their only thought was to get away, get beyond the fence. Stumbling, falling, crawling over each other, they were no longer human beings—they were crazed animals, trampling the fallen ones, running in circles, diving into any hole they could find, flinging themselves wildly against the barbed wire where they would be shot and left dangling by torn rags and flesh.

In those first brief seconds Bok was unable to move, paralyzed with disbelief. Blood was flying everywhere, people's bodies ripping apart, heads exploding, the earth near his feet kicked up with the steady impact of bullets spitting into the ground. A transformation had begun in the soldiers—a new, increasing animalism in their actions. He had a sudden remembrance of where he had seen the same behavior in the past: alone in the hills, he and his brother had witnessed a pack of wolves tearing apart one of their own injured companions. He could see the same wild, frenzied movements in the soldiers running back and forth along the fence, infected by the desperation in the refugees, hungry for more and still more killing, their eyes lit with the yellow light of blood-lust. And in all of the snarling, panting frenzy, there was but one small figure that didn't move, and his immobility made him oddly conspicuous.

From somewhere nearby, but seen in his stricken mind as coming from a great distance, running in long, slow-motion strides, the boy saw Father Scully coming toward him, the expression on his face one of immeasurable fear, not for himself, but for the motionless boy. He seemed to be yelling something above the ugly chatter of the weapons and only when the man was close enough to reach out with his hands did the boy hear his voice—

"My God! My dear God!"

The priest crashed into the boy, tumbling with him into the dug-out on top of the old woman who screamed in terror. The boy landed on his stomach, feeling the heavy "oomph" as the weight of the priest knocked the breath from his lungs.

Only when he was in the hole with the priest on top of him did Bok begin to feel something beyond his own shock, hear something other than the deafening thud of his own heart. He began to hear the soul-wrenching screams of women who saw their babies explode in their arms; he heard the gagging, strangling sounds of men who lay dying with wounds in the chest and throat; he heard the incoherent moans of others who lay dying, heard them call the names of loved ones; he heard the explosions from grenades that found their targets, spewing the contents of holes upward and outward in a blast of blood, dirt, bits of cloth and flesh. The sounds raged on, gathering together in his mind as one hellish scream. He began trembling and couldn't stop. Though it lasted only minutes, all of the hours and years of hell stretched together couldn't have been longer. Even as the evil monotone laughter of machine guns dwindled to an occasional chuckle, even then it didn't end. Short bursts of fire picked off a refugee here that raised his head, or one there that groaned in pain. Babies that sat in the midst of the carnage covered with blood, sobbing uncontrollably, were shot. Two more grenade blasts heaved the earth around him, sending trickles of moist earth onto his neck. Like the final notes of a brief, horror-filled symphony, the grenade blasts ended the massacre, leaving an unnatural, howling silence across the knoll.

He shook so hard he was certain that Father Scully would whisper for him to be still, but the priest said nothing. The old woman had clamped her hand over her mouth to keep from screaming, her eyes were squeezed shut, oozing tears of fear into the deep wrinkles of her cheeks, her shapeless old body vibrating in answering tremors with the boy. There was no sound from the compound. Nothing moved.

When he heard the engines of the trucks grumble to life,

heard the doors slamming and gears shifting, Bok knew it was finished. The soldiers had all gone and it was over. In gradually receding waves of fear he could feel the old woman's tremors lessen, then stop, leaving only brief, muffled sobs that wracked her body, but she made no attempt to rise. The boy turned his head to the side and tried to breathe, feeling the warmth of something seeping through his clothes, thinking the priest must have urinated on himself. He closed his eyes, trying not to breathe so hard—every sound he made seemed maddeningly loud. By the time he finally gathered the courage to speak, he could barely breathe.

The priest was unbelievably heavy.

"Do you think they're gone?" he whispered. There was no answer. He squirmed again, feeling the odd stickiness of his clothes. "Is it over?" There was still no answer and Bok became suddenly frantic, realizing something was wrong. He pushed and twisted, finally slipping from under the man, feeling the relief of weightlessness. He sat up, staring down at the man who still hadn't moved. The old woman pulled herself up with great difficulty, stiffened by old age and held down by fear. Together they stared at the priest, the silence between them more oppressive than the silence across the knoll.

Father Scully's torn, frayed cassock was drenched with blood from the bullet wounds in his back. His eyes were partially open, his face set in an expression of relief, an expression of accomplishment. He lay on his stomach with his head turned toward the boy, his mouth set in a half-smile as if he possessed a newly-learned secret. His pale, colorless face held the look of someone who had just been given the answer to a nagging question, and the answer was so simple, so clear, it was humorous. And though he knew the man was dead, Bok felt a curious envy as he looked at the face that was softer now, less angular. In death it was as though Father Scully had discovered something vitally important, something he had wanted to share with the boy before leaving, and now he felt oddly cheated. Bok sat very still, his body vibrating with a sense of something lost, his mind able to think of nothing other than his own clothing, soaked with the blood of the priest.

When he heard the sound, at first he didn't realize it was coming from the old woman. It was a soul-deep wailing that began as a soft moan in her throat, rising in volume and pitch until it became all the sounds of sorrow in the world. She didn't touch the man, her hands moving in slow gentle motions just above his body as she lifted her face to a sun long-since risen, and poured out her grief.

Her keening became all the love she had never expressed, all the secret hopes, all the fears and joys of a long life. It was a song of happiness so profound it could only be expressed at a moment of profound sadness. It was the ancient music of love expressed too late, of human need ignored too long. It was a sound that pulled the soul to its brink, forced the spirit to face itself and acknowledge the fact that a man does indeed die, but first—ah! But first, how he lives!

Bok climbed from the hole and stared around him. Set to the sound of the old woman's wailing, the sight before him rose in waves of heartache and desolation. He felt strangely elevated by the sound, weightless, without substance, and yet forever earthbound. He felt as though the woman's voice was telling him, "Look at him. Remember him. Look at it all, and remember..."

Of the nearly three hundred people who had survived the winter, Bok could see perhaps fifty who had survived the dawn. They made no sound, these wraith-like creatures slowly pushing themselves from beneath other bodies, from inside holes that had been missed by the grenades, from out in the open where they had pretended death to avoid dying. One by one they had come forth to reclaim their own. They too were weightless, and they too were observing the ancient ritual of healing. The old woman's wailing was a chant for all of them as they drifted about the blood-soaked knoll. Her voice was theirs, their grief was hers.

Piles of dirt and debris from the grenade explosions added an odd look of chaos to an almost-orderly scene: bodies lay flat with heads or arms or torsos torn apart; people hung along the fence like wisps of paper blown there by a humorless wind. The wind began to gust, raising its own voice in hollow accompaniment to the old woman's chant. He stared at the gates of the compound partially destroyed in the shooting and through which the refugees were leaving one by one, walking slowly southward. He thought of those first rare minutes before dawn, remembering the incredibly heady feeling of believing—truly believing—they were all going to be set free. He remembered the horrid shock of realizing they were all going to die, remembered the huge sense of betrayal that washed over him, drowning him in a sea of disillusionment.

He felt the giant, gnawing sense of having discovered a basic human flaw, a flaw that would leave him forever mistrustful of more than just one faction, one isolated group. On that morning, an inner door to the cathedral of trust that is every child's birthright came crashing shut with an echo that was almost a physical pain in his heart. Always, through the travesties of the war he had found his way to the source, had uncovered in himself a way to explain, to understand, to live through it. But this betrayal was an altogether uglier, more vicious hurt, a thing with no shape, a void in the universe of logic that defied understanding. A vital chamber in his heart had been rendered suddenly sunless.

Bok returned to the hole and sat next to the keening woman whose voice had assumed the tone of pure grief. The sound carried across the compound into the mountains and beyond. She reached every soul with her song, and the boy closed his eyes, allowing the essence of the grieving to find a place somewhere inside him, a place that was unformed, still embryo-like. Numbed from the pain and then suddenly forced to feel it in one wave of emerging emotions, he found himself unable to contain it all. Adrift in the overwhelming sensations, the boy stared down at the stiffening body of the priest. And in answer to an emotional beckoning that he hadn't heard with the loss of his parents, hadn't responded to with the loss of his brother, in a final acknowledgment of his helplessness, a helplessness he swore he would never feel again, he raised his face to the sky where Father Scully's god was so fond of disappearing to. And hoping that this god would see, he clenched his fists and wept.

By the time the keening finally stopped, the boy had been sitting motionless for hours. The sun was well into the afternoon sky and he dimly realized that he and the old lady would have to hurry if they were to have the priest buried by nightfall. Feeling the emotional exhaustion of having wept until there were no tears left, he stood wearily and waited for the woman to follow, but she didn't move. When she finally looked up, there was a serenity to her face, a long-vanished youthfulness suddenly appearing again.

"You go along now," she said, her voice sounding clear and resonant, totally unlike the croaking he had been accustomed to. "Go along with the others. I will see to the priest myself."

He frowned in concern. "You can't stay here," he said. "You'll die if you stay. Let me help you bury him and then you come with me." She shook her head calmly while he spoke, then reached up and gently pushed him away. Her smile was quiet, her eyes which he had once thought ferret-like and small were now large and soft, like the eyes of a girl. Once again he was struck with the impression that she too had learned a secret, that she had an answer to some question that he was being denied knowledge of. Again, he felt the need to find out what it was and he urged her to come with him. She shook her head and looked down at the priest, at his graying red hair moving in the breeze, at the cold blue hands.

"Leave the dead to the dying," she said softly, with a look of such love on her face the boy was astounded. She looked up at Bok and motioned him to get going. "Go along now. Your life is only beginning, the swallows have only now taken to the skies for you. Go away from this place. Go find your brother— and live. Live!"

When he had passed beyond the gates of the compound he looked over his shoulder one last time and saw her sitting there on the mound above their dug-out home, still a shapeless mass, still wrinkled and strange, but somehow no longer old.

He walked southward, lifting his eyes to Father Scully's heavens, hearing no voice from God—hearing only the distant thunder of war planes on the horizon.

VIII

In the first days after the camp, he had moved along the road south with a small group of refugees who were silent, withdrawn, immersed in memories much too raw to discuss. Though they had no food, there was little thought of hunger. Their bodies had been mercifully undemanding until they were picked up by a South Korean Army truck on its way south. It seemed that all the world was trying to find its way south. Bok climbed aboard with the others. Lying on his side on the cold metal bed of the truck he fell into a deep sleep, totally oblivious to the bone-rattling journey that bounced his body up and down. He lay with his arm under his head, matted hair clinging to his face in sticky strands, his mouth ringed with dirt, his lips dried and cracked, his eyes partially open in dreamless fatigue. Two scabbed and dirty feet hung at the ends of stick-thin, knobby legs. One hand flopped loosely against the bouncing bed of the truck as he slept, a fine-boned, skeletal hand that hinged on a skin-covered bone of an arm and resembled a small garden rake. A body that had been smooth and dimpled with the healthy fat of a baby was now a mere shadow of what it had been. But the physical emaciation was only part of the picture: there was no more softness to the child, no soft places to touch with hand or heart. His entire being was angular and boney, hard and craggy. His outward self was a mirror image of the rock forming within. The camp left him with a legacy of flint-hard perception, a cold understanding of his world. While man had bludgeoned innocent trust out of his spirit, nature had filled the ruins with sharpened instincts, bequeathing him to herself as she did all of the inherently strong of the species.

Amid the clutter of dying, hopeless countrymen, the seven-year-old boy pushed onward during the months of summer, finally separating himself from everyone as they stopped by the wayside in weariness, unable to move on. He shed himself of the burden of memories and thrust forward in simple, unfettered pursuit of food, taking advantage of everything nature placed within his short reach.

He spent several weeks in a deserted bunker on the shores of the Hwachon Reservoir, nursing swollen, infected feet while surviving on crayfish that lived in the shallow water close to the shore. Evidence of a gigantic battle earlier in the spring still littered the miles of shoreline around the huge lake, the angry whispers of men's lives lost still hanging in the air at night, floating over the water and dwelling in the tree tops.

With the first chilled winds of autumn, his feet healed and wrapped in layers of a shredded army blanket bound with strips of canvas, Bok set out again in single-minded drive toward Kangnung, feeling the persistent prodding of instinct urging him to push southward through the mountains before the heavy snows fell. Three long, empty months of trudging forward along roads pounded deep and hard by the heavy vehicles of war; months of hiding from passing patrols of Chinese soldiers, or rushing forward anxiously toward units of ROK soldiers who would offer bits of their own rations, pieces of clothing, and on one cherished day, a small pair of canvas sneakers that were inches too big but made wearable by rag stuffing.

On he moved, deeper into the Taebek mountain range, upward, upward, keeping the rising sun to his left shoulder and the north wind to his back, stopping by rare streams to fill a battered canteen. Nights were spent huddled under pine trees and listening to the voices that searched him out on the wind, whispered to him through the branches, nights of shivering loneliness punctuated by the distant howling of wolves that stiffened the hair on his neck and made him grateful for sunrise. Onward, onward, in a primal race against the heavy snows, staying mere steps ahead of starvation as he approached the summit. On he moved, even after losing his race with the snows, moving downward now, huddling in caves at night and during blizzards, pushing himself harder as the snows got deeper.

Eventually the hills began to smooth and flatten, eroding finally into the brown foothills of the Eastern Taebek range that stretched outward almost to the sea. The boy's gaze began to intensify and deepen as he stared into the distance, seeing a destination he had come so far to reach. Without understanding how he knew, Bok realized suddenly on a frozen morning in early spring, that he had made it. The undistinguished outline of houses in the distance was the village of Kangnung.

IX

So this is it, Bok said to himself, walking slowly down the main road. A journey of two and a half years ends here, in a village of empty streets.

It was a fishing village; much like Sok-Cho only larger, better maintained. Fishing nets were hung neatly on the outside walls of houses, everything was orderly and clean—but he saw no one. The docks were strong and well-repaired, with dozens of small, tidy fishing boats moored to pylons, rocking gently on the water that licked softly at the docks. The smell of the sea penetrated deeply into his conscious mind and beyond into the simple being he was, making his hunger even greater—he was close to the source of it all, and his body responded with insistence.

Still following the scent, he rounded a corner in the oddly-deserted streets and walked directly into a man who startled him out of his prowling, nearly knocking him off his feet. The man stood calmly staring down at the boy, digging at his teeth with a thin sliver of bamboo. Bok said nothing as the man casually scrutinized him, his deliberate examination beginning at the scraggly hair, before moving gradually down to his feet.

"What're you doing here?" the man asked sharply, but the twinkle in his eye belied the sternness in his voice. Bok cleared his throat. "I was looking for food," he replied, feeling the peculiar strain of using his voice for the first time in so long. "I know that," the man said, smiling. "You look like a skinned rat. I mean what are you doing in Kangnung? How did you get here?"

In brief, choppy sentences, Bok explained his year alone, his trek through the mountains, feeling as he spoke the familiar vacant sensation that was the accompaniment to starvation. His legs were weak and he longed to sit down, but the smell of food was so close the aroma alone kept him buoyed on an invisible film of hope. The man's nose occasionally twitched, his frown deepening, and when he finished speaking the man turned and walked into his home, returning moments later with a huge bar of lye soap and an old army jacket.

"Go wash yourself," he said, his nose wrinkling. "Get rid of those rags and put this on. If you're going to join me for dinner, you're going to have to smell more like a human."

At the mention of a meal, Bok suddenly discovered a reserve of energy he wouldn't have thought possible. Thanking the man for the jacket, he stumbled to the nearby shore, hugging the bar of soap and the clean jacket close to his body. "And be sure to scrub your head!" the man called. "It smells like a pelican's ass!"

At the shore, he tore off the remains of his shirt and was removing his pants when he remembered the photograph. Carefully removing it from a pocket, he placed it under a rock to keep it from blowing away. Totally naked for the first time in months, the skinny, foul-smelling boy ran into the ice-cold water, gasping in shock. He rubbed the heavy bar of soap over and over his body, scrubbing his skin until it burned. He ran his fingers up and down his ribs, feeling the odd prominence of every bone, aware of the bones of his pelvis and buttocks with the same distant curiosity. He soaked and rubbed his hair, soaked and rubbed it again and again. He sat at the water's edge and worked sand into his feet to remove the worst of the crust, realizing with some surprise that he still had toe nails. He ran back into the water and rinsed, splashing and diving, feeling once again the marvelous texture of clean skin. Though he knew he would be covered with a thin, dusty layer of salt when he dried, he didn't care—the salt was clean.

Shivering with chill and hunger, he slipped into the jacket

which hung to his knees, feeling the rough warmth next to his skin. He rolled the sleeves as high as he could, making a heavy roll at each wrist. Slipping the photo into a pocket that he could button, he picked up the rags he had worn for over six months and with one last glance he tossed them into the sea.

"There used to be many people here," the man was saying between mouthfuls of rice and fish. He seemed pleased to have someone to talk to, and he tried pushing his conversation out over the mountains of food in his mouth. "Most everyone is gone now, just a few of us left." He took several more gulps from the wine bottle, his eyes twinkling with the gentle haze of good-natured drunkenness. He looked from side to side in mock conspiracy and motioned the boy to lean close. "You're not a spy, are you?" Bok shook his head emphatically, his eyes wide with the absurdity of the question. The man laughed and winked. "Good! Then I'll tell you a secret." Another huge pinch of rice popped into his mouth, followed by wine. "The reason you don't see anyone on the streets is because we all work at night..." another chopstick load of fish and kim-chee "...and we sleep during the day. Today is my day to stand watch while everyone sleeps. We take turns..." more wine "...lots of money. We all make lots of money," he boasted, throwing his hand wide in a magnanimous gesture, indicating all the food and drink "...if the Communists don't catch us and kill us—or worse, sink our boats!"

Even through the rolling waves of drunken fog, the man knew he had gone far enough, that he had told the boy too much already. He would have enjoyed telling it all: about the island a day's trip off-shore where he and the others smuggled supplies to a South Korean Army outpost under cover of night. Instead, he hiccuped and suppressed a yawn, reaching for another bottle of wine, settling himself back with a satisfied belch, scratching his belly. "And you," he said, "you say you think your brother might be here." The man shrugged and shook his head. "Hardly anyone is here anymore."

Bok reached into his pocket and showed the man his photo. He squinted in the light of the lantern, rubbing his chin in thought. He finally handed the photo back, shaking his head. "No one here like that. And so many refugees pass through here on their way south I wouldn't remember if I ever saw him. I know there's no one here like that now."

Though it was an answer he had expected, Bok felt the familiar sense of sinking he always felt with the answer "no." He put the picture away.

The man watched him with a smile, the wine making him drowsy. "You say you're from Sok-Cho?" Bok nodded without looking up. He was concentrating on each soft, sticky grain in his third bowl of rice. "The Americans are there now," the man said, and the boy's head jerked up. "That's right. There was a lot of fighting up there, lots of people killed, but the Communists are gone now and there is an American army compound there. Americans..." the man sniffed, with a sneer on his amiable face. "They laugh too loud, they drink too much, they all smell like a boat bilge..." then he grinned broadly and held his bottle in the air "...and they're all as ugly as a pelican's ass! Americans!" He belched loudly, scratched his crotch and pointed with the wine bottle to a sleeping mat rolled in one corner of the room. "You can stay the night if you like, as long as you don't snore like my poor dead wife, may the gods keep her."

The boy slept that night in a pleasant fitfulness, a comfortable agitation from having food in his stomach for the first time in so long. His veins and nerve endings sang with the remembered sensation of satisfied hunger, keeping him just below the surface of wakefulness most of the night. The man fell into a slumber deepened by the wine and snored in huge, resounding snarls until dawn.

Awakening with a hunger made larger by the previous evening's meal, Bok sat up with a stiffness in his muscles caused by the sudden jolt to his digestive system. The man was gently nudging him with his foot.

"Wake up my friend. The sun is up and I have slept too long again, such a lazy dog! I have to do some repairs on the mistress." Bok stood up, pushing the sleeves of his jacket up above hands that reminded the man of chicken's feet—pale yellow and meatless. "Now," he said in a voice that was accustomed to giving orders, "come with me. I have something for you."

In a shed next to the man's house, hanging from the ceiling in several neat rows, were dozens of dried mackerel. The pungent, papery aroma of the sea filled the hut and the ravenous boy felt his stomach begin an insistent rumbling. "You'll need some food when you go—it may be a while before you reach Sok-Cho." The man untied a fish that was half as large as the child himself, wrapped it in a cloth that smelled of old fish scales, and tied it with a length of twine. He presented it to the boy, whose eyes were wide with gratitude. There had never been a mention of Bok leaving, but with the understanding of human nature derived from years of watching people, the man had known the boy would be going. And with a kindred knowledge, Bok had known he would not be staying, had known he must return to Sok-Cho in the feeble, persistent hope that his brother might have found his way there. With the enemy gone and people returning perhaps Yoon was already there. He took the fish and bowed, thanking the man for his generosity.

"I have no money to pay you for the food and the jacket," Bok said, "but I'm a good worker and I can help you on your boat. I can help do repairs or clean up for you." The man laughed and roughed up the boy's hair. "Your offer is a big one and I thank you," he said, "but I have no need of a skinned rat on my boat, and you have a long journey ahead of you. You need not concern yourself with debts you do not owe. You need only to be on your way."

Bok bowed again, and the man shouldered a heavy canvas bag of tools, striding away toward the docks. Stopping suddenly, he turned and grinned. "And take the soap with you!" he called.

It didn't occur to the solitary traveler to puzzle over the strange village of Kangnung in its emptiness and quiet, with its windows and doors closed against the hordes of desolate refugees that passed through her borders. He gave no more thought to the men of Kangnung who lived only at night, like subterranean creatures who took their boats and their lives to sea during the darkness, leaving an empty harbor that kept its secrets well and waited for dawn.

Though he was alone again, he felt no sense of loneliness. Freedom and all its attendant possibilities pulsed around him, through him, fluttered along the road with him like the beating of heavy wings. The silver mantle of the sun rushed before him, warming him, welcoming him. The same evil wind that had terrorized him before became a breeze that stroked his face with a loving hand, bringing with it all the heady fragrances of an expectant world ready to burst into bloom. A weary world, ready for any kind of new beginning.

X

Where before there had been a hollowness, a shapeless unhappiness whenever he came upon a blackened, bombed-out house, he faced these shattered structures now with a calmness of spirit that even prompted mild curiosity. A full day's walk from Kangnung he came across one of the gaping phantom homes sitting like the square skull of some giant creature left eyeless and toothless by an indescribable disease. He approached the house with interest, taking into account its roof which was still partially intact, and most important, a nearby well with a pump. Even after being fiendishly conservative with the bits of fish he ate that day, he was now terribly thirsty and the well pulled him forward like a fleck of iron to a magnet.

The pump worked with no priming, letting the boy know it had been used recently, which was no surprise. The house sat only a short distance off the main road and the ground around the house was trampled smooth by countless rag-bound feet. The interior of the house had been pushed smooth of clutter, and there were small blackened circles here and there across the dirt floor that had been cooking fires. In its destruction, the death's-head house had served to shelter far more people than it ever had while alive. And now there was one more, a single presence. For the moment, he had food, he had water, he had the remnants of a roof over his head. He settled himself against a wall that sheltered him from the wind, curled into a tight ball and fell asleep.

It is a sense that exists in wild animals, seldom finding

place in the distracted, unfocused mind of a human. This sixth sense, a sense of proximity, awakened him later that night with a quiet alarm through his nerves. He opened his eyes without moving, allowing his eyes to swivel and roam as they scanned the interior of the shack. It was too cold yet for crickets, too soon for the owls. There was total silence, disturbed only by the boy's breathing. His eyes glinted in the dark as he searched the blackness looking for whatever it was that had awakened him. There was no moon and only scant light from the stars. The inside of the shack was in total blackness, the world outside bathed in a deep contrasting blue and within the blue, framed like a portrait in the entrance, was the figure of a young woman.

She didn't move, made no motion to enter, but he instinctively felt she had seen him and he sat up slowly. Her head never turned and he knew she was staring at him. "Are you alone?" she asked softly, her voice brushing his ears. When he didn't reply she stepped into the house and walked toward him, her movements smooth and sweepingly soundless. She dropped a small bundle on the floor as she approached with the weary, road-sore movement of a refugee, and Bok felt himself unbending the coiled spring of caution as she sat next to him. "You're alone then," she said. He saw the tiny flash of white teeth as she leaned her head back against the wall and smiled. She pulled her legs up, making a tent of her long muslin skirt; then with a sigh she dropped both arms on the tent between her knees. With her thin legs outlined in the fabric, drawn up like a little girl's, she moaned with fatigue and wrapped her hands around her ankles. It was an unconscious, natural movement, and as simple as it was, it disarmed him and made him begin to relax.

"I've been walking for hours," she said in a soft breathless voice that soothed and pleased him. "I saw the house and decided to get some rest. I couldn't see anyone and was about to come in when I saw your eyes glint in the dark and I just about turned and ran—I thought it was an animal at first." She smiled again and pulled a heavy woolen shawl tighter around her slender shoulders. "But it was a different sparkle and I knew it was a person. I stared at you until I could see you were just—just you!" And she laughed. A tinkling, rippling sound that began at the top of her voice and trickled downward in cascades of soft merriment. It was a sound he hadn't heard for many, many months. It fell like rain all around him, a sweet, unfamiliar rain that quenched something parched and vacant inside him and he listened to the sound with the open wonder of a remembered secret.

She talked for a while in the same pleasant resonance, telling him her name, Sook, and of her long walk from Kangnung, of how she hadn't seen a vehicle on the road since leaving the village. She knew there were military trucks headed north to the American army compound and she had hoped to catch a ride on one of them. As she spoke, Bok watched the barely-perceptible outline of her profile, delicate, with high, smooth cheekbones and a thin, narrow nose, unlike many of the girls he had seen. Her hair hung in loose wisps that had escaped a tight roll at her neck and she used a fragile-looking hand to push the hair from her face as she spoke.

"Do you live in Kangnung, Sook?" he asked, wondering if he had just discovered one of the elusive denizens of the village, but she shook her head and stared at the blue darkness beyond the entrance.

"I came to Kangnung on an army supply truck from Pusan. I've just spent the last two weeks on a little rock island about a day's boat trip from Kangnung. And now—well, now I'm going to Sok-Cho, but I hadn't planned on walking all the way, goodness no. Just look at my shoes, they won't last another day at this rate."

"What were you doing on the island?" he asked, interrupting her steady prattle. She didn't look at him, kept her eyes somewhere in the darkness.

"I went there with the boats," she answered, "and just look at my skirt! All frayed on the bottom..."

"Yes, but what were you doing out there?" She began to sniff the air, straining her head forward. "Is that fish I smell?" she asked. He reached beside him and produced the mackerel, offering it to her. He saw her teeth again in the dark as she smiled and talked while she ate, her chatter filling him and pulling him upward to a strange, peaceful place in himself. He fell asleep while she talked, dreaming of boats in the Kangnung harbor, and rock islands in the sea, and questions that she never answered.

In the morning sun she was even more beautiful than he had imagined in the dark. As they walked along the road he kept stealing glances at her, trying to examine her. Sook smiled under his furtive scrutiny and tried to make it easier for him: she kept her face forward and continued to talk. When they sat beneath a tree to share more of the fish, she produced a cloth bag full of cooked rice and broke off a generous portion for the boy.

"From Seoul," she said in answer to his latest question. "I came from Seoul. I left during the first evacuation and I've never been back."

In her voice he could hear rivers and streamlets, the sound of water chuckling over sounding stones, some smooth, some sharp and pointed, her expressions flowing and bubbling in a duet with the expressions in her eyes. Exotic and shaded, like winged birds that would take flight at the slightest thought, flying upward in a flurry of long lashed and arched eyebrows, he believed her eyes to be the most beautiful thing about her, other than her voice. They were set between fine cheekbones that were covered with sleek, ivory-toned skin that flushed a shade of tawny pink when she got excited. He had an inexpressible urge at times to reach out and touch a finger to the tip of her delicate nose, just to see what it felt like—it seemed so small and ineffective. Her mouth was set in a permanent upturned expression of gentle amusement with a thin, pale upper lip underlined by a full, sensuous lower one. She was an uncommonly beautiful creature in an uncommonly ugly world and Bok found himself staring at her continually. The sight of her kept leaping into his mind, jostling something in his memory that had been far away but now rushed forward again with incredible force. When he looked at her profile with her hair done up in the heavy knot he remembered so well, this girl reminded him of his mother. Everything about her was a huge remembering—beginning with the laughter.

She spoke of simple things, of her childhood in Seoul as the daughter of a doctor. Only 13 years old when her father had been sucked into the jaws of the conflict, she and the remainder of her family had been forced to flee Seoul with the thousands of others that choked the roads heading south. She spoke about his death only briefly, flying away from the subject as easily as her eyes would flutter to new expressions. "That was two years ago," she said quietly, a gentle distance forming in her eyes. "Almost a whole lifetime ago." Sook looked at Bok and smiled wistfully. "I have a brother, too," she said. "In fact, he looked a lot like you, only not so skinny. When I saw you in the shack last night I thought of him. He was smart and so much fun to be with, but oh!, how he hated getting his hair cut, and he hated taking a bath. I used to scrub him myself with a big bar of soap like the one you have in your pocket—where did you get that anyway? Soap is so hard to find..."

He loved her way of doing that—changing the subject so effortlessly. He told her of the man in Kangnung, of his nearly being starved and of the man's kindness. "He gave me the soap," he said innocently, "because he said I smelled like a pelican's ass."

She stopped still in the road, threw her head back and laughed with total abandon. A delicate hailstorm of mirth that tapped and rattled against his heart, making him smile with pleasure and bewilderment. He was glad he had made her laugh, though he had no idea what had been so funny. Sook reached out and took his face in her hands and rubbed his cheeks vigorously.

"So he gives you a big fish and tells you to fly away." This sent her into a fresh wave of rippling laughter as she wiped the tears from her flushed cheeks. "My little pelican," she said, pinching his ears. "My funny little pelican."

Her laughter touched a part of him that had been deserted for so long that the feeling at first was almost a hurting. But it was a tender thing, and as they walked up the coastal road under a sky thickening with impending rain, he felt a part of him turning to her the way a sunflower follows the sun.

They felt the grumbling vibrations from the truck before they heard it coming from behind them, and Sook took his hand and stepped to the side of the road. The truck was still somewhere in the distance. She watched and listened intently.

"An army truck," she said simply, her voice still soft but somehow more firm.

"That's good!" Bok said. "Maybe we'll get a ride." Her face was still the same, the same skin, same smile; but something in her eyes had changed and the boy looked at her curiously.

"Oh, we'll get a ride, pelican," she said as she reached up and removed the pins from her hair. "If it's an army truck, we'll get a ride." Her long, jet-black hair tumbled down her back in soft deep-blue waves, fraying out just below her waistline. She removed the heavy shawl and tied it around her tiny waist and unfastened the first few buttons of her cotton blouse. Pushing the hair pins into her little bundle, she calmly walked up the road, her body moving with a slightly altered rhythm. Her head was tilted in a different way, her arms no longer moved freely. The alterations in her demeanor were so slight, and yet they seemed to change her completely. She had assumed a totally different form in a matter of seconds—especially with her eyes: they no longer resembled birds in flight; now they were the eyes of a refugee.

The truck came closer and Sook kept walking. When it rolled rapidly past them, sending up a swirl of dust that made him cough, his heart sank. "They're not stopping," he said. The amusement on her lips had been replaced with a quiet cynicism, a gentle smirk. She said nothing. She had seen the soldier's face in the rearview mirror on the passenger side.

There was a squeal of brakes, a clanging of empty fuel drums toppling against each other, and the truck momentarily disappeared into its own gorge of dust as it came to a heel-digging stop. Sook's smirk deepened. "Come on, pelican," she said softly. "Let's go meet some Yankees."

The soldier on the passenger side had stepped from the

truck by the time the dust settled and he stood with his hands on his hips as the two approached. "Helloooo, mama-san!" he said with a side grin. Dressed in the warm brown wool uniform of the American army, the man looked massive standing next to the truck. His skin was pale, reminding Bok of Father Scully, and his eyes were blue, but not the gentle blue of the priest's. These were a hard, ice-chip blue that didn't smile when his mouth did. Bok was uneasy in his advance toward the American, but Sook gripped his hand and walked smoothly forward, her hips swaying.

"Hey, mama-san," the man said, using awkward hand gestures as he spoke, "you go Sok-Cho?" He indicated northward. "Sok-Cho, yes, baby?" The girl smiled a type of smile she had never shown the child and nodded her dark head. The man grinned and stepped aside to let her into the cab. As she stood on the running board the soldier placed a huge hand on her rump and rubbed. "Oooo, nice kung dingi, baby!" Bok stared with wide, intense eyes at the soldier, who turned and scooped him up in his arms. "You ride in back, boy-san."

"It's all right, pelican," the girl translated, "they want you to ride in back, that's all."

As the truck lurched forward Bok situated himself close to the cab of the truck out of the wind, looking up at the sky between the steel rungs that reminded him of the skeletal ribs of a huge cow. The back of the truck was uncovered, the empty fuel drums clanged with irritating regularity, and the whole truck smelled of spilled diesel fuel. His discomfort was compounded by the incomprehensible change in the girl, and he leaned his head back with a feeling of dejection he could neither explain nor shake off. And on top of it all, he thought sourly, it's going to rain.

It was the first few raindrops that awakened him. He opened his eyes and dimly realized they weren't moving. The truck was stopped beside the road and he thought at first it had broken down. He stood up and peered over the wooden slats just as Sook and the two soldiers were emerging from the woods next to the road. One of the men was concentrating on the buttons of his pants while the other one—the one with ice-chip eyes—walked a few paces in front of the girl. He jumped a wide ditch that separated the road from the woods and left her to carefully pick her way across, gripping her skirt in one hand and bracing herself on the banks of the ditch with the other. When she reached the truck he motioned with his head toward the back. "You ride with boy-san now, honey. You understand, ride with boy?"

Sook looked at him with a cold stare that was at once alluring and derisive. "I understand very well—honey," she said, and took a distinct pleasure in the shock on the man's face.

"You speak English?" he asked thickly. She didn't reply, climbing smoothly into the back of the truck. The bewildered soldier tossed her bundle in after her and she began twisting her hair into its former roll. She was fumbling for the pins in the bundle when Bok spoke. "What were you doing in the woods?"

She smiled with a rapidly returning semblance of the smile he thought so beautiful. "I was paying for the ride," she said.

She didn't look at him, her slim white hands working skillfully with the heavy handful of hair until it was secured expertly at her neck. By the time this simple chore was completed and she had wrapped her shawl around her shoulders, the truck was moving forward again. She turned to him with a smile that belonged only to him and pinched his chin. "I'm hungry, pelican. Let's celebrate our ride into Sok-Cho and eat the last of my rice with some of your fish."

They huddled together for warmth as they nibbled on bits of food that suddenly tasted so good. And as the rain started to fall from a late afternoon sky, Sook pulled the shawl over the top of them, her wind-chime laughter mingling with the rain on her upturned face.

XI

"Oh! This will do just fine!" she said, as she looked around the hut with bright, determined eyes. He had looked at the one-room mud structure, one of the few left undestroyed in the battles that had practically leveled Sok-Cho. The place was littered with debris and dirt, and there was no oven. It was nothing but four walls and a thatch roof, but Sook saw it the way a young bird sees a possible site for a nest. Bok watched her as she set out to work, the back of her skirt drawn up between her legs and tucked into the front waistband to form balloonish pants, and a red rag tied around her hair. She turned and smiled at him. "Go!" she said, motioning him away. "Go find us some blankets and maybe something to cook with. I have work to do here."

Only when he was back out on the streets of Sok-Cho did the full impact of where he was finally settle in. At first all he had been able to comprehend was the huge military compound that covered what had once been open field. The base sprawled and hummed, growled and sweated with life, a continual din of activity in direct contrast to the pace of life he had known in the village. But the village no longer existed for him; there were no familiar faces, none of the neighbors he had known. There were different people here, refugees who had drifted into Sok-Cho after its liberation, looking for sustenance and protection in the shadow of the American army. They were all different, these people with no names and no past. He wandered the alleys and roads searching faces, looking for anyone he might have known before, showing the photograph to everyone he saw and asking, "Have you seen him? Is he here?" He was awash in a pool of shaking heads and terse frowns, feeling the sliding sensation of futility, familiar and heavy. He became almost manic in his search, stopping anyone that was old enough to speak and thrusting the photo at them. He searched in empty houses, examined any structure that looked even partially intact. His earlier memories of Sok-Cho gradually submerged in the reality of the Sok-Cho he searched now. The childhood Sok-Cho was gone and now he was frantically trying to find the one and only thing that would make the village have any meaning for him at all.

By the time he returned to the hut he was emotionally spent, physically hungry and painfully tired. But he had found two discarded military blankets that were only partially ragged and he found two woven sleeping mats. The hut was almost unrecognizable. She had cleaned and swept, had arranged some stones for a cooking fire, located a few cooking utensils in deserted homes, and when he walked in she hugged him.

"You did well, pelican," she said, taking the blankets and giving them a brutal shaking. For the rest of his life he would have a vision of her like that: a red scarf on her head, her skirt tucked into ridiculous-looking pantaloons, her small bare feet covered with dust. He would remember her face, shining like an ivory coin on a background of mud and firelight as she shook the dust from those first torn blankets scrounged from the wreckage of someone else's life.

He experienced a mix of emotions when they ran out of food after the first couple of days and Sook found a job at the bar. Though he knew they would be hungry soon and he knew she would be able to buy food with the money she made, he still felt that sensation peculiar to close attachments: a small, nagging sense of abandonment. She would be working only at night, she explained, so she would be with him during the day. He was quick to assure her that he was glad she found the job, that he'd be fine during his nights alone. It never occurred to him that he might be young enough to warrant protection.

So Bok watched her prepare for work every night, quietly enjoying the ritual of bathing herself as best she could with a bucket of water, standing naked and shiny in the firelight; then the chore of using the same bucket of water to wash her hair, brushing it vigorously until it dried in a long black drape shimmering down her back. She hummed to herself as she washed and brushed and tucked herself into worn-out clothes, a soothing melody that had no words, only feelings. By the time she was ready to walk up the road to the bar constructed for the American GI's, the look in her eyes had changed and that same incredible metamorphosis had taken place in the atmosphere around her. It was a change Bok never could justify or explain and there were times when he didn't wait for her to finish dressing. He would leave the house and wander the streets or head for the rocks by the sea, not returning until the small hours of morning. Sook would come home just before dawn, smelling of cigarette smoke and liquor, though he knew she neither smoked nor drank. She would smile weakly, remove her smelly clothes and fall into a deep sleep on her mat next to his. She never discussed her work and he never knew what she did to earn the money she brought home night after night, and after awhile he stopped wondering.

"The Yankees are usually generous," she offered once. "They smell horrible, they drink until they pass out, not one of them has even the manners of a goat—but they laugh easily and they spend lots of money." She didn't seem to hate the Yankees; she seemed not to think of them one way or the other. She simply disappeared into the mysterious, gloomy sanctums of the wood-and-canvas building every night and re-appeared before dawn. She was a closed world, an unreadable record of existence from the hours between nightfall and sunrise. She kept her night world and her day world in two separate chambers, never allowing them to collide with each other. Her nights were cast in shadows, away from prying eyes. Her days with the boy were her return to sanity.

She was a persistent well-spring of energy and she hounded him about things he had put aside as unimportant long ago: "You need a bath again, pelican, and you need your hair cut...look at those fingernails! Get me the scissors..." They spent their days together on the beach looking for shells—she loved the tiny ones, the perfect ones with no cracks or chips—and they hunted for crabs. They stretched and expanded inwardly during the warm months of summer, rediscovering during those sun-bathed days a few of the freedoms that are the exclusive rights of children. It was on one of those glimmering days when they sat on the rocks staring out to sea that she decided to tell him about her work. Having said very little to each other since morning, though she had been cheerful, she was quiet and preoccupied and he glanced at her often, watching her expression. "So this is where you ruined your brother's ear," she said, smiling and nudging him.

"I told you," he said, "it wasn't my fault. He got in the way. She laughed at his defensiveness, then sighed deeply and gazed out to sea.

"Pelican, I want you to know something," she said softly. He believed in that instant her voice could command the sea to be still or send it roaring to the corners of the earth. Bok looked at her profile, at her neatly-bound hair shining in the sun, at the unsmiling honesty of her face. "The things I do...," she began haltingly, "...the work I do at the bar...these things I do because I have to, not because I want to. Do you understand?"

He looked at her in bewilderment and she tried again.

"There are men—most men, in fact—who get a lot of pleasure from...putting their penises into a girl. They get so much pleasure from it that many of them are willing to pay girls for that feeling..." She hesitated, feeling clumsy and inarticulate. Bok came to her rescue. "You mean like the girls in the concentration camp? The ones who got sold to the guards all the time?" She nodded and tried to continue.

"Yes, something like that. The difference is, my parents aren't selling me—I'm selling myself." There was a part of this, she knew, he was understanding and she wished she had the courage to tell him the rest of it. But this boy, this intelligent, innocently hardened child was the one clean thing in her life and she wanted him to continue to think of her as something other than what she was. By telling him the truth, she felt she would be sacrificing the one look of adoration in her life, the one face of welcome, the one face she knew would never twist in contempt when she walked by, spitting in the dirt at her feet and muttering "Yang kal bo"—Yankee's whore. She ignored the spurns and derision of other people, none of it reaching her in the least. She knew what she was. She knew that by servicing American soldiers she had become, in the eyes of her people, worse than a whore. It made no difference. From the moment she had assumed her role in order to survive, Sook had considered herself a step below human. As far as she was concerned, it made no difference who she decided to service—men were men and a whore was a whore.

But this boy, she realized, didn't think of her as a Yang kal bo. He thought of her as family, a special link to civilization. She loved that feeling and wanted to keep it, but the duplicity of her two worlds was becoming an emotional burden; her innate sense of honesty was harassing her into sharing this with him. I may be a whore, she thought, but I'm no hypocrite. Sook straightened her shoulders and breathed deeply.

"Someday when you're older you'll remember what I said today, pelican, and you'll understand. On the day you remember what I am, please remember there is a price for everything. You'll always remember the price you paid to stay alive during this war. When you grow up and think of me, remember that I, too, was only paying a price."

They left the rocks that day and walked together in an isolated vacuum apart from their surroundings. She was unusually quiet, but she seemed more at peace and he was glad for that. By the time she had dressed and left for the bar, walking away in that strange, swaying walk, he knew she was feeling better.

He was surprised and curiously pleased when she came home early that night, knowing she'd never done that before. She was carrying something under her arm and he noticed she was limping. "It's called toilet paper," she said dryly in answer to his question about the roll under her arm. "The GIs use it to wipe their rear ends with after they finish in the latrine."

JOE PORCELLI

Bok was amazed. He'd never seen toilet tissue before. He began chattering about inconsequential things, but she seemed not to hear him when he asked her another question, and he wondered if perhaps she was getting sick. Her movements were slow, incoherent as she unfastened her skirt. Sook stood in a corner, and by the light of their one candle he watched her take a length of the strange paper, wipe it carefully across her bottom and between her legs. When she held the paper into the light he could see it was covered with blood. He said nothing, feeling a cold, unfamiliar sensation cross his heart. She cleaned herself for a few more minutes, moaning once, grimacing in pain. She finally moved toward her sleeping mat, which he made sure was ready for her. She collapsed onto the blanket in a thin, trembling heap. And after a few silent moments, he heard her softly begin to cry. Bok lay frozen, not knowing what to say to comfort her, not having any idea what could possibly be wrong. In all their months together he had never yet seen her cry. Feeling helpless, he floundered in the sound of her muffled sobbing. He didn't move, didn't touch her, just lay on his mat close to her, watching the dim contours of her naked body.

Long minutes passed within the gentle, aching sound of her weeping, until gradually, like the wilting of a flower, the weeping stopped and there was silence—a hurting silence only disturbed by their breathing.

"I know you're not asleep," she finally whispered in the silence. "I told you," she continued, "I tried to tell you..." Her difficulty in speaking was something else new to him. He could sense her isolation, could feel her reaching for an understanding that she knew he couldn't offer. But in the urgency born of raw human need she turned painfully and faced him, needing not so much his understanding or his caring. Right now she only needed to be heard.

"There are some men," she began, "who don't have any idea they are animals. They aren't bad men, not all of them. They're simply ignorant, less careful. They think that gentleness is weakness and they treat everything with brutality. I was with one of these men tonight. A big Yankee, bigger than most, took me behind the bar, bent me over, and forced his penis into my anus." The simple telling of the incident was fueling her, calming her, and after a moment Sook continued. "I know why he didn't take me into one of the back rooms where the girls usually take the men. At first I wasn't sure why, but I soon discovered the reason: he was sure I'd start screaming and he didn't want the bartender to get mad and throw him out." There was a frail, cold smile on her lips, a dim iridescence to her eyes that made them look pale. "I tried to pull away from him, because it hurt so much. I've never had anything like that happen to me before. Not in the entire three years has anyone ever done that to me. His hands were massive, big, ham-like things that gripped my shoulders so I couldn't move."

Her voice had lost all expression, no more rising waves or falling cascades. Now there was only a monotone sound that was barely a voice at all as she continued her story of pain and fear. The man had forced his way deeper into her, the pain becoming so horrid she thought she'd faint. But where the GI had expected screams of agony, he found clenched silence. Where he had expected tears of pain, he encountered dry cheeks and eyes squeezed shut to avoid the tears. She bit her lower lip and tried not to squirm because any movement increased the pain.

"I could feel it tearing," she said calmly. "I could feel the flesh around the opening separating, feel the sting in those cuts from his sweat. And you know something, pelican? It was at the very moment the pain was at its worst, at the moment I knew I couldn't stand it any longer because I would pass out from the agony—it was at that moment I knew I was going to make it, that the pain was finished, that it was over. And though he took his time with me, it was done. I could feel the blood running down the insides of my legs, but the pain was finished. I felt—nothing."

When the GI finally pulled away from her she was in an altered state, her mind retreating into itself on panic-stricken waves. He released his hold on her and she melted to the ground where she lay shaking and sick, listening to his heavy breathing as he wiped the blood from his penis with a corner of his shirt. She heard him groan with satisfaction while buttoning his pants, stuffing the soiled shirt inside. He turned to go back into the bar, hesitated as if remembering something, then dropped a few coins beside her in the dirt. He turned and walked away, hacking loudly and spitting.

"I don't know how long I was there," she said, and Bok found himself wishing she would blink her eyes. "When I finally got up, my legs were shaking so badly I could barely stand. The latrine was nearby and I..." She paused, her mind seeming to wander. He tried to see the expression in her eyes, but could only make out the two opaque ovals he had seen earlier. They were cold. They granted nothing. "I think...I think I came home after that. Yes, I came home. I realized he was only my first...my first man of the evening and I would be expected to entertain several more before the night was over. I couldn't do it. I just couldn't go back into the bar and pretend everything was fine. I stole the paper from the latrine because I knew we didn't have anything here for me to clean up with." Her lips twisted in a grimace that tried to be a smile, and she laughed in a way he had never heard—high-pitched and dead-sounding. "Can you believe it? Don't you think it's funny—the first thing I ever stole in my life is a roll of paper used to wipe shit from men's asses."

He had heard her swear before, but there was a profanity to her last words, a debasement so uncommon to her it was as though it came from someone else. He remained still, feeling suddenly that he was in the presence of a stranger. Sook sensed his withdrawal, and more than anything right then she needed him to stay close, just to be there in spirit if not in understanding, and she reached out to him, pulling him to her. She began laughing and weeping at the same time, laughing at how absurd her story must have sounded, and weeping because she had to. There was no place else for the hurt to go. Bok allowed himself to be drawn to her, wanted to be drawn to her, wanted somehow to help in a situation where he was helpless. She hugged him to her and began rocking back and forth. Everything he wanted to say got trapped somewhere between his heart and his mouth.

"It's all right, pelican," she whispered above the tears. "It's going to be all right. Don't worry anymore...nothing's wrong...it'll be all right..."

Neither of them realized she was singing a lullaby to comfort herself. They lay there together, a prostitute and an orphan boy, giving comfort to and taking refuge in their only resource—each other.

XII

There was a music box somewhere in her memory, a box made of teak wood from Japan. She could feel its gleaming lacquered surface when she closed her eyes. When she opened the lid in her memory, she could see glimpses of her past dancing just behind her eyes in smooth time with the fairy-like music floating from the box— sunshine through rice paper, rain in the garden, snow sparkling in moonlight, smooth silk dresses and soft patent leather shoes that glowed in candlelight as she danced, whirling and laughing with the whisper of silk rustling in the room. It was a childhood song, a simple melody with words she had long-since forgotten. It played over and over in her mind, carrying her deep into herself where she was alone in the fragrant world of her youth, away from the chaotic center of things that flailed around her like a maddening ring of jeering demons. Sook discovered she could open the music box anytime, anywhere, and drift away on the sound of elfin harps and be alone again—alone in the music.

The music box muted everything about the bar with its blaring, static-crusted radio, its bare-bulb lights shaded by empty coffee cans, smoke-and-liquor air, tables made of 55-gallon drums and wood tops, its artificial laughter, drunken groping hands, false kindness, its dingy backroom cubicles with their metal cots and sagging mattresses and their gruntings and slobberings and poor crippled substitutions for the act of love. In her mind, she whispered to herself that the world of the music box was real and the bar was exactly what it appeared to be—make-shift, thrown together from pieces of junk the way her life was now constructed. It would never occur to her that the soldiers approaching her for their purchased moments were attracted first by the gentle, far-away look in her eyes; and the soldiers would never know that what they were seeing on her winsome face was the memory of a child's song from a music box. So she didn't look back. She moved with a spiritual sluggishness through her days, slipping into the role of a Yang kal bo at night and furtively hurrying for the confines of the music box as she sat and waited for the next GI. "Hey soldier," she heard someone say, "you lonesome? How 'bout you buy me a drink? When heard from within the music box, she was always surprised to discover the voice was her own.

Spring came and went on stealthy green-wet feet, hardly stopping in Sok-Cho long enough to wake her up before kissing her good-bye. Summer thundered into Korea on the boiling backs of cloud-bursts, laughing at the sweltering soldiers in their sick-green, warm-weather uniforms as the rain tore long, jagged gullies into the roads. Summer laughed as the giant, grumbling trucks heaved and rocked across the gullies in a steady parade in and out of the compound, stirring up choking, sticky dust fogs that turned their uniforms from sick-green to dead-green and turned their skin to clay. Summer seemed to have a jolly sense of humor, knowing that the war had ended a whole year before, in the torrid July of 1953, knowing the compound was still there, more active than ever. Summer found it highly amusing that life for Sok-Cho hadn't changed just because men's minds had changed.

Autumn brushed the hillsides with shades of red and gold, threw open the doors to a cool north wind and swept the village as it fussed up and down the streets. It brought the smell of pine and dying leaves and settled in with the short-lived self-assurance of an elegant transient.

It was the north wind that scuttled a herd of leaves in the door when Captain Charles Rutledge pushed his way into the bar on a chilly October night. Autumn was beginning to lose its sense of propriety as winter tapped its foot impatiently, waiting for the usual grand entrance of at least six inches of snow. Autumn dallied, winter threatened, and the nights turned colder.

Captain Rutledge burst through the door in a flurry of leaves and wind, enhancing his imposing posture with a deep growl of dissatisfaction: "It's cooooold out there, boys and girls! Best wear your long johns tonight."

The crowd in the bar turned to look at the rumbling bear of a man, all recognizing him, all smiling and calling out greetings. "Hey, Cap'n! What'sa matter? You lonesome tonight?" "The good life starting to get you down, Captain?" "Hey, Cap! Little Suzy over here says you look like 'big lotta GI.' Wanna warm your tush? My treat."

Captain Rutledge smiled and shook his head as he moved up to the bar. "Thank you, gentlemen, thank you, but I'd rather not ruin my image by having the local ladies discover my inadequacies."

A chorus of laughter rose as the Korean bartender joined him. "Why you come this dump, Captain?" he asked, a look of friendly curiosity on his round face. "You never come here before."

Rutledge was scanning the crowd, his large gray eyes peering from under a Neanderthal brow jutting over the bridge of an uncertain nose, a nose broken so many times it appeared to have lost direction in the ruddy, pocked face. "I'm looking for someone, Moonshine. A girl..."

The barkeep's face lit up with surprise. "You wanna girl, Captain?" Rutledge shook his head. "No, no, I need to talk to one of the girls, Moonshine, just talk, no hanky-panky. I think her name is Sook. Is she here?"

"She here okay," he replied with a disinterested shrug. "She busy now, you wait. Maybe wanna beer?"

He settled for a Coca-Cola, ambled across the cramped, smoke-hazed room to a table and sat down. The other GI's turned back to their conversations, knowing that whatever the captain was doing in the seedy bar, he had good reason.

Respect from a military man was a hard-fought thing to come by, and Captain Charles Rutledge had earned every ounce of respect he received. He had accepted his commission in the Army with full possession of his abilities as a fighter, and with full understanding of his polished Southern upbringing, and his belief in God. His was not a pious, arm's-length belief, not a reverent, distant, mystical thing that could only be spoken of in whispers or exercised in chapels on Sunday. His was an open, passionate, brawling faith, freely expressed, no holding back. He met any disobedience head-on like a linebacker in the ultimate championship game, and he welcomed antagonism. His was not the cheek to strike in idle threat, because he wasn't likely to offer the other one. He feared no man physically and that made his leadership responsibilities much less complicated. Time was important to him, his command was important to him, and he didn't waste opportunities. He understood men, loved them in their weaknesses because he had them himself, and he realized that in struggling with the flaws in his fellow men, he was facing and often conquering his own. Though his soft, cultured Southern voice reflected the magnolias and jasmine and crystal chandeliers of his youth, his rough exterior was a direct exhibit of the rowdy cheerfulness within. And if the men in his command didn't always understand him, without exception they all respected him.

Still, there were some situations for which he felt grossly unprepared, and this was one. He sat and nursed the bottle of Coke, eyes roving the crowd from under the cliff of his forehead. To the uninformed he would have appeared to be scowling. Those who knew him understood he was anxious, wrestling with a problem that was inwardly as large as the outer man. The bar, the booze, the girls, the whole sleazy atmosphere of the place—none of it affected him in the least. These were men like him, and the girls were children who were making choices dictated by hunger. The nervous drumming of his hammer-like fingers on the tabletop wasn't spawned by a discomfort in locations. It was inspired by a fervent need to do the right thing. A boy's future was in the balance.

She smoothed her dress before walking out into the bar,

111

feeling the slick, sensuous glide of silk under her hand. She checked her face in the cracked mirror hung on the door and straightened the line of her lipstick. She didn't see a face in the mirror; only the vague image of someone she might have known once, some strange girl that was neither pretty nor ugly, young or old. Opening the door, she moved out into the light of the barroom and stood looking at the crowd of men, having no idea of the visual impact she created. Ripples of light reflected from the blue silk dress clinging to her slender body, flowing like water when she moved; her long hair shimmered in contrast to the dress, her face pale and stunningly beautiful in its lack of expression. Heads turned, conversations were interrupted by whistles of approval, appreciative gazes were emphasized by liberal strokes to her backside as she slipped gracefully through the crowd and up to the bar.

Captain Rutledge watched her when she entered the room, his soda strangling off in mid-sip. He followed her with his eyes, knowing this had to be the girl. The boy had described her well; even in his stilted Korean, Rutledge had been able to understand that she was lovely. The boy was right. He watched as Moonshine spoke rapidly to her, gesturing in the captain's direction. He watched the girl turn slowly, fluidly, watched her appraise him carefully. She moved toward him through the crowd in a smooth, unified sway, trying not to show her nervousness. Something is wrong, she thought. Something is wrong with Bok.

"You must be Sook," he said, standing to take her hand and offer her a chair. Unaccustomed to being treated with deference and poise, she blinked once before smiling in her mocking, alluring way.

"You may speak in English, Captain," she said in her soft, penetrating voice. "I understand you quite well." He smiled in relieved surprise. This was something the boy had never told him.

"What can I do for you, Captain?" she asked, and for the first time he noticed the slight nervous movements of her hands, the imperceptible frown around her eyes. "Is Bok in trouble again? Is that it?"

Rutledge shook his head and leaned forward, his massive frame making the chair seem small and inadequate. He looked at her closely and under his scrutiny she began to unbend her rigid expression, feeling the disconcerting honesty in his eyes. For the first time since entering the bar, Rutledge felt calm and in control. "No, the boy isn't in trouble," he began. "But this does concern him."

He could see her visibly relax, the relief in her eyes flickering briefly, then passing away. Her exotic lack of expression returned and she leaned back in automatic seductiveness, then leaned forward again, not knowing how to present herself to him. She looked nervously around the room, noticing the occasional amused glances. She toyed with her slender fingers, watching Moonshine from the corner of her eye as he stood with arms folded across a bulbous chest, watching her sternly.

"I hope you'll forgive me for coming to your place of work, but I've gone to your house twice and no one was there."

She shook her head and waved off his apology, glancing again at Moonshine. "I am gone most days. The boy takes me to the beach. Please, Captain, I don't intend rudeness, but you aren't a paying customer and Moonshine keeps very close tabs on my time."

His face flushed with embarrassment and apology. He stood immediately and took her arm. Out in front of the building, he released his hold on the girl and looked at her. "Tomorrow, then? At the chapel on the base, say, ten o'clock?" She glanced at him oddly. "Why the chapel?" she asked. He smiled slowly, his gray eyes warm under his brow. "Neutral territory," he said softly. She nodded nervously, hugging herself in the stiff, cold breeze. "Shall I come for you?" he asked.

Sook shook her head. "No, meet me at the gate. If this concerns the boy, I don't want him to know." He nodded and turned to go, feeling the hollowness of an unaccomplished task mixed with the anticipation of having a second chance. She stepped back into the bar, slipping gracefully back into the world of smoke and booze and an old Japanese music box.

Standing at the gates the next morning, Captain Rutledge inwardly chastised himself for the hundredth time. He had known it was a bad idea to try and see her at the bar. He paced slowly, glancing at his watch, grateful she had consented to meet him on territory he was more familiar with. It was better this way, he assured himself.

When he saw her hurrying toward him he glanced away, thinking it was someone else. He jerked his head back when he realized it was her, striding toward him in a plain cotton skirt and blouse, a pair of ordinary one-piece rubber shoes, a brown scarf tied loosely around hair bound up on her head. He smiled as she drew closer, noticing she no longer wore lipstick, smiling because she was still so incredibly lovely.

"Thank you for coming," he said, reaching for her hands and shaking the two of them together in his over-sized paws. "I was afraid you'd change your mind."

Her returning smile was warm and relaxed, though not cheerful. She no longer pretended the seduction, no longer assumed an air of alluring flirtation. She was a young village girl now—only more so. When she entered the chapel, her face seemed to be lit from beneath her skin as she stared around in satisfaction. Captain Rutledge led her to the front row of seats, motioned to one for her and sat facing her, his arm stretched across the back of several chairs like a fallen log.

"I haven't been in a church for a very long time," Sook said softly, staring around her at the pictures, the podium, taking pleasure in the manufactured sanctimoniousness of the place. Rutledge tilted his head and looked closely at her.

"You're a Christian?" he asked, and she nodded without returning his gaze.

"My parents were good Presbyterians. They used to see that we all went to church. It was expected…" Her voice dropped away, following her eyes downward to her lap.

"And your family—where are they now?" he asked, sensing a small opening into the closed room of the girl's life. For the next half hour she haltingly described the conscription of her father into the military in Seoul, of his death, of the evacuation of Seoul that separated her from her mother and brother. "My mother was not well," she said. "She wouldn't have lasted very long without food or shelter. It was hard enough for me, and I was already thirteen years old. I was healthy and young and still I nearly starved to death before..." her face twitched slightly, "...before I decided I didn't have to. My brother...my brother was only six. He had been pampered and spoiled all his life. I don't know if he..." she sighed and stared down at her hands. "He was not as strong as..."

Rutledge cleared his throat, not wanting her to get distant. "I'm sorry about your family, Sook. You must miss them very much."

She looked up at him with the first glimmerings of tears in her eyes, and nodded. "I used to. But I'm older now. It's been four years and much has happened. Life goes on and prices are paid." She straightened her shoulders. "Now," she said firmly, "what is it you want from me? If the boy is being a—what is the word? —nuisance, if he is becoming a nuisance, I'll speak to him."

He was shaking his head, pulling his hands into his lap and staring at them. He remembered the failure of the night before and decided to get on with it. This was his only hope.

"Sook, you remember when Bok was arrested last spring, when he was taken to jail on base and interrogated."

"You mean when he was beaten. Yes, I remember." Her eyes were cold, accusing.

"They thought he was one of the children used as spies by the North Koreans, Sook. When they picked him up inside a secured area, a place he had no business being, and when he refused to tell them anything, I will admit they were much too harsh with him and..."

"Harsh! He could barely walk when they finally released him," she said, her voice reflecting an anger she still keenly felt. She could still see his bruised face, swollen lips, the battered legs. "He was fishing from the rocks, that's all. He had no idea he was inside a secured area; the seashore has always been home to him."

"I'm not defending what they did, Sook. I'm trying to explain something that happened as a result of that incident."

Her eyes flashed a cold, penetrating fire. She folded her hands and listened.

"The second day of his imprisonment, I found out the boy was in jail and being questioned. As commander of the base, I had to find out what it was all about. When I went to see him, I found the guard kicking him in the ribs, furious because he wouldn't answer any questions, even with an interpreter. Of course, I put an immediate stop to it."

She sniffed and rolled her eyes as if to say, how very kind of you—since Bok was nearly unconscious anyway.

Rutledge ignored her displeasure and continued. "I tried to speak to the boy myself through the bars, hoping to show him how sorry I was and to find out who he was and where he lived. Bok walked up to me, clenched both fists above his head and brought them down as hard as he could on the bridge of my nose."

Rutledge was unprepared for the reaction he got. He had expected a gasp of shock, a look of apologetic surprise. What he got was the rippling cascade of laughter that had become almost a stranger to her. She threw her head back and laughed freely, with the abandonment of the young girl she was. Captain Rutledge watched her with his mouth open, finally giving himself over to the incredibly infectious trills of delight and together they laughed, filling the chapel with their mingled, mismatched voices. "Did he hurt you very badly?" she asked between hiccoughs of laughing.

"Yes, as a matter of fact," Rutledge said, "the kid broke my nose. Blood everywhere. Really quite shocking." His face belied the stern tone of his voice, and they both began laughing again. "At any rate...," he finally continued, wiping tears of mirth from his eyes, "...at any rate, I let the boy go, told him not to go playing around the docks inside the fenced enclosure anymore, and, well, I suppose you know how the two of us have become such good friends these past months."

She nodded, remembering the hours and hours he would spend on the base; remembering the excited prattle he would greet her with when he would return in the evenings. She would wash and dress while he followed her around the hut, chattering about "Captain Chawdi," typically mispronouncing the difficult "r" and "l" sounds, rolling them on his tongue until they became "a"s and "d"s. She never corrected him, never had enough interest in his daily activities to encourage him with newly-found English words. He had learned two English names and he repeated them over and over again, practicing them on Sook: "His name is Captain Chawdi and he calls me GI Joe." The names became a constant litany, pushing Sook into an irritability she was at a loss to explain.

Her lack of interest in all the time he was spending at the army base didn't surprise her. She had become removed, steadily, uncontrollably removed from the small everyday wonders that had brought her pleasure before. In the wake of the spiritual crushing she had suffered the night so long ago, she had felt all the false hopes crumble around her like the shattering of a porcelain shell: all the hopes, dim and distant as they might have been, for some sort of life after the war was over; all the feeble dreams for a man, a home, a family she had harbored and guarded and clung to, hoping that things would be different for her after the war. She thought of the ending of the war as a beginning of everything wonderful in her life, a re-birth of the most profound and magnificent proportions. She was a tiny boat on the ocean of cruelty that had become her homeland and she bobbed forward, using her body and her wits, never looking back, keeping a bright horizon in her eyes. It kept her going, kept her hoping and living and laughing.

But on the night of the soldier behind the bar, she had finally broken. It had taken the pain and disgust of the act itself to tear away the last illusions, the last dearly-held dreams, and she knew her life would never be any different. Even when the war was over, no respectable man would want her. On that horrible night, once and for all, she turned squarely in the face of what she was and acknowledged it, accepted it, embraced it. On that night she stopped struggling in that turbulent sea, dropped her arms to her side, and lowered her eyes. On that night, she became what everyone said she was and she never truly believed herself to be. And the moment she said it to herself—and meant it—a feeble, hungry light on the shore went out. She was a whore. Lower than the low. A simple vermin feeding on the lust of animals. She was less than nothing. She was Yang kal bo.

Sook sat quietly and listened to the captain explain the boy's relationship with him, hearing his words with a curious detachment. Most of it she already knew from Bok's prattlings: the days spent in the captain's office, wandering with him all over the base. She knew of the packages being sent regularly from the captain's wife in America, all the new clothes, toy guns and candy. It was all nice and it took up his free time during the day. Beyond that, neither Captain Charlie nor Bok had any real shape in her mind. She bought him a few clothes with the increasing amounts of money she was earning and made sure he always had food, yet she never noticed how the emaciated, hollow look had left his body, never noticed the healthier shine to his hair, the increasing richness of the color of his skin. She only saw him in brief moments of recognition while the months of summer eluded her as mysteriously as had spring and winter.

Sook was only dimly aware that Captain Rutledge had stopped speaking and sat staring at her with an odd concentration. When she noticed his gaze, she sat straighter and tried to assume an attitude of listening, though she wasn't certain what all this had to do with her. Rutledge smiled slowly, looked away and began speaking again.

"I will be leaving tomorrow to go back to the States." The captain's voice came back to her in a slow crescendo. "My father passed away last week and my tour was cut short in order to handle the arrangements at home." For the first time, Sook noticed the bright, flickering light of uncertainty in the captain's eyes, knowing that he was struggling with something. And for the first time, a small alarm began to sound in her heart, and she instinctively clutched her shawl closer to her as if suddenly feeling a chill. Rutledge leaned forward and braced his elbows on his knees, his hands clasped in a huge fist of prayer-like supplication. "Sook," he began softly. "Sook, I want to adopt Bok. I want to take him back to South Carolina with me and give him a real home."

For a moment it was as though she hadn't heard him. Her face seemed chiseled of pale white stone. Then, like a sculpture of soft clay set out in the rain, her face began to change, everything sliding downward, her features melting into each other in an expression so helpless and defeated Rutledge reached out and closed his hand over both of hers. They were cold, dry, unnaturally still.

"So what do you want from me," she said. He knew it wasn't a question. It was consent. It was resignation.

"Bok doesn't want to go," he said evenly. In her resignation, he sensed an odd challenge. By simply giving up, he felt an unexplainable tightening of her claim to the child and he was rising to whatever contest might be ensuing. With the keen perception of the human soul, he could see her acquiescence as the most powerful bastion of defense the girl would employ in her desire to keep her companion. Though he had no wish to view this delicate, likeable girl as an adversary, he quickly reminded himself of his ultimate purpose. Mingled with his compassion for her, the single-mindedness of a military man pushed to the surface and, like a trained commander, he knew he was facing a worthy opponent, someone who was as determined in her possession as he was in his conviction. She would not whine and weaken, would not use any of the lesser tactics in her defense. Discarding all these, she had called in the largest of her armaments—total indifference. And this was exactly what he was prepared for.

"Bok doesn't want to go," he repeated. "He doesn't want to leave you. He says you have no one, just like him, and you need him." His voice was calm, his gray eyes glowing from under their protective cliff held no anger, no criticism. "He says America is too far away and he wants to stay here. But he loves me, Sook, I can feel it. Even though he doesn't speak English, I know he was crushed when he found out I was leaving. But he's afraid. He's been through too much and he's uncertain. And there's you. He's extremely attached to you and at this point he's refusing to leave, even though I know there's a big part of him that wants to go."

"I'll ask you again, Captain," she said, her voice deepened and withdrawn. "What do you want from me? You know the child is not mine, that I have no claim to him. If he wants to go, he'll go. If he wants to stay, he'll give you a fight, but you and I both know that the authorities here can do what they want with him. I don't see where I need to enter into this at all."

He smiled, feeling the satisfaction of having sniffed out the enemy and the confidence of knowing how to deal with it. "Sook, you know I can't drag him onto the airplane kicking and screaming. If he flat refused to go, all of the work I've gone to, all the formalities, red tape, paperwork, special diplomatic permissions, all of that will mean nothing. I won't force him to go and you know that. You also know there's nothing here for him, Sook. In America, Bok has a chance, he has a future. He's an incredibly gifted boy and now he has a rare opportunity to progress, to get an education, to grow up in a home with a mother and father. He has a chance to live, Sook, to live! There's nothing you can offer him..."

"Except love," she said bitterly. "What about love, Captain? Doesn't that mean anything?"

"Is it love?" he asked in an intense half-whisper. "Is it love, Sook? Or is it selfishness? Are you thinking of how much you love him and want to do what's right for him? Or could it be that you're thinking of yourself and how much you'll miss him? Can you really be considering the idea that your lonesomeness for him is more important than his entire future? Love is it? Or your own selfish need?" He had moved closer and closer to her face as he spoke, not to intimidate but in a sincere effort to make her see. He was no longer the military man. He was suddenly a guerrilla fighter armed with nothing but blind faith, scaling the walls of her defenses and standing on top, waving a flag in a wild hope that she would look up and know that she had been discovered. He held her gaze, refusing to let her retreat into the safety of lowered eyelids, refusing to let her hide from him any longer.

She stood up, pulling the brown scarf tighter around her.

He noticed that her hands were shaking. "You have no right to judge me," she said coldly, trying to keep her voice level. "What do you know of loneliness and selfish need, you in your warm barracks in your warm clothes and your warm life, you who have never known a single day of hunger? What do you know of need? You have no right to presume..."

"You're avoiding the issue," he said, pressing the attack. She whirled away and walked to the podium, staring up at the garish crucifix on the wall behind it. When she turned back, he knew the wall had been scaled. Tears were rolling down her cheeks.

"I'm not avoiding the issue, Captain," she said, her voice loud and trembling. "I'm trying to tell you that you don't even know what the issue is. It's not me that keeps the boy here. It's not me and it's not Sok-Cho. It's his brother."

In a blinding flash of light, Rutledge could feel the guerrilla fighter lose his footing on the wall and come tumbling down into the thorny briars at her feet. He had no idea Bok had a brother. He never said a word about a brother, saying simply that his family was dead. He stared at the girl with the mute, helpless expression of someone who has just been struck from behind. She returned to her seat, her movements no longer fluid, merely exhausted. With a heavy sigh she briefly explained to him about Yoon, about the separation after the loss of their parents. He listened intently, his shoulders rolled forward in a bulky mass that looked as weary as the girl's fragile frame. They made an odd statement in contrasts, these two—differing shades of light and dark, large and small, differing cultures and races, opposite sexes. To the outward eye, there was nothing of similarity in the two; to the inner eye of understanding, they were the same. Equals in spirit, equals in strength. And with the equality came an end to the conflict. Her soft voice waved the first flag of truce.

"He watches for every stranger," she almost whispered, "he waits for every new face in the village so he can show them the picture. It's an obsession, and it's bigger than you, or me, or America. It's not his love for me that keeps him here and...I guess I've always known that." She felt him turn to her, felt his hand on her shoulder as he moved her around to face him. There was hurt in his eyes, an apologetic plea for forgiveness mixed with inexpressible frustration.

"Sook," he said, his voice soft and uncertain. "Sook, I need your help." She closed her eyes and shook her head, trying to move away from him, but he held her firm. He turned her to face him again. "Sook...please!"

She dropped her face into her hands and for a few moments she wept soundlessly, with only her shoulders moving slightly with each sob. When she raised her face her eyes were red and swollen, wet with tears, but her face was calm, set in a mask of non-emotion. "What do you want me to do?" she asked, and the lonely soldier inside him leaped in relief.

"Talk to him, Sook. Talk to him and explain to him that his future is in America. Explain to him that his search for his brother may go on forever. Tell him it's useless to stay here and wait for someone who may never show up. Tell him you know it's a good idea to go to America. Tell him...oh, I don't know, tell him what you think you need to, but please talk to him! He'll listen to you. I know he will."

"You don't understand how strong Bok's desire is to find his brother, Captain. I don't think anything I say to him will make any difference."

"Please try," he said, genuine pleading in his voice. "Please, Sook." His eyes burned into her with a white, intense pain. "I love him, Sook. I want him with me."

She stood slowly, turning away toward the door. He followed her, wondering with terrible anxiety if he had been able to reach her. At the door she stopped and turned, her red-rimmed eyes finally dry, strangely narrow and lifeless.

"I will speak to him, Captain. I will do what I can. That's all I can promise."

The burly hulk of his frame moved forward and closed its tree-trunk arms around her, holding her close with a gentleness common only to very large men. He spoke softly, his voice rumbling in her head against his chest. "It will have to be enough. It's his only chance. And mine."

It took three more days for her to gather the courage to talk to Bok, and in those days she knew without looking in the mirror that she had aged. With a deep sense of irony, she realized that she was not so afraid of the fact that he might flatly refuse to go. Her fear lay in the fact that he might not.

Bok walked in that morning after spending several hours combing the beach, and was delighted to find her awake already. She seldom rose before noon. When she looked into his wide, black eyes, his shining seriousness, she realized for the first time that he hardly ever smiled. She rubbed her hand through his hair and suggested another walk on the beach, which he immediately accepted. Strange, she thought, as they walked along the narrow sand at high tide. Strange how I've never noticed how small this beach is, this town, this country. Sook felt a comfortable numbness surround her, subduing even the sound of the ocean. She watched Bok scramble along a few steps ahead of her, picking up shells and stones, tossing them at aggravated sea-birds who squawked angrily and fluttered up, only to land a moment later a few paces away. She saw everything without hearing, knowing that her senses were shutting down, pulling in, bracing her for what was to come.

"I have something to talk to you about, pelican," she called, and he hurried back to her. She found a dry spot on the sand, barely noticing the coolness through her skirt. He plopped next to her, tucking his legs up under his chin, wrapping his arms around them to keep warm. With some surprise and disappointment she realized that autumn had escaped her also, and the first chilly winds were beginning to haunt the beach. "I had a long talk with Captain Rutledge a few days ago," she began, and she noticed a definite stiffening in his back. The last time she had gone to the base was when he had been arrested. "Oh, don't worry," she said with a slight smile. "You're not in trouble. The Captain wanted to talk to me about you and...about America." Though she knew he was no longer tense, she saw a quickening distance forming in his eyes. He put it all together in a matter of seconds and was preparing himself for the questions. She sighed and pushed on. "It's the right thing to do, pelican," she said softly, watching his profile as he stared out to sea. "You have a wonderful chance with Captain Charlie—school, clothes, a mother and father. This is something I want you to do. It's a very special thing you're being offered, and I want you to do it."

"I don't want to," he said simply. "I like Sok-Cho. This is my home, and if Yoon comes back and I'm not here, then..."

"I'll stay here and watch for your brother," she said quickly. "I'll keep track of everyone who comes here and I'll keep asking about him. I meet all kinds of people at the bar and if anyone sees him I'll have them tell me. If I find him, if he comes here, I'll write you immediately and let you know."

He creased his forehead in a frown of confusion and disarmament, feeling the discomfort of being stripped of a fair excuse. Bok shook his head. "I don't want to go and leave you here alone."

She smiled and put her arm across his shoulder. "I'll be all right, pelican. I'm used to being alone. And when you learn to read and write, you can write to me all the time. It won't be like we don't still have each other. Captain Charlie is waiting for you in America, and he said to have you go to the chaplain on the Army base whenever you're ready to join him there. The chaplain will make all the arrangements. It'll work out just fine, you'll see."

"I don't think it's a good idea," he insisted. "I like it here. I don't want to leave you. I won't leave you," he said firmly, and she felt the familiar helplessness she had experienced before when he made up his mind. There was a finality to it, a solid grounding from which, in the past, she was never able to move him. In his own way he was as strong or stronger than she, and in most ways he was more persistent. She felt a growing sense of futility and with it a sure and painful understanding of what she had to do.

She rose slowly and stood in front of him as he sat staring up at her with eyes that were open and accepting. She saw his look of bewilderment as she braced herself. She was the image of determination, of aloof, solid power as the wind billowed her skirt and freed her hair from its pins. She was a striking ivory statue on the beach staring down at a boy who met her gaze. There was a tangible transmission of electricity between the two, opposing poles of push and pull finally colliding with all the accumulated energy inherent to the victims of war.

"What do you mean, you won't leave me," she said in a voice as cold and rushing as the wind. "What makes you think I want you to stay with me? I don't even know why I kept you around all this time, you've been such a pain in the ass, getting arrested, staying gone all hours of the night and day, eating all the food. What makes you think I want you, you little shit! You don't belong with me. I never asked you to follow me here and then stay. You've used up your welcome with me, and I don't want anything more to do with you!"

His vision of Sook at that moment was a horrible one, a vision that would haunt him unmercifully: her narrow, flashing eyes; her long hair blowing like a nest of writhing snakes around her head; her skirt swept wide in the wind showing two thin white legs like fence posts in the sand supporting the cold, hateful creature above them. He stared at her with his mouth open, his heart shattering like glass under a hammer.

She whirled in the wind and walked away, her skirt and hair seeming to pull her from him down the beach. Bok jumped up and ran after her.

"Sook!" he called into the roar of the sea. "Sook, wait!" She turned and faced him as he caught up with her. Her breath stopped in her throat as she looked at the stricken expression in his eyes and she felt her heart grind painfully in her chest. But what the boy saw was a deepening of the ice in her eyes as she jerked her arm from his grasp.

"You don't belong here," she said frigidly. "There is no home for you here. You blew it up, remember? There are no more parents, no more brother, no home. No one wants you here. I've got my own life to live and I don't need a kid hanging off me all the time, so why don't you do us both a favor and just don't be here when I get home from work tonight?"

That's how she left him: standing alone on the beach of Sok-Cho as she strode away in a flurry of blowing hair and clothing, never once looking back. And in her mind she heard none of it—not the sea or the birds or her own harsh, destructive voice; she saw nothing—not the agony of hurt in his eyes, not the silent tears on her own cheeks. As she walked blindly up the beach, she could feel herself crawling, clawing, dragging her weeping soul backward, backward past Bok, past Sok-Cho and all the places since her youth. She felt her twisted, shattered spirit wrench the music box open, heard the maddening, distorted tones from the fairy harps as she anxiously, gratefully plunged inside.

The waves drummed against the shore that became the edges of his soul, a continual wash and pull, tides and currents that gave, took back, added to and destroyed coastlines and submitted themselves, exposed themselves to the birth and death that was the ocean. There was constancy here, no falsehood. A man's spirit had no need for pretense when facing the sea. She loved and hated with equal intensity, and she had no favorites. She gave what she would and took what she wanted, and Bok loved her because he understood her. He recognized in her the mother from which all life once emerged, and he had no choice but to be a devoted son.

The rocks of Sok-Cho held him out over the ocean as in the palm of an offering hand and he sat in enormous serenity, listening to the familiar voice of endlessness. The autumn sun had gone down, leaving the sky illuminated from somewhere within the sea. He kept a gentle inner hand on his memory, which insisted on jumping away from him, darting and laughing as it coaxed to be allowed to wander freely. The lights of the village behind him began to wink on, resembling eyes flying open in surprise, and he knew he should get back to the hut. Sook would be getting ready to go to work, and he felt he wanted to see her off tonight.

The thought of her sent shafts of warmth and cold across his memory and he sighed, grappling with the perplexity of her. Perhaps it had been the relief of her, coming into his life after a long, silent year spent alone in the wilderness. Or the impish ray of sunlight she brought with her that first day after leaving Kangnung. He wasn't certain. He knew only that he was hers and she was his in a permanent whimsical bond he was at a loss to define. She filled one of the many caverns that had been blasted into him by the war and he never struggled with any explanations of where she belonged in his life. Not until tonight.

He searched his limited resources for possible answers to the questions she had made him ask, and he found nothing. Sitting on the friendly rocks of his childhood he felt his spirit tethered inside, felt the sinewy bonds of his own lack of understanding holding him trapped and angry, beating furious wings out across the sea. All the negatives of his short life had drawn him inexorably to the rocks where he had always found, if not the answers, then at least the peace to move forward without them. He was certain that no one ever felt as lost, as singular as he did at that moment. He was totally, miserably confused and he had no way of knowing that the pounding of wings he felt inside was the sure and certain emerging of a conscious man. It was a reluctant acceptance, like a gift from a battered, dying, crippled thing, a gift of the larger person this crippled being had protected. He was growing up, and his soul was feeling the strain of trying to keep up with his mind.

He kept trying to tell himself that this was her fault, that his confusion was a direct result of her, but deep inside he knew this wasn't true. When he thought of her laughter, of her light, girlish movements during those first weeks together, he knew this was not her fault—she had made him feel only sunshine at a time when there was no sun and he could not blame her for this new discomfort.

Bok sighed and closed his eyes, feeling the soothing drum of the sea on the vast coastline behind his eyes, and he set himself free among the memories, running barefoot and giddy among the flowers of laughter rising and falling in cadence with the sea.

He could remember tiny things that became large and luminous in his mind: the unconscious, natural touch of her hand on his hair; a look of intense concentration while she skillfully sewed pieces of clothing for him by the light of a candle; her comical antics as she chased a rat around the room, pounding it with a scruffy old broom while cursing it under her breath and squealing involuntarily every time the thing turned on her; and her waterfall laughter. Always he would remember her laughter.

He had tried to convince himself that it was another betrayal, tried to force her rejection of him into the same dark category as the massacre. He pushed and tugged and tried to form this into something he could understand as he sat on the rocks at sunset, looking either for the answers or the serenity to accept the silence. But there had been something so unpremeditated in her words that the pall of betrayal didn't fit; even in her profanity, she had been too spontaneous. He sat and searched the face and breadth and heart of the sea for hours, and, as always, the sea stroked, petted and soothed him until his violently heaving emotions had settled.

This was all his own fault, he decided as the chill of evening began to nudge him from his perch on the rocks. I've done something to make her angry. This has nothing to do with me going to America or Captain Charlie or any of it. He jumped from the rocks and headed back to the house, ignoring the buzzing uncertainties that still lay formless on the floor of his mind, whirling and spinning like trapped flies waiting to upright themselves and take shape. He didn't know what he had done to create the wild, angry thing he saw on the beach today, but he had no doubt that some sort of apology from him would make things better. She hadn't been herself for a long time. He saw her outburst as an extended form of her melancholy distance these past months. Nothing serious. He would apologize and make it right.

Hurrying toward the hut he passed the gates of the compound and thought again of Captain Charlie. A sharp, distinctly painful stab of longing slowed him down and made him stare through the fence at the lights and drums and crates and buildings. Captain Charlie was a warm, empty place in him now that surprised and dismayed him. He had never expected to miss Charlie the way he did. He wondered where Charlie was, what he was doing, what his wife looked like. He wondered if Charlie would miss him when he found out he wouldn't be coming to America.

He pushed away from the fence and hurried on to the house. Before he could enjoy the bitter-sweet memory of Charlie, he would have to make things right with Sook.

He stepped through the door and knew something wasn't the same. The house was dark, but that wasn't it. He thought it was the disappointment of having missed her before she left for the bar, but it was more than that. There was a hollowness to the room, a cold vacancy that made the hair on his neck rise. He moved automatically to a corner table and lit a candle. When he turned to the room again, his heart wrenched with a pain that surprised him with its violence.

The room was empty—completely empty, except for his own basket of clothes and his sleeping mat. All of her things were gone and the room vibrated with her absence, sending tremors of shock and grief up and down his spine. The morning on the beach came hurtling with ugly force back to his mind and he knew that everything she said she had meant, and with that understanding came the same pounding sense of betrayal he had battled down on the rocks. And one screaming question: WHY?!

He burst from the house and ran as fast as he could to the bar, and though she had never allowed him to set foot in the place, he burst through the door in a storm of dirt and leaves kicked up by the wind. He was in the midst of a forest of legs muted by cigarette smoke, surrounded by uniforms, bewildered faces, girls in strange, shiny dresses, the same sour smell of liquor that she brought home with her every night, loud music coming from somewhere.

Bok searched the murky interior frantically, ignoring the surprised shouts and hoots of laughter that followed him on his desperate search. Finally collared by the bartender, his legs pumping furiously as he felt himself lifted from the floor, he heard himself calling her name. "She not here, kid," he heard somewhere in the distance. "She quit today...not here anymore...gone...haven't seen her. Gone...gone...gone..."

When he finally felt anything again, heard anything, he was walking aimlessly down the road toward the hut, automatically, instinctively headed—where? Home?

It was a nearly audible snap and he stopped, turning his senses inward to listen. It was the final separation of his bonds to Sok-Cho, to a destroyed home. He stood in his interior, gazing at himself with curiosity. He saw himself isolated in a hopeless land where no one was offering solutions, no one was taking a hand in his direction. All the grief, all the melancholy in his life he saw as shapeless bogs that served only to slow him down, pull him under. He stopped in the middle of the road and looked around him, listening inwardly and outwardly, feeling the wind and the emptiness. He looked up at the sky, imagining he could see the wasted remains of something inside him drifting up through the darkness.

He felt his smallness like a fragile paper kite suddenly released on the air: dry, easily torn, forgotten on the wind. He felt the gathering of rasping loneliness around him, taunting him, laughing at his thin nothingness in the road. He was tired, soul-weary and defeated, wanting only to rest someplace where the memories would let him go...just let him go.

Sok-Cho was nothing now, a paper shell, just like him. There was no one, no family, no Sook, no brother, and he was too weary to continue the search. He felt the last of his emotional resources dwindling into the atmosphere like blood from a wound and he knew he had to rest.

He needed to be wanted, needed to be where he could marshal his strength, patch the gaping holes, regroup. He knew he couldn't give up...his brother was out there somewhere, but he was too distant, too far away to feel, and the weaker Bok became, the more his world took from him, the more distant his chances became of ever finding him. It was time to rest...to heal...to get ready to continue the search, even if it meant going to the other side of the world first.

AMERICA

XIII

"On your mark...! Get set...!"
The blast from the starter's gun shot a white puff of powdery smoke a short distance in the air and Samantha Paget realized with some disappointment that it wasn't a blast at all—it was a crack, an exaggerated POP!, a neutered thing with no bullet in its wake. The runners were off the blocks, six of them streaking around the track like startled gazelles. At first they moved as a solid unit, their legs pumping in furious syncopation. They were an odd machine in the wind, their bodies one motor of pure energy, their legs the pistons. Half way around the track she saw them separate slowly, saw the motor begin to fragmentize as some parts moved ahead and some fell behind. Arms pumped in longer arcs, heads rolled farther back, legs gradually lost their tensile strength under the grueling sprint and the pack stretched wider.

And in the end, was there only exhaustion? she wondered. They exert and push and extend themselves beyond their farthest limits against each other; and in the end the winner stumbles over the finish line with arms thrown wide, hands dangling like odd grape clusters, sweat running in his eyes, with his nearest competitor only split seconds behind him. As if in confirmation of her own bewilderment of the contest and its rewards, the meager crowd in the stadium clapped and cheered with praise that was more proper than congratulatory.

Slouching back on the bench, she stretched her long legs and propped her back on the bench behind, the slender lines of her body forming a smooth, graceful angle against the lines of empty stadium around her. The late April sun heated the fabric of the chinos against her legs, gleaming softly off long blond hair. She was a luminous image in shades of pastel from the pale, glowing skin of her face to her sandaled feet. There was a sultry grace about her made more elegant by her deliberate casualness. Her movements were slow without being tentative, languid without being lazy. She exuded a natural tautness, a fluid purpose to every shift in her posture. Lifting her face to the warmth, she smiled behind sunglasses with heavy dark lenses, feeling the satisfaction of a shared secret. Just you and me, right, sun? He doesn't need to know I'm here—it wouldn't make any difference to him anyway. Ah! the things I do just to catch a glimpse of him. A track meet. Ridiculous. I deserve a good sunburn.

She sighed and closed her eyes, knowing it wasn't ridiculous, not any of it. This was all a part of the process of healing. She took pleasure in her secret appearance at a track meet where she knew he was competing. It was the sense of the ridiculous, the almost juvenile nature of watching him without his knowledge that made her feel young again. It was proof to herself that she was salvageable. It had been three long years, years of crushing disappointments, soaring successes made small by monstrous emotional fraud, and she hadn't been certain she was still intact when she returned to Charleston. Now, sitting in the fragrant spring sunshine of the Carolinas, watching a young man who didn't know she was there, she knew the old Samantha Paget was finally home. She had made it back alive.

The next event was announced and she opened her eyes, carefully scanning the contestants stepping up to their blocks. This was *his* event—the hundred-yard dash. She sat up, moving to the edge of the bench with her hands clasped between her knees. When she saw him approach his starting position her back became rigid, every muscle tightening. With the sight of him, none of it mattered anymore: all the time lost through the stellar black hole that was New York. It was all so unimportant now, soothingly distant. When he turned slowly at his mark, the familiar sensations churned the air around him, simmering with silent electric warmth, and she opened herself to the vibration, to the delicious pain of simple wanting.

She wasn't even vaguely aware that other runners were taking their marks along with him. Five other human beings, young men with faces and names and lives, suddenly never existed. He was out there alone, singular, uninvolved. And she knew her image of him was reinforced, wholly justified by his own instinctive solitude at that moment. She saw him alone because he was convinced he was alone. There was only the man and the run. She understood in those first moments, as he peacefully submitted to the tingling nervousness of muscles prepared to exert, that the contest was not against other runners. He moved with the volatile assurance of a man who knows his only competitor is himself. Shaking his hands, trying to coax warmth into them as he stared calmly at the cinder track, he lifted his head and gazed up at the fathoms of rich blue sky, and he smiled. Tall and slender, his body hardened and deceptively lean under a skin already tanned to a rich brown by the springtime sun, she knew his visual impact was only part of what she was seeing. She had known handsome men before. She had worked with some of the most physically handsome ones in the country, professional models from around the world. But placed in the balance with this one man, they became suddenly ordinary and bland. She had seen shoulders like his before, heavily muscled and shining brown in the sun; she had seen legs like his, long and solid and ready; she had seen blue-black hair and confident smiles. But the consummate collection of everything he was became startlingly different from other men. All of the mystery, the heartache and joy, all that was unspoken and deeply held—everything he was—found safe harbor in his eyes. Exotic and secretive, they were at first glance the unmistakable eyes of the Orient. But to Samantha Paget, they were the crystals of other worlds, other universes, other lifetimes. His eyes were everything he was—the unassailable power, the unsolved mystery.

"Runners, take your marks...!" She heard the starter's voice through a metallic tunnel, heard the words in drawn out, exaggerated slowness. Space and time perception slowed to a hollow drift, a dimension in which everything became unnaturally clear, where every sight and sound pressed into the mind with a deliberate insistence on being received. No detail was lost. She saw him bend his body, doubling with liquid ease until the tips of his fingers pushed into the cinders; saw him stretch his legs and settle his stance; saw the toes of his track shoes snug into the block.

"Get set...!" His hindquarters lifted smoothly away from his haunches, the muscles in his thighs tense as his dark head lifted. His eyes concentrated on a destination somewhere down the track and she had the odd, swelling sensation of yearning, wishing it was she at the focal point of his eyes.

She felt rather than saw the muscle in the starter's finger begin to tighten, putting a gentle, constant pressure on the trigger, and she knew that the runners felt the same thing. In that microscopic fragment of a second when the starter's hand flexed against the gun in the act of pulling the trigger, his body was already propelling forward. When the white puff rose from the eunuch weapon, his move was already being made and his foot left the starting block in that brief milli-second before the pop was heard. To the naked eye, both actions occurred simultaneously. To the runner and Samantha Paget, the first contest—between pistol and runner—had already been won.

She saw the minute puffs of cinders startled up by the toes of his shoes, leaving small craters of precise, measured dimensions like the tracks of a deer in wet sand. She saw the muscles in his legs pulse and ripple, saw his hands curled into fists that appeared to grip the invisible reins of the thing inside him begging for untethering, and she found herself wishing he would open his hands and let go.

The finish line seemed never to have existed for him. The run hadn't been toward a tangible goal, hadn't been against any mortal clock or being. The run had been for him. The run had taken place *in* him and the motion of his body had been a mere extension of his soul's playful push for wings.

When he crossed the finish line she saw his eyes cast upward again in that same joyful expression, and this time his arms, his head, his entire body joined the celebration. She saw his fists open, saw his face burst into a smile so clean, so full of the raw, uninhibited delight at living, that she felt herself ache to be a part of it. She heard someone laughing, and suddenly realized it was herself.

The moment he crossed the finish line and smiled, her comfortable time warp dissipated as abruptly as it had formed. She felt the sun again, heard voices again and knew the race was over. People were cheering and applauding and someone was yelling something about "a possible new NCAA record," that The Citadel had reason to be "proud o' that sum-bitch!" It had all taken less than ten seconds.

She heard it all in brief, jumbled segments, feeling herself rise slowly from the bleachers and walk past several cheering spectators toward the exit. She watched him as she walked with her hands in her pockets. She saw him stop in the midst of his cool-out jog, saw him turn abruptly toward the stands as if someone had called his name. She felt a peculiar lurch inside her chest as she continued to move across the bleachers, a breathless moment when she believed he was looking for someone in the stands—a leaping sensation that was a fear he might see her, and a gasping disappointment that he might not. She kept moving, gliding smoothly around and over spectators until she reached the break in the bleachers and stepped down. He was surrounded now by teammates and well-wishers, with coaches and friends. Though he seemed to be straining around the throng to see into the stands, she knew he was delightfully swamped and would never see her leave. She walked out of the stadium toward her car while he was propelled in a tight, giddy crowd toward the locker rooms.

In the wake of his winning run, Joe Rutledge was anxious to detach himself from the furor of friends and teammates and be off into the intoxication of a Charleston weekend in spring. With an important win flooding his veins, he wanted to be out of the showers and through the Lesesne Gates, those brooding jaws that spanned the entrance to The Citadel. He endured the sweaty-socks-and-soap-lather ribaldry of the locker room, responded to congratulatory shoulder punches and butt swats for only as long as it took to get in and out of the shower. Gathering his track clothes into a damp wad and stuffing them in a bag, he hurried to his car. Turning the key and hearing the answering purr of power from the engine, he felt the familiar vibration that every young man feels behind the wheel of a true "muscle machine." He gently gunned the engine, snuggling himself into the contoured seat with the same deliberate motion as settling his foot against a starting block. He was folded in the powerful embrace of a sleek, silver Jaguar XKE. Together they streaked through the gates and burst into Charleston, like a heat-seeking projectile, while he raised his voice in one joyous shout of "Yaahoo!"

To all outsiders Charleston was a freak, a strange idiosyncrasy the nation allowed itself. With its meticulously restored homes belonging to another era, its irritating tangle of one-way, dead-end cobblestone streets and its peculiarly aloof residents, Charleston was a bit of puffery that outsiders tolerated the way they would a pretty, spoiled child. It wasn't that people didn't like Charleston when they first saw her; they just couldn't understand what she was doing there. All other cities, towns, suburbs, hamlets, road-side stops and pig-sties in the country had a reason for being where they were. But in her ancient, aristocratic insistence on claiming a life of her own squarely in the face of the twentieth century, Charleston was defying an unwritten law of civilized man—she was refusing to be cannibalized by progress. Outsiders poked and pawed and tried to see beneath her warm Southern welcome like peeping toms trying to catch the neighbor's daughter with her clothes off. They were always caught in the act and pretended disinterested effrontery when Charleston swished her fragrant Southern skirts in their faces and closed the window on their fingers, all the while whispering seductively, "Y'all come back now, y'hear?"

But there was more to Joe Rutledge's possessiveness of

Charleston, something that went much deeper than his irritation with tourists who regrettably came every spring and thankfully went home in the fall. It involved blood, destruction and rebirth; it involved a kinship without lineage; it was a matter of heritage. Though impossibly mismatched, Joe and Charleston were irrevocably joined through composite heartaches and triumphs running parallel courses until they converged on each other. Their lives had been the same—one life had merely been longer. Three hundred years longer.

Moving in a zigzag pattern through the crazy maze of streets, Joe could feel the anxious machine around him urging for a trip down the old Savannah Highway just to blow out its pipes. But today he had a restless, spine-tingling urge to be with Charleston, his Charleston, the world around and below Broad Street. He watched the hordes of tourists scuttle back and forth across streets at indiscriminate locations, all wearing the same dazed, disoriented look of children who just discovered they had wandered into the wrong house. Once in a while his good manners escaped him and he would honk his horn, just to see them jump and scowl as they scooted away.

If he breathed deeply and half-closed his eyes, he could smell the kitchen of Rutledge Hall even from here. He could feel the happy fat of Shady Mae taking up space in the aroma as she rolled out dough for dumplings. The sound of her humming mingled with the scent of collard greens and ham hocks, the scent of rising biscuits and the scent of Shady Mae, which were all one pungent, spicy-sweet odor. By now, she would be putting together a favorite meal, and he was going to be late, as usual. She would fuss and fume and rotate toward him when he finally got home, her shiny black face trying hard to suppress the grin that always made her eyes disappear. He would dance around her, untying apron strings and dodging two big hands that reached for him in an effort to strangle or hug him, both actions being the same for Shady Mae. It was a ritual of contentment they had performed since his arrival in the States, and one he was loathe to leave behind, even as a man about to graduate from military college. It was a rite they performed religiously every weekend and which was just as surely interrupted by his mother, who would push into the kitchen without greeting him, begin checking into boiling kettles and under cloths spread over rising dough.

"So," Eva would say, and he knew her German accent would be heavier than usual, "you are late again, Joey. And why is it we go to such work to make your favorite meal when it sits here and gets cold..." And on and on. This too was a ritual, marked by Eva's flashing blue eyes, the worried black eyes of Shady Mae, and the impassive opacity of his own. He would bend and kiss Eva on the cheek, apologize appropriately, and the ice would thaw just enough to allow Eva another trifling victory and allow Joe to escape past her into the orderly spaciousness of the house.

But that would all come later, he thought. Today he had other plans. He drove toward the Battery—that part of town where life had begun for him in the States. It was there he had seen his first indoor plumbing and his last dirty toenails; where he had tasted his first ice cream in Shady's kitchen and his last bite of kim-chee ("Gawd awmighty, whassat smell?!") and where his one jar smuggled from Seoul went flying into the trash; where he had seen his first Fourth of July fireworks from Fort Sumter out in the harbor and where he had floated his last leaf-boat out into the Ashley River; where he had fought his first fist fight in the days before he could even speak English and where he had spent his last days of boyhood; where he had ridden his first bicycle, attended his first day of school, kissed his first girl, and spent his last night before entering into the mystifying, delightful world of sex. The Battery provided a laying-aside and a rebirth.

It made no difference to him if Charleston loved him with such intensity as this. It made no difference to him if she loved him at all. She belonged to him as surely as a woman from a conquered tribe would belong to him, were he Ghengis Khan. He often thought of himself that way: the conqueror among pillows of magnolias, riots of azaleas, floods of gardenias, and cascades of wisteria. Charleston couldn't hide from him; he knew her coquettish ways, understood that her intoxicating perfume was a lure that drew people to her to worship at her

140

columns, pay homage to her agelessness and Southern charm. He knew how she took delight in turning away even the most ardent pursuers, allowing no one access. Only those who approached her with hat in hand and a list of six generations of Charlestonian relatives in their back pockets were permitted within her fragrant bastions of society. It was a world where money meant a lot, old money meant even more, and old Charlestonian names ruled supreme.

He had appeared in a virtual snow storm of newsprint, a tidal wave of publicity and flashbulbs, and the residents of South Battery had taken a special credit for having as a neighbor the first Korean orphan to be adopted after the close of the war. They crooned and petted, gasped with delight at this odd little creature who stalked their neighborhoods until he knew every garden, every tree, every carriage house in the area, and they all spoke of him as "that darlin' thing Charlie Rutledge brought home from Ko-rea." It never once occurred to any of them that this "darlin' thing" had fallen hopelessly in love with their city, with their society, and that he fully intended to be a part of it. That would have been out of the question. So they all watched him with casual, tolerant amusement, applauding in all the right places as he grew older, none of them realizing that someday soon their pet Korean was going to storm the fortress.

He parked on East Bay Street across from the old Masonic Temple and hurried across the busy street to the raised walkway along the sea wall.

And finally, there was the sea. This was a sea different from other seas, though she bore the name Atlantic; because this portion of the Atlantic was graced by Charleston. And this, too, he realized, was a matter of heritage. The harbor, Charleston and Joe Rutledge—they had seen it all, heard it all, lived through it all. They were the authors of war, of death, of new life. They had each in their own time been orphaned by war, separated from loved ones and country. They knew of dying and now, in joining vast landscapes of heritage, they shared the secret of being reborn.

At the apex of the sea wall, with the wind blowing salt spray against his face, Joe felt he was at the top of the world. This is all of it! he thought. This is Sok-Cho, where the rocks by the sea held me out in offering to nameless gods. The market is here, adorned with different produce and graced with different villagers. The time-honored reverence for ancestors is here in the persona of a different society. "This is mine!" he said to the sea, loving the sound of his voice in the wind. "And I'm yours! We earned each other!" He could feel the forces of past and future gathering together around him like a huge boiling wind, lifting him, supporting him, sweeping him up and beyond the glorious city where he looked down on the world in which he would stake his flag. Turning his back to the shimmering water, he threw his arms wide and lifted his face to the sun. He was standing up on the wall itself, his form cutting sharp, clean angles against a backdrop of deepest blue. In a voice heard across centuries of ballrooms and bloodshed, he embraced the city with his whole soul and yelled, "Stand by, you pack of magnificent bigots! I'm here to improve your bloodlines!"

Several startled tourists nearly strangled themselves on their camera straps trying to get a picture of the screaming man on the wall. Joining in the madness of the moment, they captured this bit of lunacy to take back to their friends in Illinois and Maine and Utah, proving they had seen "the real South" and to laughingly tell their friends over cocktails that it was the spirit of Osceola haunting the sea walls of Charleston. With arms spread wide, a grin still on his face, he scanned the flocks of tourists below him, and with one sweeping gesture that included each of them, he opened his arms and yelled, "YA'LL GO HOME!"

XIV

There had been no mystery to America. The country was one huge banquet, a continual feast of pleasures and discoveries, a persistent bombardment of the senses, but no mystery. Much was missing from America that Joe had been accustomed to in Korea, but nothing that he didn't almost instantly replace. There were only two cavernous vacancies in his new life as he plunged into the world South of Broad. The first was the missing struggle for survival, a struggle that evaporated in the opulence of old Southern money. The second was the bottomless pit of yearning for his brother. One cavern he filled happily and constantly, beginning in Shady Mae's kitchen. The second was a gaping hole he maneuvered carefully around to avoid being swallowed in a morass of longing. There was no prominent struggle to adapt. Weighed in the balance with the savagery from whence he had emerged, he gauged everything by a different standard. American discomforts, anxieties, hardships and fears were viewed through distinctly altered lenses. He had arrived from Korea with a raw innocence of spirit that placed him beyond trivialities. In nearly stripping him of his very life, Korea had stripped away the social clutter of ideologies that are the stumbling blocks to learning, and he burst upon America with only one voracious, fathomless hunger: a starving mind.

Public school was out of the question—he was now a Rutledge—and private schooling, in its quiet Southern sluggishness, had quickly proven unable to keep up with the absorption rate of his mind. After the boy's first week in school, Charlie hired a full-time tutor who began teaching him the basic subjects of the first grade.

In his mind, there were chambers for everything: all the fundamentals of a blossoming language skill were isolated in one sunny parlor of his brain where he settled in to learn simultaneous English and German. There was a place for math, which he loved, and writing, which he didn't. He instantly opened a large spot inside for music, which he had so seldom heard in Korea, and he allowed a secluded place for art. He would bounce eagerly among all the chambers, concentrating, thinking, absorbing, asking for more. His tutor brought in special aides and advanced materials as quickly as he saw the boy was ready, keeping himself in a constant state of breathlessness with the boy's ability to consume it all. By the end of his first year in Charleston, Joseph Ashley Rutledge was in the fifth grade.

During those initial years of discovery, he felt the wild unleashing of his abilities, both mental and physical, and he felt equal to a captive falcon whose leather hood is suddenly removed. He was wild and hungry, and with a shout of impending conquest that echoed through the chambers of a startled Rutledge Hall, he was free at last.

Rutledge Hall had been childless for years, and with the arrival of Joseph Ashley Rutledge, the grand old house preened and warmed itself, taking on a new life. It was a house constructed for the rearing of large numbers of children, and their children's children. Carlisle Stanley Rutledge had fully intended that all the male Rutledge off-spring would bring their brides to this house, where they would contentedly settle in and have veritable litters of children whose men would grow up and bring their brides to Rutledge Hall...and so on into infinity.

During the golden years of Charleston, before the Civil War, the sparkling new facade of Rutledge Hall graced the Battery with stateliness that all other homes in the area were forced to try and duplicate. She was one of the elegant old dowagers of the city, having survived the great fire of 1861 and the bombardment of the city by Union ships lasting 587 days.

She stood proud and shaken as General Sherman burned his way toward Charleston, her cracked columns holding firm, her verandas unbroken, waiting for the final humiliation that would bring down what remained of a way of life. When Sherman shunted his forces away from Charleston, Rutledge Hall, along with the rest of Charleston, began the slow, painful process of rebuilding. A new wing was added after the war to replace a destroyed servant's quarters and provide more room for what the now-ailing Carlisle Rutledge was certain would be an expanding family. When he died in 1870, out of thirteen sons and daughters he left behind only two sons, one of whom died of tuberculosis a year later. The war had taken all the rest.

The next three generations proved uncommonly fruitless, with only seven more direct male heirs raising their raucous voices in the nursery in nearly a hundred years. Of these, Captain Charles Drayton Rutledge was the last, bringing to the child-hungry wings of Rutledge Hall a young German bride who was unable to have children. But the house was undaunted, maintaining her smooth, matronly lines, her solid mahogany good looks. Her polished and gleaming hardwood floors remained in unwarped preparedness, waiting for the rowdy tramplings of children, if not from this son, then from Charlie's adopted. She was elegantly patient; she had survived over a hundred years. She would yet see her longed-for brood.

When the wide-eyed, silent Joe Rutledge first walked through the twin solid oak doors to the reception foyer, the house seemed to whisper excitedly to herself, seemed to catch her breath and watch as he stepped into the foyer, feeling dwarfed by everything. She sparkled a welcome in the breeze through Swedish crystal chandeliers offering a tinkling greeting as the house-wind whispered through the droplets of glass. Rutledge Hall opened herself to him, gave herself to him, and took immediate possession of him. He loved her instantly.

The enormity of the house had dictated over the years that it be graced with enormous people, either spiritually or physically—preferably both. In accordance with that unwritten denominator, there appeared Reuben Calhoun, husband of Shady Mae. Nearly as much of an institution as Rutledge Hall itself, Reuben had answered the door on that first day, grinning down at the boy with blindingly white teeth shining in a handsome, aging face. He was the biggest man the boy had ever seen, and he stood gaping up at this giant, speechless and slightly frightened. Images of the sooth-sayer's hut in Sok-Cho flapped around in his memory, and he knew that the goose-flesh on his arms was the same chill he had felt then. He didn't try to back away, didn't try to hide, but when the giant's head began descending toward him, the boy felt his heart banging around in its cage, looking for escape.

"Lawd, Lawd, will you look at this! You sho'nuff one fine-lookin' l'il man, an' tha's a fac'! Mista Chawlie, this here am one fine boy!" The man's face was close to his and the boy could smell the faint, clean aroma of Bay Rum lotion mixed with another distinct aroma he would come to know as Shady Mae's kitchen. Reuben's eyes opened and closed with rapid scrutiny, and Joe was forced to smile through his nervousness. When Reuben straightened up and extended his greeting to the returning Rutledges, the boy craned his neck back and watched the man's huge eyes. A lighthouse, he thought with a grin. He looks like a tall, black lighthouse with his beacon-eyes signaling ships all the way out in the harbor.

In his role as butler and overseer of the estate, Reuben swung an iron fist of authority that was famous along the Battery. His father and his father's father had been with the Rutledge family, accompanied by a scattered assortment of family members that alternately made up the gardeners, cooks, maids and maintenance staff of the huge home. But Reuben was acknowledged as the best of them all. He asked no forgiveness for his own mistakes and gave none for others if it involved the discrediting of Rutledge Hall. He was fiercely loyal to the family and was determined that young Mista Joe was going to have the best the home could offer. In his own way, Reuben was a confirmed racist; he understood the class system of the South as only a black man could and he understood the traps and pitfalls a person was beset with if his skin wasn't white. He had heartily disapproved of Charlie Rutledge's decision to adopt a Korean boy, and had said as much to Eva Rutledge. He had spoken freely about the difficulties the boy might face from neighbors and schoolmates, and he expressed his sincere concern for anyone being subjected to the harsh realities of discrimination. Eva had drawn herself up to her full diminutive height, faced the man in the centuries-old posture of royalty to peasant, and had told him it was none of his concern. This was the wish of Master Charles, and Reuben's job was clear—treat the boy as a member of the family and mind his own business.

So the boy arrived and was swept into the house by welcome, concerned arms. But Reuben was not obliged to "mind his own business." The boy's first lessons in the sociology of the South were learned from Reuben and Shady Mae; his first glimpses of the double standard of prejudice were offered by them; and the first raw, grating disillusionments were softened and made clear in the warmth of Shady Mae's kitchen. Under their skilled parenting, Joe developed a deeper love for Charleston and its people than Reuben had intended. And with every passing year, Reuben reluctantly acknowledged the boy's disregard for "the system", and grudgingly admired the adaptability that allowed the boy to excel under the dark tutelage of people who tolerated him as being "only a step above a nigger." Reuben knew the boy was accepted because he was a Rutledge, and knew the boy survived because of himself. The Calhouns nurtured the parts of him that allowed nurturing and left the rest to himself. Joe's life was a direct antithesis to Korea except for the sea—and the jagged ice-flow that was Eva. The sea was a return to the serenity of his youth. Eva was a continual reminder of the mistrust he still carried as part of his legacy.

Rutledge Hall was a skilled old hand in the art of making the Rutledge wives exude a grandeur they never possessed before entering her twin doors. Eva, however, understood grandeur and demeanor. She was elegant and haughty in her own right and needed no help from her surroundings. Though she only stood five-feet-three, she was a woman for whom heads turned and eyes stared when she entered a room. It had nothing to do with her looks, which were the delicate cream pastels of the Aryan race: blond hair, pale complexion and sharp blue eyes. Small-boned and finely-built, she was what everyone would call "a lovely woman". But that wasn't the term they used when she entered a room. There was no word to describe her at a first meeting—elegant, yes; beautiful, yes; poised, most certainly. But that wasn't all of it. She was a woman other women feared, even women more beautiful than she. She could wither someone with a glance or create kings from paupers with one smile, and her ability to manipulate was instinctively feared in a society where the women were master manipulators. When it came to ambition and achievement, Eva was a skilled in-fighter, a street-wise operator. Nobody ever won a verbal slug-out with Eva.

The women in the homes South of Broad would have delighted in spurning Eva— "Why, my dear, not only is she not Charlestonian, she's not even American ! I declare, I'm so glad Charlie's mama isn't alive to see what he brought home from the war..." But there was an unwritten law passed by Eva herself and branded into the honeysuckle-scented heads of her neighbors: no one, but NO one shunned Eva. She might not be American and she most certainly wasn't Charlestonian, but she was a Rutledge, and she knew how the Rutledge fortune intertwined the peninsula society like the morning glory vines on their trellises, and, by God, she would be treated accordingly. Children had never been a part of her plans when she met Charlie in Berlin at the close of World War II. And when emergency surgery removed from her the possibility of ever having children of her own, she greeted the situation with a hidden contentment, though she assured Charlie she was heartbroken. She loved Charlie the way she had never loved anyone, and would have had his children had she been able because there would have been few alternatives, but she was secretly relieved that the possibility of competition for Charlie's love was removed.

She greeted the news of Charlie's intention to adopt a Korean boy with the stunned, frozen expression of a store-window mannequin. Charlie assumed that she was delighted with the news and pushed ahead with the arrangements. Eva threw herself into the excitement, even promoted it, keenly sensing that to challenge Charlie on this issue would be one time she would lose. So, like the master head-player she was, she saw to it that everyone knew of the wonderful thing she was doing: she was adopting a poor Korean orphan boy. The results were calculated and expected: all of Charleston smiled on Eva.

The boy found himself being pushed in front of cameras with Eva smiling sweetly and hugging him; he found himself petted and pawed by perfumed women at lady's clubs while Eva accepted their applause with graciousness. Joseph Ashley Rutledge was a big hit. And Eva was a star.

There was a great deal of his life in which Charlie Rutledge took an impish, perverse pleasure, always for reasons only he would understand. He was a gentleman of honor and good nature, creating admirable friends and few enemies of any consequence. He was the image of decorum, never having given anyone cause to criticize his ability to carry on the Rutledge name. But Charles Drayton Rutledge had one basic flaw that was inadvertently bred into him by his upbringing on the Battery: he could never stand to be told "no."

When he found a woman he loved and wanted to marry, he took a pseudo-innocent delight in bringing her back to Charleston, flags flying, enjoying immensely the sputterings and clucks he surely knew were taking place all over town. Eva, he knew, was enjoying the challenge on a completely different level, but for himself it meant the pure delight of flying in the face of tradition. He would no more deny himself a woman he loved for the sake of tradition than he would deny himself anything he truly wanted. He knew he was a deeply selfish person and he never tried to deny it because he knew that his was a selfishness that began with the generous giving of himself.

There was no way, however, that he was able to verbalize his feelings for Joe. He wouldn't even subconsciously cheapen his reasons for wanting the boy as being caste-related or a blatant challenge to society. It went much deeper than that, and when pressed about his reasons for adopting a "foreign child" as opposed to a "white child," he was at a loss to find the right words to reply. Though he didn't think of himself as a prejudiced man, he knew that he was. His racist tendencies were brought into full, ugly focus for the first time in Korea where he was bludgeoned over and over again with the sheer naked bravery of the Korean people. He was never again able to look himself in the eye and pretend that there was, indeed, a superior race. Korea had destroyed that concept in him forever. And Joe embodied all of them: he was the soul and spirit of a hopeless people who remained in touch with themselves, people who had struggled, suffered, starved and learned how to laugh again. The boy had turned Charlie's gaze inward, introducing him to something wonderful and unseen in himself. He forced Charlie to see his kinship with the world and its people, enabled him to understand that love is the least segregated of emotions and that courage has no color, no race, no age. In that first magical moment when Charlie hugged him with the strength of genuine affection, felt the boy's returning hungry grasp, and saw the open need in his eyes that flickered like a match flame, Charlie knew that he was simply caught in the wondrous, mystical world of loving a little boy.

A vague perplexity surrounded his observance of Eva's behavior toward the child. There was a driven atmosphere to her acceptance of him, an almost frantic desire to present the boy in all the best circles, make him prominent and visible. Charlie even went so far one evening to suggest that maybe she was carrying things a bit too far. "Charleston never did like anything shoved down its throat," he said with a slight smile. Eva had whirled on him, leveled the weapons in her eyes, and fired.

"Charleston doesn't even deserve to lick the mud from his shoes—if I could ever get the little heathen to leave them on."

She walked briskly to the door with Joe in tow. Charlie chuckled with mystified amusement as she left. Joe sat silent and still in the car, knowing exactly what she had meant and knowing full well for whom her venom had been intended.

When he looked back, Joe always saw his life that way: brief cameos of moments that said nothing, yet said it all. It was difficult for him to remember Eva without those moments of bitterness. He had been entranced by her pale, sparkling beauty, never having seen skin so translucent and white as hers, never having seen eyes so blue. He wanted to be able to love her for her beauty alone, to lose himself in the wonder of her fragrance. He wanted to touch her hair, stroke it, squash the lustrous waves with his hands just to see how it felt. He wanted to love her for her devotion to Charlie, for the continual court she paid him, forgetting the times he heard her try to diminish Charlie with the rapier of her tongue. He wanted to dwell on the flickering moments of laughter when he had done something that amused her. He wanted to love her for the good that he knew was in her, to tell her they were both refugees in a land of ancient families who had no real place for either of them. If she could find it nowhere in her heart to love him, he wanted her to at least be his ally. But she was too desperately insecure and she saw Joe as a bigger threat to her position with Charlie than even their own children would have been. She took up arms in her own defense. She waged a subtle, deadly battle in a war of her own making. Joe quickly gave up his longing and did all he could to rescue his snagged emotions, freeing them from the ice-flow that was Eva.

During those early years he retreated to the haven of Shady Mae's kitchen. Under the watchful, doting eyes of the Calhouns he learned of pirate ships and Rebel heroes, of songs in the cotton fields and symphony halls, of corn husk dolls and springtime regattas in the harbor. Nestled in the warm folds of Shady's lap, he uncovered the mystery of colored skin when he licked his finger and ran it firmly down her cheek.

"Chile!" she burst, and he knew another earthquake of laughter would soon dislodge him from his warm pocket. "Chile, that ain't shoe polish on there. Well go on, rub it good now, see fo' y'sef. Rub dat cheek, go on young 'un, rub dat cheek!" He rubbed and giggled, rubbed and giggled, and Shady Mae laughed until her huge breasts bounced like full water bags.

He learned the wonders of electrical appliances and spent an hour one day turning on and off every electrical thing he could find in the house. He lay awake at night and planned miniature guerrilla raids on the pantry where Shady Mae stored cookies. She yelped in surprise one night when she ambled back to the kitchen and saw the shadow of a naked boy streak past her with a chocolate brownie in each fist, and one in his mouth. He learned of hot baths every night— "Git yo' haid up outa dat water, young'n, I declare you gonna drown doin dat!"—and clean underwear every day, which he promptly discarded—"Dat's inDEcent, chile, plum inDEcent! Ever'one gotta has underwear. Where you hide em dis time...?"

He discovered the secluded beauty of the Rutledge garden, which was famous for its rare species of tulips and its immaculate topiary. He spent hours in the garden, hauling stacks of books into the topiary to study his lessons with the hedge-lions and bush-rabbits. His wanderings in the garden always pleased Reuben, who felt personally responsible for every sprig and bloom. He would watch the boy's dark head moving in and out of the green, watch the sun dappling on the black hair as he bent over his books.

Armed with milk and cookies one warm spring afternoon, Reuben decided to join the boy in the topiary—"Boy gits so serious sometimes, Shady Mae. He eatin' up dem books faster'n dat teacher can drag em in the door..." When he found the stack of books, Reuben set the tray down, careful not to spill either glass of milk, and looked around for the boy. He was nowhere to be seen. Reuben figured he would find him examining some new insect the way he had seen him do so many times, picking up the wiggling bug and turning it over and over, pulling gently on legs and wings, finally smelling it before turning it loose. "Some bugs good to eat," he explained. "Some bugs not," and he would wrinkle his nose in imitation of having smelled something bad. That boy's bug-lookin' again, Reuben thought with a smile, and he set off to find him. "He don't EAT dem critters, does he?" Shady had asked him one day. "Hell no, woman. He jes wants t' see if dey smell like

Ko-ree'n bugs."

When Reuben found the boy he stopped stone still, a sudden lurch of irritation and disgust making him catch his breath between clenched teeth. There, between the scrupulously trimmed legs of a leafy kangaroo, the boy had dug a small hole with a spade, had removed his pants and was squatting, a look of contented concentration on his face.

"Gawd A'mighty! What're you doin', boy?!" Joe jumped up, catching his shirt collar in the belly of the bush-beast. As if the topiary was in on his capture, the kangaroo held his shirt firmly while the boy stood and watched Reuben slowly approach. The look in Reuben's eyes was terrifying.

Reuben's worst moment came when he discovered that Joe had been relieving himself in the garden ever since his arrival almost nine months before. His garden! His lavish, cherished garden! Reuben clapped his hand to his chest and rolled his eyes until only the whites showed and Joe thought for a moment the man was going to faint. It took several more minutes of gestures and broken English to make Reuben understand that the indoor plumbing was distasteful to him, that he had never in his life heard of anyone relieving himself inside his own house. It was dirty and uncivilized.

The boy hung there like a raincoat in the hall while Reuben fought for control, first of his anger, then of his laughter. Before he freed the boy from the shrub-claws of the kangaroo he elicited a promise that Joe would use the toilets from now on—"You be in a heap o' trouble later on, young'n, if you keep diggin' up folkses gardens and such fo' your private toilet. You hafta have a mighty unnastanin girlfriend while you out wizzin' in her mama's azaleas!"

That night, there was another midnight raid on Shady Mae's pantry. Carefully selecting two of the ripest bananas he could find, Joe slipped soundlessly down the hall to the Calhoun's bedroom, peeling the bananas as he went.

At exactly two a.m. Reuben swung his long legs from the bed, preparing to make his regular wee-hour check of the house, a routine he followed without fail every night, checking locked doors and windows, and now that Joe was here, checking on him, too. The sensation began at the toes of his long, flat foot, spread upward through his left leg, swirled dangerously when it hit his stomach, then oozed into his brain with the same mushiness of whatever was oozing between his toes. Instant visions of the boy desecrating his garden came flashing with foul clarity into his mind and he froze where he stood. When the sound finally formed in his throat it was more a strangle than a cry, but it bore the trademarks of both, rising in a slow, panicked crescendo—"ShhaaadyyMAAAEEE!"

The light in the Calhoun bedroom blazed as Shady Mae flew into terrified motion. "Lawd Gawd, Reuben, what is it! Jesus save us, what's wrong!"

"That young'n done shit by my bed that's what! Gawd A'mighty, I don't care how much Mista Charlie love dat boy, I gonna kill dat sum-bitch! Oh Gawd, I can smell it...!"

When Reuben finally got the courage to lower his head to look at the mess squished between his toes, he heaved a huge sigh of relief. "Lawd have mercy, it's bananas!" Then the shock hit him, and the roof began to tremble with his angry bellows. And as lights flickered on in the Rutledge master bedroom and in maids' quarters in the west wing, the house came to rollicking, sputtering life as the sounds of a boy's laughter lifted above the house and floated out across the starlit Ashley River.

XV

The nightmares began after his first year in Charleston.

It took shape slowly during those initial weeks of adjustment, swirling at the boundaries of sleep in a formless gray mass that he never remembered when he awakened. The dream became a dark punctuation mark to the brief paragraphs of grammar school years, occurring at odd intervals with no regularity. It remained a constant amid first bicycles, first baseball games, first sailboat trips, first BB guns and first birthday parties. It became a brooding volcano that chose its own times of eruption with malicious irregularity, made more frightening because of its sameness: the dream was always a sinister reproduction of itself in expanding versions.

By the end of his junior high years, the dream had begun to have face and form, and with his first years in high school he experienced the first terror of a heart-pounding, sheet-twisting nightmare. He remembered these dreams when he awoke, all of them, and the sickening terror seemed to accumulate in his system like a drug overdose that his body couldn't expel.

In the summer before his senior year, a tired August breeze nudged the curtains of his window as he sat gasping on the edge of his bed. The growling mist of his dream retreated reluctantly to safer corners of his mind, the wolfish haunting slipping out the open veranda doors, back to the hillside. Moonlight bathed his skin, browned to a chestnut polish that glowed sallow and pale in the dark. The sheets were in a mad tangle around his long legs and his heart blasted in his ears as he disengaged himself from the bed. Stepping onto the veranda and leaning over the wooden banister, he waited for the sounds of night to gain access to him, reassure him, convince him the dream was over. Tonight had been one of the worst. Tonight the cloud had spoken his name.

He closed his eyes and listened to the slumbering Battery, breathing in the tangy scent of late summer. Charleston was exhausted, just like him. She had danced and laughed and flirted her way through yet another summer of tourists. She had opened succulent arms to her own, playing the perfect hostess at lavish weddings, tasteful garden parties and elegant summer teas, spending her days in humid, sweltering pursuit of laughter and her nights in the torrid, panting arms of harbor breezes. She lay now seductively sprawled on the peninsula, breathless and footsore, listening to cicadas and crickets gossip among themselves. The houses south of Broad Street sleepily fanned themselves with magnolia trees, their eyes closed, the streets silent and empty. Charleston barely stirred while he stood naked on the veranda. She slept on, never having heard the howling within him.

He dragged a patio chair across the balcony and sat with his bare feet propped against the white-painted balustrade, breathing softly now as he stared at the harbor. Fort Sumter made a small swelling at the mouth of the bay, the battered guardian of a lost war. The breeze stroked him, petted him, coaxed him into thoughtlessness.

He felt the man behind him before he heard him and he turned to see Charlie standing in the balcony doorway. His tall figure clad in pajama bottoms, his sandy hair disheveled, he said nothing while he moved a chair next to Joe's and propped his feet companionably next to his son's. "Can't sleep?" Charlie asked, his voice heavy with the gravel of slumber.

Joe nodded, still feeling the moisture on his body. He considered getting up for a towel to throw around him, decided against it and smiled. "It's hot tonight," he replied.

"Your bed's a mess. Looks like you've either been wrasslin' with some girl, or trying to strike oil in your mattress." He saw the answering grin, waited for a moment in the silence. "Bad dream again, Joe?"

"Just about the worst," he said softly, closing his eyes.

"I thought sixteen-year-old boys were supposed to sleep like rocks, especially after a whole day of water-skiing." The answering silence settled over the veranda and Charlie sat back to wait, letting the boy determine what he would share.

"Hey Charlie?"

"Hmm?"

"I have something I'd like to show you." He got up and padded back into his room, returning a moment later. He stared for a moment at the thing in his hand, then reached out and offered it to Charlie, who turned the small photo into the moonlight and squinted to study it. The expression on Charlie's face melted slowly from vague curiosity to a soft, pained comprehension. He looked up at the young man standing in the shadows. "This is what's been keepin you awake at night, isn't it?"

Joe sat on the edge of his chair, leaning toward Charlie with his elbows on his knees. Charlie's gaze returned to the photo. It was showing signs of age, the surface beginning to crack in tiny lines. But the images were still clear: a young Korean woman with two unsmiling boys at her side.

The sounds of the city settled over the two, falling on them like invisible rain, and from deep in someone's garden a tree frog added his voice to the rumors on the night air. The decision to show Charlie the picture had been long in coming, and now the ocean of night sounds made it seem like a simple thing, an act of no consequence, made it ultimately right.

"This is your brother here, and your mother?" Charlie asked, and Joe nodded.

"That picture's the only thing I brought with me from Korea."

"And the dreams?" Charlie pursued. "Are they about your family?"

"Just my brother," he said. He looked up at Charlie intently. "He's still alive, Charlie, I know he is! And I know that's why I have the dreams—he's alive somewhere and he...with my parents it was different. I saw them die, I knew they were dead, I was able to adjust. But with my brother..."

"Tell me about the dream."

"What?"

"Tell me about the dream you had tonight. Maybe it'll get some of this off your chest, make you feel better."

"It'll sound real weird to you," Joe warned.

"Go ahead. Most dreams are weird."

Joe settled back into his chair, fixing his gaze out beyond Fort Sumter, and for the first time since the dreams began, he shared the nightmare with another person.

"I'm in the back of a truck, the one leaving the indoctrination camp. I see the camp looming behind us, all green and speckled with white muslin. I have my brother's hand in mine and he's running to keep up with the truck. He has a smile on his face—we're going to make it! Then I see the cloud. It isn't dust from the road; it's growing up out of the camp, boiling out over the fields and racing toward us. It sees us! I can hear the thing inside the cloud. It's snarling, gnashing its teeth, growling as the cloud rolls faster and faster toward us, and I yell at my brother, 'Run! Run! It's catching up! Don't let go!' He looks over his shoulder and sees the cloud, then turns back to me and the look on his face is different. His eyes say it's over, he's not going to make it, it's no use. His eyes are terrible and I feel them right next to mine, feel his face in front of mine, wild, helpless, pleading. I feel his hand slip from mine. I'm hanging onto his curled fingers, he's stumbling, the truck is going faster. The cloud is almost on him and something in the cloud is screaming, howling. My brother's eyes are terrified. The cloud is lapping at his feet, making him stumble, finally dragging him to the ground. I scream his name as the cloud swallows him. I try to scream again, but no sound comes out, my throat is tight and I can't breathe. And then I can feel that whatever is in the cloud has seen me, has heard me trying to scream and now it wants me too. I fall back into the truck, scooting backward, trying to get away from it. It's crawling up over the tailgate, and I hear the sound deep in the animal's throat. It's looking at me, I feel it looking at me..."

Joe took a deep breath and blew out slowly, feeling an odd ringing in his ears. Charlie said nothing, sitting still in the heavy silence.

"Tonight," Joe continued, staring out to sea, "tonight was different. Tonight was the first time I heard the thing speak. It said my name, my Korean name. Just once. That's when I woke up..."

There was no sound, no movement in the world. The breeze had stopped, the water in the Ashley was barely moving. Even the insects seemed to have paused in their chattering to listen to the hauntings of the dream. Charlie's voice startled the night into sound again and the noises began, whispering this time, hoping not to miss anything.

"You're right," Charlie said. "That's awful damn weird." Charlie shook his head and sighed. "I'm sorry, Joe. I'm sorry about your brother, about everything that happened in Korea." He handed the photo back to Joe, who stared at the four feet silhouetted in the moonlight and smiled.

"I've made a decision about college," Joe said abruptly, and Charlie blinked in surprise.

"You have?"

"Yup. And since you were stupid enough to come out here at three in the morning, I'm going to tell you about it." He looked at Charlie's anxious face and grinned. "I'm going to be a professional gigolo and increase the Rutledge fortune by exposing myself to grateful old widows who die of ecstasy, leaving me all their money."

Charlie kicked the boy's feet off the balustrade and smiled at Joe's short burst of laughter. "Speak, son, or I'm going to bed."

"I've decided to go to The Citadel, Charlie."

He sat up and stared at the boy, the expression in his eyes saying everything he was unable to voice. His eyes spoke of pride so real, so deep it was almost painful. He swung his legs around and faced Joe, searching for the words. "When did you decide?"

"A long time ago. I just haven't said anything. If I keep up my performance at school they're going to offer me a scholarship and I've decided to take it."

"You mean to tell me you've let Eva rant and rave about Harvard all this time and you've known all along you were going to The Citadel?"

"It doesn't do any good to argue with Eva, you know that. I figured the real battle would come when I actually accept the scholarship. Believe me, there'll be plenty of time later on for blood-letting."

Charlie threw his had back and laughed, squeezing Joe's bare shoulder until it hurt. "Goddamn, son, you know how proud I am. You know what a tradition The Citadel has been for this family. But are you sure, absolutely sure you want to face what you'll—we'll get from Eva? She has her heart set on Harvard and you know how she is when she makes up her mind."

Joe sat quietly, a look of placid distance on his face. He knew. And he was ready.

"Congratulations, Joe," Charlie said softly. "I'm mighty damn proud." Charlie stood and walked to the veranda doors, paused for a moment, then turned and walked back. "Joe, I wanted to tell you that I knew about your brother."

Joe's head jerked up, and Charlie sat back down slowly. "The girl you lived with in Sok-Cho—Sook. She told me about your family."

At the mention of her name, Joe felt a maelstrom of emotion stir within him, felt himself careen dangerously off the rocky shores of his past where he still stood on a sandy beach, calling her name. He was amazed at the powerful effect her image still had on him, like a nasty bruise that is nonexistent until someone touches it. Her face rushed at him across the waves, her hair snaking crazily in the wind, then retreating on the fading sound of her laughter, leaving him hollow and weightless on the veranda. He was suddenly very tired, tired of memories that delighted in reducing him to twitching masses of heartache.

Charlie scratched the back of his hand, rubbed behind his ear and under his nose with the nervous fidgeting of a man who rarely expresses emotions. When Joe said nothing, Charlie reached out and patted his shoulder, standing to leave. "I just wanted to let you know I understand about your brother. I know how you must have loved him."

"Charlie?" Joe's voice was quiet, "Do you know where Sook went, what happened to her?"

"I never saw her again. But you know how those girls were—they never stayed in one place too long. Why? Was she someone special?"

Joe's eyes were dark and silent. There was no expression on his face to indicate any emotion whatsoever.

"Apparently not," he said.

"Why don't you try to get some sleep, Joe, you must be beat," Charlie said as he moved to the veranda doors. "I just realized," he muttered, slapping at his neck, "that I'm getting chewed up by goddamn mosquitos! If you're going to sit out here, you best put something on—don't these little bloodsuckers bother you?"

"Naw," he replied with a slight smile, "they're Charleston mosquitos. They want bluer blood than mine."

In brooding silence after Charlie left, Joe leaned his head back and stepped into the slip-stream of his past, listening to distant voices against the background of the night. He saw her turning to him in the hut, her face radiant and young; he saw her running barefoot in the surf with her skirt hiked up above her knees; he felt her wonderment and insatiable sense of discovery as she examined an odd shell or a stranded living sea thing; he swam in the lagoons of her eyes.

Was she special? Charlie had asked, and the question echoed through that peculiar, hurtful tunnel of ice inside. Closing his eyes in order to see her better, to hear her more clearly, he struggled to push away the image of a deserted little boy on the beach, fought to rise above the murky cloud-cover of betrayal that accompanied her memory—and somehow it never worked. In the end he knew there would always be a secluded, tender place reserved in his heart for the prostitute who was loved by an orphan boy.

XVI

This was one of those days, he knew, when he pulled himself deliberately into the joy of being alive, surrounded himself with it, using it as armor. He would be arriving at the hospital in a few moments and he knew he'd need all his resources, all the positive presence he could summon. The last thing Charlie needs right now, he thought, is a hang-dog, pitying person coming through that hospital door.

Roper General Hospital identified itself with the calling card of all hospitals: the acrid, unpleasant odor of an institution of healing. Hospitals, he decided, were the only places in the world that intimidated him. They were unsettling, unfathomable with their labyrinths of corridors lined with crypts containing the sick, the recovering, the dying; their inner workings of scalpels, needles, tubes, banks of blinking, humming instruments attached to human bodies. He had a chilling vision at times, a fantasy that the machines were quietly sucking the life out of people, disobeying some computerized order and reversing their processes. Staff members matched their surroundings: cold, white-and-green stares as they pushed in and out of the crypts, their voices modulated to the whisper of a dialysis machine. But most pervading of all was the idea that these were places designed for the final days of human life. He could smell it: that tiniest odor of hopelessness when a human body finally gives up.

From the top of the corridor he could see the tall, immobile figure of Reuben at his usual post outside Charlie's door as he waited for Eva to finish her visit. Reuben's eyes scanned the hall when he heard Joe approaching, and Joe warmed himself under the lamp of Reuben's smile.

"That's better," Joe chided. "You looked like a paid pall-bearer at a New Delhi funeral, and it's such a shame 'cause yer so perty when you smile."

Reuben laughed and clasped his hands behind him and Joe thought if Reuben was any other color, he'd be blushing. "Gwon wit you now, young'n, I don't need none o' yo sass today. I jes wanna know one thing—did you win?"

"Reuben, Reuben," Joe said, shaking his head in mock dismay. "You are a continual disappointment to my sense of dignity and accomplishment, and I find myself highly incensed that such queries have to be made, especially by one so astute and perceptive as yourself."

"Hot damn, boy, you done it again! You done plucked them skinny-ass Gamecocks!"

"Damn right."

"Mista Chawlie's gonna be mighty glad t'hear dat—he ain't done so awful good today."

"How long has Miss Eva been here?"

"Most o'the mornin', as usual, Mista Joe. Poor woman hates to leave long enough to even eat anything. Shady Mae's goin' crazy thinkin' she gonna plumb dry up t'nuthin."

The door to Charlie's room flew open and Eva stood framed in the sanitary white light from behind her. Her face was pale and drawn, and Joe had the fleeting impression that if she moved too quickly her reading glasses would slip off the snowy texture of her nose and drop to the floor. "I thought it was you!" she said in her perpetually agitated voice. "Come in then, you're late, Joey, and Charlie's been asking for you. I was getting ready to leave soon, and didn't want to go until you arrived, but here you are. So..."

Joe looked up at Reuben while Eva's words tumbled over each other, and Reuben shrugged as if to say, it just gets worse as the weeks go by. He leaned down and placed the obligatory kiss on her cheek, then walked into the room, making a great effort not to let his eyes show how disappointed he was at Charlie's continued degeneration.

"Hey you ol' lounge-rat, that nurse out in the hall told me all about how you been chasin' her all over the room. So what're you doin' still in that bed?"

The skin of Charlie's face had become a powdery gray, making the sparkle in his eyes seem more brilliant, more painful. His hair was almost completely gone, making his head look much too large for his shriveled neck, and when he laughed, the skin slid down his throat like a loose stocking slipping into a shoe. "Hey Bubba Joe, I've been waiting for you, and you can tell that nurse next time I'm gonna let her catch me."

Eva stood on the opposite side of the bed, fussing and smoothing covers while they talked, her lips moving soundlessly while she tucked here and folded there. Her eyes glanced sideways at Joe every few seconds as though he were going to make some sudden move she needed to prepare herself for. Charlie became suddenly self-conscious, like a child who is accustomed to being spoon-fed but doesn't want his friends to know. He reached out and patted Eva's hand with a firm, gentle pressure. "Thank you, honey, thank you, but if you keep that up there won't be anything for the nurses to do." She smiled down at him, leaning over and touching his parchment cheek, her eyes no longer darting and furtive. She concentrated on him with a look of consummate love. "I don't mind," she said softly, her German accent falling like flower petals on the sheets. "When you get home, you're going to be glad to have such service. No more nurses..." She turned and reached for her gloves, staring at Joe as she fumbled on the night stand. Joe cleared his throat to break the silence.

"Hey Charlie, did we ever pull off a big one against Carolina today!" He went into an animated explanation of the track meet, starting from the beginning and including all the ribald bits of humor he knew Charlie would appreciate. Charlie watched him intently, the words taking him out and away from his room, away from the disease that was destroying him in slow chapters. Right now, in this one moment, there was no hospital, there was no cancer. He was a father again, young and healthy, sharing the triumphs of his son.

"They're talking about a new NCAA record for the hundred yard dash; it's not official yet, but everyone's pretty certain. You shoulda seen me, Charlie! Man, I was flyin' today! I knew I was gonna win before the gun went off."

The wispy texture of Charlie's skin assumed a faint glow as his dry lips separated into a smile. His eyes were alive with pride and an odd, distant yearning. Eva had slipped on her gloves and was standing close to the head of the bed, gently tapping Charlie's shoulder in a furtive effort to get his attention without appearing to interrupt. When Charlie ignored the faint butterfly tapping, she suddenly pulled her hand away and glared at Joe.

"And so who ever notices a track star from The Citadel?" she asked with a clear, uncut acid in her voice. "A Harvard man, yes, but who pays attention to ANYTHING that happens at The Citadel? Who cares about a bunch of glorified bellhops?" She opened her handbag and began rummaging inside. "My goodness, look at the time! I'm late again for the Garden Club, what they must think of me..."

Joe put his hands in his pockets and walked to the window while she said her lavish good-byes to Charlie. "Oh, and Joey, don't be late for supper, dear. Shady Mae's preparing all your favorites."

"I won't be home for supper, Eva," he said without turning away from the window. "I have a party planned at the beach house tonight with some of my friends from school. I'll most likely spend the weekend there."

"All right, my dear, but please be careful in the water." She sounded almost kind, and he was tempted to turn around, thinking that he might see something different in her eyes this time. He waited patiently for her to leave. When the door closed, he turned back to the bed and pulled up a chair like a child who has discovered himself alone with a favored friend.

Words spilled out and over themselves as they talked freely of school, of girls, of days gone by. They quenched themselves in a relationship that had never been a genuine father-son exchange. They had acknowledged each other from the beginning as two comrades from a shared trench; not as man to boy, but as person to person. They had seen each other as equals, ageless and disembodied, uniquely suited to each other through mutual needs satisfied. They feasted on the relationship now, giving and taking while they knew they still could. Together they linked spiritual arms and faced the largest enemy: the faceless, relentless soldier of Time.

"I want you to do me a favor, Joe," Charlie said, and Joe could see he was growing weary. He looked like a creature placed in a freezer to die, little by little, his movements becoming slower and slower. "Sure, Charlie."

"I want you to be patient with Eva. I want you to do everything you can to understand her, especially now."

"I understand her, Charlie, I always have," he replied, trying to keep the faint note of bitterness from his voice.

"No," Charlie said, slowly shaking his head against the pillow. "You need to really reach her, reach out to her to understand what she's going through right now. You see, even though she's got everyone else fooled, including all these Charleston fish-hens, she hasn't fooled me. I know how she needs me, and I know what it'll do to her if she loses me. Though she comes across as tough and capable, she's a frightened, insecure little bird trapped in the psyche of a female tiger. She's facing the worst catastrophe of her life and she's scared. All these years, she's had me to turn to, to lean on, to feed on. There were times when she sucked me dry of every sensible strength I had to offer, and all she had to do was take me by the hand, say a word or two, and I was panting at her feet, ready for her to plug into me and begin the drain all over again. I've known all that, you see. It's been a pattern that I understood, maybe even welcomed, but you never did learn how it was played with Eva. It was some sort of sick game to you, and you never were willing to learn the rules. I've known all that, too."

Joe looked at him in amazement. "How could you stand it all these years, Charlie? If you could see what her game was, how could you stand it? Why...?"

Charlie looked at him, his eyes gleaming like sunken marbles at the bottom of a well. His smile was wistful, patient.

166

"Because some people need to be needed that badly," he said softly. "I guess maybe I needed the game as much as she did."

Several precious minutes went by when neither of them spoke. Charlie never took his eyes from Joe, who sat staring at the patterns of blue lines on the backs of Charlie's hands. "What do you want me to do, Charlie?"

"Take care of her, Joe. Don't give up on her. I know how you feel about each other. I've always known how she felt about the adoption, how she used it because she knew she couldn't fight it. And I knew that *you* knew. I've seen all of it. I've brought you two together out of circumstance, like two animals who are natural enemies, finding themselves sharing the same cave during a flood. They know they're in it together until the water goes down, so they sit in separate corners and glare at each other, showing their teeth now and then. I want you to put all that aside now and help her. She's losing what small foothold she had in this world and it's affecting her badly, you can see that."

Joe's largest emotion at that moment was an amazement with himself for not having seen Charlie's perception sooner. He felt small and shamed, realizing what Charlie had willingly suffered at her hands all these years; when all was said and done, Charlie was a man in love.

"Stay with her, Joe. Till the water goes down."

"I'll take care of her, Charlie, if she'll let me."

"She won't let you. But take care of her anyway. Please."

Joe smiled and nodded, squeezing his shoulder. He wondered briefly if Charlie fully understood the depth of Eva's enmity toward him, wondered if he truly knew the extent of the animosity in the cave. He also knew that it didn't matter. He didn't believe he needed to be needed the way Charlie did, and especially not by Eva. But he needed to be loved and respected by Charlie. And he would face even Eva for that. He turned and walked to the door.

"Hey sandbagger," he said, turning as he opened the door, "you gonna get your lazy ass outa that bed long enough to come to my graduation? It's in five weeks."

"Depends on which nurse is on duty that day," Charlie

replied, shifting tracks as easily as Joe had. "If it's Miss Goodbody, then you can graduate without me; I'll be busy."

On the way to Folly Beach, Joe couldn't help wishing it were true. About Miss Goodbody and being busy. God, how he wished it were true! It was going to be a dark, lonely cave with Charlie gone, and he had visions of a pair of eyes gleaming in the dark—sharp blue eyes, frightened and irrational, hiding in a corner and refusing to live.

XVII

The beach house was one of the eccentricities Charlie had allowed himself in his younger years, simply because it was so perfectly suited to his "no" syndrome.

Open rebellion wasn't in Charlie's nature and he insured that no one would ever be able to accuse him of being a total maverick. His infrequent flailings at Old Charleston dictates were always tasteful, always fringing on acceptance. Even in marrying Eva he had merely walked the tightrope without jumping off. Eva was undeniably an elegant lady. She was, therefore, borderline. Joe was a larger break, a larger rebellion for Charlie because he was not only a "foreigner" but because he was also a different race. However, Joe developed academic and athletic skills that gained him a limited entrance into Charleston's society in his own right. Though a more flagrant deviation from tradition, Joe, too, was now marginally acceptable.

But the beach house was something else again. One of the best homes on the beach, it still bore the unmistakable hallmarks of degeneration endemic to all Folly Beach houses. No one south of Broad Street ever seriously considered owning a home on Folly Beach. It was a run-down, dirty, forsaken little backwater that was referred to as a "resort" only by people who'd never been there. Charlie had bought the house while he was in school at The Citadel over the exasperated objections of his parents, and had defended his ownership of it even in the face of mortar-round objections from Eva. She had wrinkled her nose in disgust when Charlie first took her to his hideaway; she had planted her feet in the sand, refusing to go inside, and had pronounced her sentence of death on the place. "Mein Gott, Charlie, why has no one burned this—this termite farm—to the ground?"

The house was now under the sponsorship of another Rutledge, and Charlie took a secret pleasure in the fact that Joe had taken possession of it. It was a perfect alliance of solitary natures. The beach house was a hobo version of Rutledge Hall, and she took a special pride in her shabbiness. She loved laughter, loud and boisterous, and didn't mind the clink of beer bottles or the shrieks of naked girls running through her hallways. Her raucous love affair with the sand and sea had taken their toll as the harsh lovers they were, and there were times when she appeared to droop in exhaustion after a storm. But soon the makeup of a new paint job would revive her bawdy spirits and the bottle-raising, butt-slapping laughter would begin again.

The house kept her interior a secret, and visitors were always surprised to see modern elegance adorning five large bedrooms, a spacious living room that overlooked the ocean, and a fully-equipped kitchen. She was a crusty, hard-bitten old hostess but she made certain everyone was comfortable when they crossed her threshold. For she too, after all, was a Southern lady.

Folly Beach itself was "Land's End, USA" and Joe was wild about the place. It was one of the few areas in the world that would have accommodated the beach house in such a perfect atmosphere of isolation and earthiness. When standing on the beach and gazing out over the water at sunrise, he could see himself at the boundaries of civilization, at the very brink of creation. He could sit on the beach and imagine Father Scully's god looking out over the vast expanse of nothingness, deciding to add on to the thin strip of sand that kept him from being sucked into the sea. He could imagine this god feeling a need for something to balance out the beauty and solitude of Folly Beach. So he created Charleston. After that, this god must have become bored; that's when he created the rest of the nation.

Joe smiled as he drove along the beach road toward the house, enjoying his version of Genesis. The drive, he realized, was almost as important to him as the beach itself. The houses brought to mind a long row of huge elephants that had wandered onto the beach, weathered and wasted, looking for a place to die. They stood now on truncated pylons, frozen in a glacial field of sand, staring out at the sea in perplexed disappointment and realizing they were in the wrong place, but too tired to move on.

They stood in dry, gray silence, never really dying. They simply erased themselves through the years, fading to the same color as the sand, and Joe had a vision of them vanishing into the dunes someday. Gone forever.

He reached the house and pulled into the driveway, cursing good-naturedly under his breath when he saw two cars already parked in the port under the house. The automatic sensation of warmth that accompanied his motley collection of friends began to settle over him as he dragged the first case of beer from the passenger seat of his car and headed toward the stairs, giving Simmons' '61 Chevy a swift kick to the fender as he walked past. He pushed through the door and was immediately greeted with a chorus of welcome from four classmates littered in various positions around the living room. "Hey, Rutledge! Who the hell invited you? And where's the beer..." "Well, there goes the neighborhood...!" he smiled and pushed past them, dropping the beer in the kitchen.

"Is this it?" he asked, looking around. "Where is everybody?"

"Durrell is coming after he picks up his girlfriend," Simmons offered, "and Carver stopped to pick up some more food. Debbi's bringing her roommates later on, and then it's every man for himself! Too bad, Rutledge. With this expanse of gorgeous manhood you don't stand much a chance." Simmons was a thin, sallow character that girls dated out of pity and stayed with because of his unconscious, spontaneous wit.

"You're right, Simmons, I never have any luck with girls

171

when you're around," Joe smiled. "I used to wonder why, until Debbi told me you can lick your eyebrows."

"You're just in time to join in our intellectual discussion, JoJo," Hampton said as he popped open another cold beer from the refrigerator. He was a hulking, knock-kneed powerhouse of a man attending school, like Joe, on an athletic scholarship. Hampton had singled Joe out during the first week of their freshman year, a week justifiably referred to as "Hell Week;" he had lumbered into Joe's life—and simply stayed. "We've been discussing the political philosophies behind the Vietnam war, planning strategies and solutions."

"You been figuring out how to go AWOL without getting caught," Joe said.

"Damn straight."

"Not me," Eberhardt said as he tightened the string of his bathing suit. "I'm gonna be a jet jockey, rainin' death and destruction on all those skinny-ass little Viet Congs; the avenging angel, John Wayne in an F-4! All them gooks are gonna see me flyin' toward em and they're gonna burn up their Ho Chi Minh sandals all the way to Laos!"

"Ha! With your luck you'll get shot down your first day in Vietnam," Hampton chided. "What a waste of good airplane! You better do the Air Force a favor, Ever-hard. Resign before you do any real damage."

"Hey, asshole," Everhardt said defensively, "I ain't no Sneed."

There was a flickering silence in the room as Joe continued to shuttle beer into the fridge, ignoring the conversation.

"What ever happened to that dip-stick, anyway?" Simmons asked, and Joe had to smile, hearing the comment from the only person in the room who truly resembled a dip-stick. "Who knows?" Hampton said with a loud belch. "Maybe he got lucky and married a dairy cow from Clemson. He sure ain't around here anymore."

"What about you, Joe?" Morelli asked. He had been sitting in customary quiet, listening to the conversation with muted amusement and offering little more than occasional smiles and nods. Tall and dark with brooding Italian handsomeness, Morelli and Joe were more instinctively drawn to each other than any of the rest, and yet Joe saw Morelli the least. It was a friendship of unspoken acceptance, a friendship of simple concretes. "What are your plans when you graduate and get your commission?"

"He's gonna be a goddamn Green Beanie!" Eberhardt chimed. "A kick-ass-take-names-sure-as-shit Green Beret, right Rutledge? He's gonna be down there in the jungle tryin' to strangle them gooks one at a time while John Wayne of the airways here comes along and...hey, JoJo, where you goin'?"

"I'm gonna let you guys fight the damn war by yourselves for awhile. I'm heading out to catch some rays before sundown. Y'all help y'sevs to the beer." He pushed through the living room and into his bedroom where he quickly changed into bathing trunks and grabbed a large towel from the bathroom. He didn't like discussing Vietnam. He had definite opinions about the war and usually ended up sending his hawkish friends into a lather of righteous indignation with his pacifism. He kept his own counsel where Vietnam was concerned, viewing all his friends and classmates as babes in the woods when it came to war. They were like ten-year-olds trying to discuss sex—they puffed and they postured, but they knew nothing. They went through the ludicrous bumps and grinds of valor, not having the faintest idea what bravery really was.

He spread his towel on the sand and lay back, closing his eyes to the sun and his mind to Vietnam. Behind his eyelids the world was a hazy pink, a perfect place to be on a day like this. Oh God, the tourists are going to be crawling out of the woodwork this year. It's going to be a long, hot summer. His mind skipped from one inconsequential bit of trivia to the next in a game of lazy mental hopscotch, until it jumped into a puddle that had almost been forgotten: Sneed.

Joe could never recall Marion Sneed without thinking of the fifteen-year-old Ginny—Shady Mae's niece. The two of them were inextricably woven into the fabric of one violent curtain in his mind and he pushed the curtain aside now, staring at the memory behind it with detached curiosity. He was glad to find there was no more anger when he thought of Sneed, and only a residue of pity for the girl. That's good, he said to himself. After a whole year, he knew it was time to let the anger die.

He felt no pity for Sneed, no remorse. When he thought of him as an individual, Joe thought of a magazine ad for tennis shorts, a slick eight-by-ten glossy photo with no substance. A senior upper-classman in Joe's junior year, Sneed was the consummate cadet: president of the debate club, a member of the prestigious rowing team, captain of the elite Summerall Guards. His blond, gray-eyed good looks were made more striking by his smile: dazzling, they called it. Charming, they called it. Joe thought it was feline, the sly grin of a Cheshire cat. Sneed was the youngest in a long line of Sneeds who were Citadel graduates and promised to be the most brilliant of all. He was elegantly perfect. They called him El Cid—a moniker he wore with arrogant pleasure. He was Mr. Citadel.

When he thought of Ginny Ann, Joe thought of a willowy slip of a girl who would spend Saturday's at Rutledge Hall with Shady Mae, helping out in the kitchen or doing odd cleaning jobs around the house. He saw a painfully shy smile with white, even teeth. She had grown from a timid little girl into a retiring, slender beauty, and Shady adored her. Joe could remember frequent trips with Reuben into the black sections of Charleston, into the row houses and projects where Ginny Ann would take quiet delight in showing him her world. He remembered hours in the dust with a bagful of marbles. He remembered an innocent worship in her eyes as she looked up at him.

Through the pink behind his eyes Joe could still see the week of spring break the year before, a week of blooming tulips and rainy nights. He saw himself walking into Shady Mae's kitchen with a bucket full of fish he had just caught. If he concentrated hard enough, he could still feel the weight of the bucket in his hand, the handle across his palm. Every detail of that day became sharply outlined in his memory: the smell of the kitchen, the friendly bulk of Shady Mae, the wooden spoon in her hand, the swollen, red-rimmed eyes. He remembered the clunk of the bucket as he dropped it to the floor.

"What's the matter, Shady Mae?" he asked. He had seen her cry before, but only at funerals and while chopping onions. "Shady?" She shook her head and tried to turn away from him. He grabbed her shoulders and turned her to him, his eyes narrowed with concern. "Where's Reuben?" he asked. She shook her head, holding her hand to her mouth and staring at him with tear-filled eyes. He turned and ran from the kitchen, searching the garden and calling Reuben's name. There was no answer. The door to the garden shack was open and he rushed inside, feeling an unreasonable fear. Reuben sat on a stack of fertilizer bags, his hands clasped in front of him, his elbows on his knees. A shaft of sunlight pierced the darkness, shining on the bowed head and lighting the twisted threads of gray. "Reuben, what's wrong? What's happened?" There was still no answer. Joe knelt on one knee in front of him, realizing the man was weeping, and Joe felt a sickening sense of helplessness, never having seen him shed a tear before. "Reuben...Reuben, we been friends a long time. Tell me—tell me what's wrong."

Reuben's lips began to tremble and Joe gripped the man's shoulder. "Mista Joe," he said, his voice cracking with emotion, "It's Ginny Ann." The tears spilled over the reservoirs of his lower lids, adding to the flood on his cheeks.

"What about Ginny Ann? What's wrong with her?"

"She..." he sniffed and wiped his nose with the back of his hand. "She been workin after school and weekends at the Sneed place. Shady Mae got her the job." He lowered his head and stared at his hands for a moment, seeming to search inwardly for words to go on. "She was there alone last night gettin ready to go home. Young Mista Sneed, he come in jes as she leavin' and grabs her, takes her out back..." Reuben broke down again, shedding soft, painful tears. Joe let him cry, feeling the numb, dizzying sensation of anger rolling up his spine, spreading through his body. "She fought like a wild thing, I guess, and he beat her up something bad. When he done with her, he beat her half to death, say he kill her if she tol' anybody. She laid in the bushes all night, Mista Joe, all night! She too hurt 'n too scared to go in the house this mornin', so she manage to walk over here, where Shady foun' her on the back porch."

Joe had risen slowly to his feet, a languid movement that belied the rumbling anger stretching and gnawing at his insides. "Where is Sneed now?"

Reuben stood quickly, wiping his nose again. "Mista Joe, it ain't gonna do you no good to go gettin' riled. Young Mista Sneed, he ain't gonna admit to a damn thing."

"Have you called the police?"

Reuben's expression was incredulous, as though he were looking at an imbecile. "The po-lice! The po-lice ain't gonna do shit, Mista Joe. Dis here happen to a nigger girl at the hands of a rich white boy; dey ain't gonna lif' a finger to hep. It be her word agains' his, and ain't no one gonna take the word of a nigger girl over the word of a Sneed. Dey own haf the goddman worl'!"

"And the Rutledge's own half of *them*!" Joe said sharply, his eyes glinting with a narrow, amber light. "Where's Mister Charlie? At the office?"

"Yassa, at the office. But I done spoke wid 'im awready. He agree, dey ain't nothin' to be done but grieve..."

Joe never heard Reuben's insistent pleading that he stay out of it, never knew how he reached his car or how he managed to make it all the way to the corner of Church and Broad Street. When he was able to see again, he was pushing his way through the second-floor office, walking resolutely past a receptionist, past banks of secretaries, past a sputtering, protesting executive secretary and through the heavy mahogany doors of a board room where another secretary tried to intercept him. "Please, Mr. Rutledge, your father is in a very important meeting and can't be disturbed. If you'll just wait over here..."

He put his hands on her shoulders and gently, firmly

moved her aside, then pushed beyond the doors. The room smelled of expensive wood and cigarette smoke. Morning sunshine spilled in through large, airy windows and struck green plants overflowing window boxes. The room echoed with half-spoken words cut off in mid-phrase when Joe entered. Nearly a dozen men—government officials, bankers, attorneys—sat around a huge oval table lined with coffee cups and littered with papers. Joe had met all of them at one time or another at Rutledge Hall. They all looked at him now, surprised recognition on all their faces. Charlie stood at the head of the table, impeccable and professional. He stared at Joe with a flicker of open amazement that vanished almost instantly into complete understanding. He looked nervously at the gathering, then back at Joe as if to say, please, not now. Joe strode smoothly across the room and stood next to Charlie, then turned and spoke.

"Please forgive me, gentlemen, but a matter of extreme importance has come up within the family. This will only take a few moments if y'all would be so kind as to wait." His voice was clear and certain in odd contrast to the way he was dressed. Still wearing the faded dungarees and loose-fitting T-shirt, there was no escaping the air of assuredness, of dignified strength in him. Standing face to face with Charlie, there was an energy pulsing from him, a power that would not be denied. Charlie turned to the group, his eyes intense and apologetic. Please excuse me, gentlemen."

They didn't speak until they reached the street and began walking toward East Bay Street. "Important meeting, Charlie?" Joe asked tightly.

"We're planning a new container ship facility on the Wando River. Lots of dollars, lots of red tape. Today is the final decision—yes, it's an important meeting. It's going to mean a lot to..."

"What are we going to do about this, Charlie?"

"Nothing, Joe," Charlie said, calmly shifting tracks. "There's nothing we can do about that little girl. I'm as sick about it as you are. I'm very fond of Ginny, but believe me, there's nothing we can do."

"There has to be something!" Joe's voice was impassioned, his fists clenched. "This is supposed to be a civilized country, and there's a girl who gets raped, we know who did it, and no one can do anything about it? I can't believe that."

"She's not just a girl, Joe; she's a colored girl," Charlie said, and Joe turned to him, looking at him with a strange, frightening intensity. He was seeing an image of Charlie he had missed, and his expression reflected his amazement at not having seen it before. It was so simple, so unavoidable, and yet he had missed it. He was seeing Charlie for the first time as a deeply Southern man, a man who was, in the end, inspired and motivated by the roots from which he sprang. Charlie was from the South. And Ginny was a nigger.

"There's something you can do," Joe said flatly. "You can yank your holdings out of their bank, you can crush that rat hole in one swoop. You can tell that little pissant Sneed that he's going to turn himself in or his old man's bank is going to sink into the sunset. You can do that, Charlie."

"I'm not going to do that!" Charlie said in a rare moment of anger. "You're talking about an entire family's future here, generations of business and family ties. You're talking about ruining them all, and for what? The deed's done, it's a disgusting thing, but life goes on, Joe. You're tilting at an unbreakable windmill here and I want you to drop it, understand? It'll be his word against hers, there's nothing to be done. We'll take care of the girl—she'll have a job with us when she recovers, but beyond that there's nothing I can do..."

"Nothing you *will* do," Joe corrected.

"Come on Joe, be sensible. You're no bleeding heart sentimentalist. You saw things like this with those girls in Korea all the time..."

The moment the words passed his lips, Charlie knew he had made a mistake. He had no way of knowing, however, just how large that mistake was. A sudden, violent flash of memory exploded in Joe's brain and he could see Sook limping into the hut with a roll of toilet tissue under her arm. He glared at Charlie, feeling the hot, formless worm of disgust curling his

178

insides with the memory of a situation so many years ago when there was nothing anyone could do.

"Well, it's different this time," he said, speaking to Charlie, speaking to the memory. He turned and walked away, retracing their steps back to Church Street. Charlie followed him but said nothing, knowing a judgment had been made in which he no longer had any part, knowing that no more words would help, if they ever had. When they had reached the office, Joe kept walking as if the building no longer had any significance for him, leaving Charlie standing at the entrance, wanting to say something, anything to bridge the fathoms of distance separating them at that instant. There was no sound other than the city traffic, and the bells of St. Michaels tolling the hour of high noon.

Marion Sneed enjoyed life. He had the best of everything and he knew it. There were times when he tried to convince himself he should want to do things the hard way once in a while, make a few sacrifices for his rewards, but the notion lived a short, aborted life in his mind, dying a quick death at the soft hands of opulence. On his way home from a particularly satisfying date with yet another "lovely Southern belle," he draped his wrist over the steering wheel and smiled with half his mouth. Southern belle, my ass—she's nothing but a social climber, figuring on gaining something by getting cozy with a Sneed. Well, there was something gained, all right, but not by her. She'll probably figure that out in the morning. Marion Sneed was pleased with himself. He was in love with the world, and his whole world was Marion Sneed.

He pulled into the driveway and jumped from the Thunderbird convertible, whistling to himself and tossing his car keys in the air as he headed for the side entrance. The huge old vine-covered house was silent and dark, the only light coming from two ornate gate-post lanterns at the entrance to the driveway that automatically went out at two a.m. He was searching the key ring for the house key when the lights went out and he cursed under his breath at the sudden blackness. He never saw the figure move soundlessly up behind him, never saw the tight brown fist as it slammed into the back of his neck, sending a violent flash of red into his eyes in the second before he lost consciousness and dropped like a stone into two waiting arms. He didn't feel himself being propped in the passenger seat of his own car, was unaware of the brief ride down Lockwood Boulevard to the yacht basin.

There were night sounds, the sounds of a sleeping dock. There was moonlight on the water reflecting between sleek, extravagant boats. There was a soft lapping sound as the figure of a man was lowered into a smooth-lined Donzi, and the quick gurgling of an engine coming to life, a subdued sound of restrained power as the boat moved away from the docks and out into the Ashley River. But Marion Sneed saw nothing, heard nothing as the boat gained speed and began its solitary flight across the dark water.

At first, all Sneed could do was smell. In those numb, swirling moments of returning consciousness, his mind tried desperately to sort its senses, to resume logical functions, and his mind told him he must have vomited. There was no other ready explanation for the foul odor all around him, and his mind told him he must be drunk because he felt so horrible— hot and bloated. His ears were ringing. His head pounded viciously and the skin of his face felt slack. Vaguely at first, then with increasing intensity, he was aware of a painful pressure around his ankles. He opened his eyes slowly and the sense of disbelief at first out-weighed a mushrooming fear that threatened to squeeze his heart through his throat. He was, if anything, a logical man; he believed in an explainable order to all things, and in those first seconds after opening his eyes, his mind kept stubbornly insisting that this couldn't be, that what he was seeing was part of a nightmare. But there was a sickening reality to the smell, to the feel of the air, and his logic was forced to give way to reality.

The candle he saw was burning upside down. When his struggling mind tried to tell him the whole world was upside down, he blinked his eyes and swallowed, forcing himself to realize that it was *he* who was upside down. In the dim light of the candle he looked around quickly, tried to move his arms but couldn't. He looked down—up—at his ankles wrapped tightly together with his own shirt and bound with a rope. His hands were tied behind him and secured with a rope that led from his wrists to the rope around his ankles. His eyes widened as he followed the rope down—up—where it disappeared into inky blackness. He was hanging from his ankles like a plumb-bob over a bottomless black nothing, an open hole in the world that had no end. He began to squirm, hoping to awaken himself from the nightmare, but he was hopelessly bound. He made a small sound like a trapped animal, and with the answering echoes all around him he realized he was in a structure, a building of some sort and the understanding sent a nauseating chill over his naked body. He could no longer hope this was only a nightmare; it was real, all of it.

He turned to the candle flame burning only a couple feet away and saw a face in the light, saw the shadowed brown skin blending into the muted glow of muscles on a bare chest and arms, saw the grim set of the mouth. He saw the eyes reflecting two points of flame that became blazing forests as he stared, burning civilizations. The man was sitting calmly on a stairway, holding the solitary candle between them and saying nothing while Sneed tried to comprehend what was happening.

"Rutledge?" he said, his voice bouncing off surrounding walls of granite. "Rutledge, is that you?" The man said nothing, his face seeming to change shape and move in and out of the flame gyrating in an updraft. He moved the candle out and away from him, watching Sneed's terrified eyes bulge as he stared at the damp, guano-streaked walls, the rusted iron stairway where the face in the candle was sitting. The foul odor coming from above, from below, from the walls, filled Sneed's lungs. He squirmed again and felt his dangling body sway at the end of the rope like a piece of meat in a smoke-house. This has got to be a joke, some crazy-ass cadet prank. My roommates, he thought wildly, my goddamn roommates put him up to this, those bastards.

"Rutledge, what the hell is this? Where the fuck am I?

JOE PORCELLI

Did Reynolds and Platt put you up to this? Goddamn
Rutledge, my ankles are about to break, get me down from
here." His voice fell into the emptiness around him, leaving a
hollow wake of silence. Rutledge said nothing, staring at him
with the eyes of creatures who dwell on cliffs and in jungles.
"Okay, you've had your fun, but this isn't funny anymore, that
rope could break..." Then a new, infuriating idea wriggled its
way into his mind: What if I'm only a few inches from the
floor and he's been making me sweat. "You got another thing
coming if you think you're gonna see me crack under a sick
joke like this—you set it up real well, asshole, but it's not
gonna work, making me think I'm hanging out over
nowhere..."
    Joe calmly picked up a piece of broken Coke bottle, held
it up in the light for Sneed to see, turning it slowly back and
forth while the glass glinted in the glow. Then he tossed it
over the metal railing. There was no sound. On and on the
bottle fell and there was still no sound. When the glass finally
broke, it was the sound of distant tinkling, as though from a
disturbed chandelier. And for the first time, Sneed realized he
was hearing another sound from somewhere in the darkness
below, a rushing, rumbling noise rising up and beyond him—
the sound of the sea. With the breaking glass there was
another scouring sound of a wave far below—a hissing thing
that rushed in and devoured the broken glass.
    "Rutledge, goddamn it, this has gone far enough!"
Sneed's eyes were wild now with a fear he tried to mask with a
violent show of rage. "You cut me down from here, you
sonofabitch, or I'll make you pay. I'll see you thrown out of
school, you slant-eyed bastard. You never belonged here
anyway, you and your phony Rutledge name. You're no better
than a goddamn nigger..."
    The word echoed in deafening vibrations, and Sneed's
mouth froze over the word, his body swaying slightly, like an
uncertain pendulum. The sudden realization was so profound
that he momentarily lost touch with his fear. His naked body
was sweating now, his penis dangling ludicrously while he
rotated slowly at the end of the rope. He tried to swivel his

head as he turned, keeping an eye on the beast with the candle.

"Is *that* what this's all about?" he asked shrilly, "all this is over that girl?" There was no answer, but Sneed could see a slight unconscious narrowing of Joe's eyes, could see the light reflecting a deeper shade of amber. Sneed rolled his eyes, his warped instincts telling him he had just stumbled onto a precarious foothold with the silent thing on the stairs and he pursued it in gasping relief. "That's it, isn't it? Look, Rutledge, that was an accident, I got kinda carried away. I didn't mean to hurt her. You can tell your maid—ah, Shady Mae—you can tell Shady Mae you got even with me, alright? Tell her—tell her you beat the shit out of me. Just get me down and we'll forget this whole mess."

Sneed had the sickening, bottomless sensation of hopelessness. He could see in Rutledge's eyes that it wasn't working. There was no movement, no word. Another hiss from the monster of the pit sent him into a fit of squirming. "Rutledge, this is CRAZY! SHE'S NOTHIN' BUT A GODDAMN NIGGERRRR!"

When he had exhausted himself he swayed gently back and forth, dragging in huge gulps of air, making small strangled noises in his throat. He turned and looked at Joe, his eyes helpless and wild.

"Rutledge," he said, his voice crackling with a fear hovering dangerously around madness, "Rutledge, what do you want from me?"

Joe spoke with a soft, level voice that seemed to pound like thunder in Sneed's head: "I want you to resign."

Breathing heavily, his pale sweating chest heaving with effort, Sneed opened his eyes and tried to lift his head. He was removed now, separate from all he had come to believe about the nature of human beings, and he stared at Joe as though seeing something from a deep and distant past. Crouched on his haunches in faded blue jeans, shirtless, his black hair in disarray, the candle in his hand dripping wax across fingers that didn't seem to notice, Joe seemed much too at-ease with the role of captor. Against the background of slime-covered walls, rushing waves and echoing screams, he was transported into a primal world where animal cunning is the only law and savagery reins supreme. He was early man. To Sneed, he had sprung from within this foul-smelling hell and was conducting an ancient rite of his own where Sneed was the intended sacrifice. "Resign? From The Citadel?" Sneed asked, feeling the vacancy of talking to the creature from the cliff. "I can't do that. No Sneed has ever resigned from The Citadel. I can't do that. I WON'T DO THAT!" His voice was growing shrill again.

Joe moved forward on the steps, bringing the candle close to his face. "Listen to me carefully, Sneed. The only way to reach this place is by boat at high tide. When the tide goes out, I'm going with it and it's up to you whether you leave with me or not." The act of communicating, exchanging words he understood, that small, insignificant gesture brought Sneed far enough back into his own world that he again tried to grasp the only reality he could deal with. If the thing on the stairs could talk, it could be reasoned with; it could be threatened.

"Fuck you, Rutledge. I'm not resigning for you or anybody else. I'd die first!"

The smile on Joe's face spread slowly, like cooling wax. "That's one of two options you have, Sneed." He stood up, reached out and grabbed the rope, tugged it toward him and let it go. Sneed swung out over the void, emitting a strangled cry of terror that was half-scream, half-sob. Joe walked slowly down the stairs and Sneed could see the candle receding away from him toward the pit below.

"Rutledge, come back here! You can't leave me here like this! I'll kill you, you sonofabitch, I'll kill you when I get outa here! You can't do this to me. I'm a Sneed, goddamn it, you won't get away with this...RUTLEDGE!" The candle became a tiny pin-prick of light, then vanished completely. "Rutledge..." Sneed whimpered as the dizzying arcs slowed and he closed his eyes against the raw terror as the sobs began to rise in his throat. "Rutledge...please..."

From the decrepit lighthouse Joe could hear the faint whimperings, punctuated by sudden screams of terror—that would be the bats, he thought with a dark smile. The crumbling lighthouse listed slightly now under the demise of its wooden footings. It had allowed the sea to gobble a hole from its base, running freely in and out at high tide, enjoying the sound of its own rowdy voice through a megaphone. In the moonlight it resembled a misfired rocket that had sunk back to earth in exhaustion. Once the noble salvager of hundreds of sailors' lives, its shining cap had long been darkened and deserted, now a salvager of homeless sea gulls and vagrant bats. It was alone in a century that had forgotten it, didn't need it. But tonight, it was a hall of retribution. Tonight its beacon had turned inward on itself and had become a searing candle of the first and final law.

He checked the flow of the tide with the expert eyes of instinct; it was receding. He would have to end this quickly if he didn't intend to be stranded on Morris Island all night. He checked his pocket for the lighter, reached down and retrieved the shrinking candle. Stepping carefully over broken bottles and crushed aluminum cans the ocean hadn't managed to lick up, he silently began ascending the rickety staircase.

Sneed was mumbling incoherently and breathing erratically, trying not to strangle on his own snot and tears. He made soft, high-pitched noises that resembled laughter, but died somewhere at the back of this throat. He could no longer feel his feet; he was left with a total disorientation, a floating sensation that was interrupted only by sharp shooting pains in his shoulders and a terror of not being able to breathe. He was being crushed by a nameless weight from above, below and around him, and he was without spiritual means to withstand it. His tender, opulent lifestyle had padded his senses to the point of genetic numbness and he no longer had the deep rational defenses against pure terror. He was stripped naked, body and soul.

The cigarette lighter clicked and burst into flame and Sneed shrieked with the sudden sound and movement.

"Rutledge!" he cried, his voice hoarse from the strain of yelling and weeping. "Oh Rutledge it's you, thank God, it's you, I was afraid you'd...I couldn't see you down there and I...there's fucking BATS in here...! Rutledge, for the love of

God get me down from here, please get me down from here I can't stand it..." His words flowed in one high-pitched stream with no breaks, as though he were afraid Joe would disappear again if he stopped to take a breath. His face was an odd shade of purple and his eyes were practically swollen shut from crying and from the force of gravity.

"I want you to resign, Sneed."

"I CAN'T RESIGN!" he screamed. "I can't resign, I can't resign!" His head jerked back and forth, spraying tears and sweat; he was openly sobbing. "I can't disgrace my family that way, I can't, I can't...!"

Joe stepped to the edge of the railing and held the candle next to the half-inch nylon rope. His eyes were wider now, fully open and relaxed, reflecting peacefully in the candle light. Sneed stared up at him with trembling face muscles.

"Tell me something, Mr. Citadel," Joe said softly, as though speaking only to himself. "You gonna live, or you gonna die? Which is more important: your fucking family honor—or your life?"

A nylon filament snapped, a tiny sound of no consequence but one that resounded like drum rolls in Sneeds fractured mind. "You're crazy!" Sneed screamed, his voice breaking. "You've gone CRAZY!"

Another filament snapped. Joe was staring at the flame with the mesmerized expression of a bird charmed by a cobra. Snap!

Sneed was crying, openly wailing. "Rutledge, pleeeease! We grew up together, you know what it's like, please Rutledge, PLEEEASE!" Something warm was rushing down his stomach, down his neck and into his hair where it dripped into the darkness and Sneed dimly realized he was urinating on himself.

Snap! The drum rolls were deafening.

"ALL RIGHT, ALL RIGHT, I'LL RESIGN, I'LL RESIGN, I'LL RESIGN!"

The candle didn't move. As another filament snapped, Sneed finally became the primal beast he had been from the beginning of time, finally glimpsed with pure, brutal honesty the helpless, groveling creature he actually was, and he began screaming; he screamed and screamed, couldn't stop screaming. He screamed from more than the fear of falling to his death in the chasm below; he screamed because in that instant he was convinced he was seeing the only true madman he would ever know; he screamed for the terror that the look in Joe's eyes aroused in him—a transfixed, other-worldly stare of serene animal satisfaction of the impending feast after the kill.

In the moments before Joe seemed to revive himself, to forcibly and slowly take the candle away from the rope, Sneed's life was irretrievably changed: he couldn't stop screaming; he never felt himself being lowered to the iron stairs; he didn't know at what point Joe finally cut the bonds from his feet and hands. He knew only that, from that moment on, no matter where he went in the future, no matter what he did with the remainder of his life, he was hopelessly altered. His own face would no longer stare back from the mirror, his eyes would no longer be his. He had witnessed the death of protection in a world where he had believed he would always be protected, no matter what his sins. He had been exposed to the stinking, shallow puddle that was Marion Sneed deep inside, and for the rest of his life an important part of him would continue to dwell there in fetid, fearful squalor.

XVIII

The memory of Sneed took up a small but important space in his subconscious, a place seldom called to mind, but one that tinted his life with the dye of bitter-sweet satisfaction. It was a memory accompanied by the heady feeling of a debt paid, of justice served, mixed with the sour understanding that both Charlie and Reuben had been right: the system was too old, too wide-spread, too loved. Equality was another one of those shouts of human progress that went largely unheard by Southern ears. And it wasn't wholly the fault of innocently prejudiced men like Charlie; Reuben was also a Southern man. The roots of inequality burrowed deeply into both races and perpetuated themselves, renewed themselves with each new generation. It was ancient without being honorable, automatic without being instinctive.

Stretching muscles warmed by the sun, he rolled to his stomach on the beach and laid his head on his hands. All in all, he decided, he held no one responsible, and held no one blameless. It was a social ailment shared by everyone, either by participation or by ignorance, and he settled himself into the assurance that he would ignore the disease along with everyone else—until it crawled onto his doorstep, as Ginny had done. Then, he knew, he would take on the windmill and he would bend it, if only in one spot. Sneed had been one of those dents, and there were no regrets. Even through the anguish of Sneed's family when he so suddenly, unexplainably resigned from The Citadel, even through the rash of rumors that flew about what had happened to Sneed, questions about his mental stability—through all of it, Joe had no regrets. There were only momentary flashes of irritation with himself for his ability to become so lost in the vengeance, so completely removed from the polished refinement of civilization he had worked so hard to achieve. He saw himself as a survivor, the ultimate image of adaptability, and he knew that a large part of the challenge to living peacefully in Charleston had been the mastering of his instincts. The man in the lighthouse was a man who demanded recognition, demanded satisfaction and exposure when pushed beyond the brinks of morality, and Joe found his greatest challenge in adapting his new life around that man. There was no getting rid of him; he was as much a part of his being as the color of his eyes, and just as unchangeable. There was no pretending he didn't exist. There was no ignoring him when he was set upon by broken ancient laws. And there was no denying the feeling of prehistoric satisfaction he provided when he was allowed his freedom. The man in the lighthouse was the avenger who blew up huts full of drunken soldiers; he was the exposer of crime and the hand of justice; he was the bender of windmills. And there was no place for him in a society ignorant of basic instinct. So he remained hidden, carefully concealed behind the shining exterior of gentlemanly poise and Southern charm. He could crouch in the cave behind the facade, and wait. He would endure the schooling, the grooming, the practiced civility. But when his time came, Joe knew, he would not be denied. The man in the lighthouse was a totally serene spirit, at peace with violence.

Joe allowed the late afternoon sun to burn away the residue of memories of Sneed, of Charleston and of lighthouses. He lay still, finally drifting in the aimless waters of non-thought, feeling the memories lift from him like vapor. The party at the beach house would be well underway by now, he knew. Debbi and her roommates would have arrived, and he knew at least one of them would be looking for him to come back soon. He smiled and decided to think of something infinitely more pleasant than old acts of revenge. He felt a shadow cross his face as he nearly dozed, felt the disappearance of the sun on a cloudless day. Simmons, he wondered? Morelli? It was too much effort to roll over and open his eyes.

"Hey," he mumbled sleepily, "you're blocking the sun."

When there was no answer and no movement from the shadow, he sighed deeply and rolled to his back, squinting up at the silhouette against the sky.

It was one of those rare, perfect moments that remain with a person for years. She was standing with her weight casually on one slender leg, her arms hanging relaxed and graceful at her sides. The sun back-lit her body, creating a halo of intense light that framed her long blond hair and outlined her figure in a gleaming mold of poured white heat. He felt her smiling in the way she stood, in the way she held her shoulders, in the tilt of her head. She was a thing returned from childhood memories of softness and fantasy, her whole posture emanating a peaceful whisper of greeting. In that moment he wasn't certain if her face was pretty; he knew only that she was beautiful in her bearing, that she had touched him deeply without a word.

"I have something for you," she said, and he felt a peculiar thrill when her voice matched her demeanor. It took him a moment to realize she was holding a brown paper bag out to him. "May I sit down?" The air around them felt suddenly tangy, scented, crackling with an electric current that arrived with her. He blinked and jerked himself from his trance.

"Oh, excuse me," he said, shifting his position on the towel. "Please sit down. I didn't mean to forget my manners, ma'am, but I was trying to figure out who you were and where I'd seen you before. I didn't mean to stare."

She folded herself like silk on the towel, placing the paper bag between them. The beauty of her face was, in his startled mind, possibly a thing born of legends. In those first few seconds of examination, her eyes belonged to the sea, brilliant gems of green set in pearl and framed with gull-wing brows, eyes reflecting a sweetness with no innocence or illusion, eyes accustomed to remaining level. Her nose was the narrow, upturned nose of audacity that translated into fresh, almost tom-boyish beauty on this girl. Her mouth was the mouth of every sultry, sought-after female of the silver screen, expressive, full and inviting. She was a conglomerate of myths, a gathering of legendary beauties in one entity. He was completely entranced.

Had he mentioned all of this to her, she would have laughed. She knew perfectly well her eyes were set too widely in her face, that her nose was a shade too long and her mouth was too big. She had spent a lifetime learning such things, had invested too many good years into the study of what makes a beautiful woman and she knew she was most likely not one. Her career, however, had been made with her face and figure; the photographer's camera had found a fortune in a face she had always believed was designed by a committee. The camera loved her, found her boldly refreshing and "workable." But she had no illusions about her looks: she knew the value of a good make-up man.

Though she would have laughed merrily at his fanciful wanderings concerning her face, she allowed herself the unabashed pleasure of having his eyes on her, feeling herself blush for the first time in years.

"I suppose I should tell you I'm sorry for interrupting your suntan," she said, "but that wouldn't be entirely true; I'm glad I found you."

"That's okay," he smiled. "I could tell you I was just getting ready to go in, but that would be a lie too, so we're even. And I'm glad you found me, too."

In the silence that followed, a warm breeze caught the scent of her perfume and lifted it to him, wrapped it around him like transparent silk, and he discovered a frustrating inability to converse with her. He was far too skilled in the art of polite flirting, too much the artisan of smooth Southern charm, and he found himself almost comically disarmed by her presence. He felt instantly that this girl would not be subjected to the practiced wiles of the cavalier. At the same time, he was slightly mystified with himself, wondering why he would even care, but knowing with a certainty that he did.

What do I say to a girl that drops in on me out of the sky and jolts me like this, he wondered. How do I present myself to her without sounding juvenile and contrived? This isn't a girl you leer at and say, "Where you been all my life, baby?" even though you wonder where she's been all your life; this isn't a girl you grab and throw to the sand and begin making mad, passionate love to, although you'd like to do that, too; this isn't a girl to be flippant and coy with. Under the heat of her cool green stare, all of the pretense in the boy-meets-girl phenomena was burned away. He had spent years perfecting the charming lies, and was suddenly left with nothing but himself.

And that's the way it began: two individuals on rare equal footing, beginning with each other from the inside out, instead of the outside in. Much later he would accuse her of having planned it that way, that she had deliberately contrived that vast emotional short-cut in their relationship, and she would openly, happily admit it. "Why waste time swimming on the surface," she had said, "when the pearl you want is on the bottom? I just saved you the swim, that's all."

"Congratulations," she said, and he broke through the mist of her perfume and her image long enough to blink in bewilderment.

"Thank you," he said. "For what?"

"For winning your race today. I was at the track meet and saw you run."

The connection was made in his mind like an unexpected shout in an empty room. "It was you I saw!" he said, his eyes widening. "It was you I saw in the stands. I *knew* I'd seen you somewhere before!"

Neither of them spoke of the beam of energy that had passed between them during that moment in the stands. He never told her of his unexplained sensation of believing someone had called to him from the bleachers, and she never told him of how she had hoped he had seen her. Instead, he used the subject of the track meet as a place from which to begin talking to her, a neutral territory of thought and substance from which he could begin covering that part of himself that had been so easily exposed.

But he discovered he wasn't talking to her about the competition at all. He spoke to her of crowds in the stands and how he never heard them during a run, but how he heard them when he was playing football. He told her of how a crowd is an inspiration during a football game and how they simply didn't exist during a run. He told her of pulled muscles and bad knees, of lungs strained to the limit and the joy that the straining invoked.

She spoke to him of the same things, asking questions, making deductions. She spoke softly of her silent thrill while seeing him run, of her singular transport into a dimension of slow, magnificent perception. Her eyes told him as much about her as did her voice, and he listened to both with equal fascination. He ventured at times to wander back to the protection of tangibles, of sweat and push and records broken. She spotted his flight and gently retrieved him, softly forced him back to the center with her own unfeigned honesty. He would speak of winning; she would speak of the winner. With tender, careful pressure, she would refuse to let him evade her with his well-used phrases of superficiality.

They sat alone in the world and spoke softly as the sun slipped away unnoticed, and he saw she was absently rubbing her bare legs, hugging her knees to her chin to avoid the chill. Dressed in white shorts and a sleeveless blouse, he could see the faint rippling of her thighs as she began to shiver.

"Oh, I'm sorry," he said, "I didn't realize how cool it was getting. Here, let me wrap the towel around you..."

"No, thank you," she said. "I have to be getting back. I just wanted to see you again and congratulate you on your win. There, you see? You even have me doing it: I didn't just want to congratulate you; I wanted to see you, talk to you, convince myself that I was right. It's been a long time..."

"Right about what?"

She didn't answer, getting to her feet and brushing the sand from her legs. "Hey, wait a minute," he said with a smile as he stood. "You didn't answer my question. And I don't know your name. You can't leave, just like that..."

"I brought you something," she said. "You haven't opened it."

He had forgotten the paper bag. He looked at her in mild exasperation and reached into the bag, pulling out two sandwiches wrapped in waxed paper. "Thank you," he laughed. "That was thoughtful of you, but I still don't know your name."

"Have a sandwich," she said with a grin. "Maybe that will jog your memory."

He sighed and opened up one of the sandwiches. At first his expression was puzzled—peanut butter and banana, what an odd combination...

His head jerked up and he stared at her with disbelief and unabashed pleasure. "Samantha? You're Samantha Paget?"

"Do you remember that first birthday party at my house, the first one you'd ever been invited to?" she asked. "We were ten years old, and you had never tasted a peanut butter and banana sandwich before. It was one of my favorites."

"And your mom made me one," he laughed. "My first and my last! I declare, Samantha, you sure have changed. I haven't seen you since...since..."

"Since that dance at Ashley Hall when I was in seventh grade."

"Oh God, yes, I remember," he said, running his hand through his windblown hair. "Why, you were just a skinny little thing then, all legs and eyes."

She turned and was walking slowly up the beach. He fell into step beside her, both of them smiling with the memory of a warm spring night so long ago, in a garden swing on the grounds of Ashley Hall.

That night, the exclusive, private girl's school had rocked with the sounds of record music in the gymnasium and vibrated with the sounds of young voices. They moved in the jittery, comical rhythms of adolescent dancing that was something more ritualistic than enjoyable. He had taken her hand and they left the hall, wandering around the grounds until they found the swing and sat down in it together. Her long legs dangled over the edge, protruding from a lovely green taffeta dress her mother had insisted she wear. Her blond hair bounced off her shoulders in springy curls and when she smiled she was certain her mouth would swallow her face. She was tall for her age, all her extremities were too large for her stick-like legs and arms, and she moved with the awkward grace of a girl hovering on the brink of becoming a young lady.

But that night she was beautiful and queenly. Joey Rutledge had danced with her all night, every dance, and she felt like a swan on a moonlit lake. When he put his arm self-consciously across her shoulders, she thought she would burst into tears, she was so excited. They sat there in the swing swaying to and fro, muddling their way through the clumsy, powerful feelings of adolescent attraction. Everything about him intrigued her: the sound of his voice, the touch of his hands, but especially his eyes. She wanted so badly to feel free to stare into his eyes, to go exploring there, to see herself reflected there. But when he caught her looking at him she would lower her eyes and blush, feeling she had done something sneaky, intrusive. When she felt his hand close firmly on her shoulder and pull her close, it was as though she had received an infusion of new strength, and her head suddenly cleared. She was floating, ecstatic. She turned to him, looking directly into his forbidden eyes.

"You can kiss me now," she said simply.

She would never know of the quick, delighted shock that had run through his veins. She could only guess at what he must be thinking as he stared at her and she didn't care; for in that moment, she could see herself dancing in his eyes and her happiness was making her light-headed. He withdrew his arm from around her, taking both shoulders in his hands as he placed a quick, stiff-lipped kiss on her mouth.

He had jumped up quickly and mumbled something about going back inside, but she hadn't heard him; she was still feeling the hard, hot pressure on her lips and she allowed herself to be wordlessly guided back into the dance that no longer existed for her. There existed only her mouth and the strange new tingling on her lips.

It was his laughter that brought them back to the beach where the ocean sneaked onto the shore in soft, foamy fingers. "Tell me something," he said. "Was that the first time you'd ever been kissed?"

"Couldn't you tell?" she laughed, rolling her eyes.

"I wouldn't have known. I'd never kissed anyone before."

The sound of their laughter joined with the waves as they walked. He put his arm around her shoulders in an almost unconscious movement of adult familiarity. It was a practiced gesture, an action smoothed by habit and they both sensed the difference from that first fumbling gesture of so many years before. They fell silent, moving through the emotions and memories on their own, feeling the movement of each other's bodies as they walked. When they reached his house and turned to walk across the dunes, he could hear the sounds of music and voices from inside, and he dimly remembered the group of people he was supposedly hosting. He withdrew his arm and turned her to face him.

"Are you free for the evening?" he asked softly. "Can you come in, maybe have a drink or something?"

She turned, looking over her shoulder at the house, and he could sense a brief moment of decision. She turned back to him and smiled, putting her hands in her pockets. "Yes, I'm free," she said quietly. "And no, thank you, I think I'll pass on the invitation. I...I don't think I'm ready to share you with another audience just yet."

She saw the puzzled question mark in his eyes, the disappointment. The smile left her face and she stepped back a pace. He reached out and took her arm, gripping it harder than he intended. "Then let me take you back to Charleston," he said quickly. "I'll drive you back in my car and worry about yours later."

"What about your party?"

His eyes searched her face in the near-darkness, feeling the odd fluttering of crazy wings inside him begin to settle as he nestled deeper into her calming hands. "You slipped away from me years ago," he said firmly. "I don't intend to let you get away again."

And in only a moment the XKE was humming in open pleasure as it rocketed up the road, becoming a brief streak of gray as it passed across the marshes through a Charleston night.

XIX

No one could accuse Joe Rutledge of being a novice with women. From his earliest days in Korea he had been witness to the complexities and simplicities of sexual activity and was no stranger to it. By the time he was five, he was able to bear witness to the fun-loving whispered maneuverings of his parents in their one-room house where there were few secrets. By the time he was six, he could also bear witness to the tawdriness of prostitutes servicing whomever was able to pay, and the ugliness of starvation-forced submission by young girls in the camp. He was left with a complete, tacit understanding of the act itself. It was nature; it was a simple, accepted part of living. But with all his understanding of the mechanics of sex, he had been left with a total ignorance of the complicated emotions involved with the act of loving. His sex life had begun almost simultaneously with the beginning of his teenage years, but he was to discover with Samantha that his love life had yet to begin.

He felt the magnificent urge to pursue her, to court her, to appeal to her in ways he had never been inclined to do with any other girl. He felt capable and anxious to deal with coyness or reticence, discovering with some confusion that she was neither coy nor reticent. He was suddenly the master of the game, when there were no games being played. He would awaken every morning with the hungry challenge singing through his veins, the strength for pursuit, only to realize with smiling perplexity that she would not be pursued. She had unleashed altogether new sensations in him that he, oddly, had no need for with her, and it left him grinning and inwardly breathless with fascination.

He became an unexpected new stranger to his roommates, a jovial new cadet who suddenly had trouble concentrating on his final exams and risked breaking quarters twice in his last week of school, slipping back into the room with a skill they would never have suspected, well after the "all-in" checks had been made. Morelli saw to it that they covered for him, knowing that he would have done the same for them.

He became a delightful irritant around Rutledge Hall on weekends, and it had begun with that first morning after meeting her on the beach. He had burst into the kitchen where Shady Mae was in the middle of breakfast for Reuben. She looked up at him in surprise. "Chile, what you doin up so early? You was out till Lawd know when las' night n'here you am awready." She dropped the spoon she was using to stir the pancake batter and trundled over to him. "You ain't comin' on sick, are you, chile? You look fever-shined outa yo eyes." She placed a huge, warm paw on his forehead. He grabbed her hand and kissed the back of it, making her eyes fly open. "Lawd, Chile...!" He laughed and embraced her in a classic dance grip, humming to himself and waltzing her around the spacious kitchen. "Lawd Awmighty!" she laughed, "What's got into you, young'n...stop dat now y'hear?...lemme go, fool!" He pressed his cheek to hers, his eyes closed in mock ecstasy as he whirled her around. She was laughing in loud gulping whoops that echoed through the house and it took a few moments for either of them to sense the frozen presence in the doorway. Eva stood with her hands on her hips.

"What goes on here?" she asked sternly, and Joe spun Shady Mae away from him, untying her apron strings as she whirled. He walked to Eva, drew himself up to stiff attention and smartly saluted.

"Eva, mein leibtchen, may I have the honor..." and he grabbed her to him, swinging her smoothly about the kitchen in a comic waltz. Eva looked helplessly at Shady, who was laughing again, shaking her head.

"Joey, are you drunk?" she asked irritably, trying to pull away from him. "What are you doing, du sweinhundt!" He laughed in between hums of "Swan Lake" and after a moment when she realized there was no immediate escape she began to chuckle.

"Yes, Eva, I'm crazy. I'm craaazy about a girl! I met the most gorgeous, the most intelligent, most sexy, charming, amazing girl in the world yesterday and I'm a ridiculous callow youth, a lump of Jello at her feet, and I'm inviting her over here for dinner tonight."

"Ha! So!" she laughed derisively. "So now it starts—the long line of women who worm their way into your heart and your house, turning you into a grinning idiot when all they want is your money."

He put his cheek next to hers and continued to dance. "Eva, my little sauerkraut," he whispered into her ear, "she doesn't want my money—she has more money than God!" He released her and pinched her white cheeks until she batted at him and yelped with pain, sending her scurrying from the kitchen, mumbling to herself in German.

Whatever small alienation he had felt with Charleston in the past evaporated during those first weeks with Samantha, and he found himself plunging into whole new spectrums of existence. Charleston showed him a new face, a new smile during those days. She gathered him in, made him feel that he was now a member of an exclusive Southern club. As his graduation in June approached, he would lie awake and think of her, viewing their days together in fragments, lovely patchworks of memories that warmed him and left him hungry for more.

He saw them together at the old city market as they wandered through the long, hollow buildings and marveled at what a small difference a hundred years had made in the place. The structures were the same, with their open porticos, their concrete floors and the stalls of produce from nearby farms.

He saw her eyes light up with the easy enthusiasm of a child as they examined sweet-grass baskets sold at stalls along Highway 17 in Mount Pleasant. He bought her a tiny woven grass box with a lid, and she had laughed—a laugh that rang familiar bells of memory in his mind, a laugh that danced and shimmered in the air around her.

There were spontaneous trips to the docks of Shem Creek where she laughingly bowed to his experience and judgment when it came to fresh fish. She would stand in front of him with his arms wrapped around her as they watched the fading light through the masts and nets of the trawlers. "Are fisherman lonely people?" she had wanted to know. "Only on land," he answered. "The riggings look lonely against the sky," she whispered. "Only when they aren't at sea," he assured her.

The Donzi became a sprite on the water, towing a graceful girl behind on water skis. Once the determined transport of justice to Morris Island on a dark night in the past, the boat now became a playmate, the perpetuator of youthful frolic. Joe could still feel the sizzling sun on their bodies as he made love to her there in the middle of the ocean, feeling the rhythm of the boat join with the rhythm of their bodies until they finally slept in the sunlight. He smiled when he recalled how they had inadvertently drifted into the shipping lane leading to the harbor, how they had been awakened by the bone-vibrating blast of a ship's klaxon—and the loud, appreciative applause and cheers of the crew lined along the railings as the huge freighter moved by.

It was appropriate somehow that his most striking memory of her would be at the beach house. There had been a beginning there, a joining of futures on the day of the sandwiches; and now he had been drawn back to the house the weekend before his graduation, back to the uncritical, comforting rooms of the tawdry old queen of the beach.

It was one of those singular nights when the air still breathed with the lightness of spring, bearing with it the absolute promise that summer was close by, hovering heavily in the background. There had been a storm of grand proportions the day before, and the ocean pounded the beach in relentless protest, throwing itself at the shore in a powerful, rolling tantrum.

They stood together in his bedroom, a brief silent passing

of moments when she toyed with the buttons on his shirt and he slowly pulled a thin, satin ribbon from her hair. She reached down and switched off the bedside lamp. He reached down and switched it back on. In a slow, ancient dance, they carefully removed each other's clothing, layer by layer, in exquisite deliberation. He bent and kissed the pulse throbbing against the skin of her throat as they moved to the bed.

Though neither of them were strangers to sex, there was a newness to all of it, a riotous feeling of exploring new lands of sensation, new territories of feeling. He stared at her stretched before him as though he were seeing a woman for the first time and touched her as though stroking a fine exotic tapestry, gently, using only his fingertips. He traced the outlines of her round, firm breasts, wrapping his hands around them and applying the pressure applied to unbruised, perfect fruit. He touched her, tasted her, gloried in her slender, rounded beauty. He disappeared into a world of her with his face in her hair and her hands pulling him in, demanding him. He followed her into the mountains and valleys of her hunger, feeding himself on the feast of her while she whispered and moaned and beckoned him still further on. She set nerve endings burning within him, set his skin to raw, tingling life with her insistence. He held her, freeing her without letting her go, lost in her usage of muscles he never knew existed. He was the controller and the controlled, master and subject as demanded her hunger while he satisfied his own. He was the pursuer and the prey, feeling the primal jubilation of original sensation. She engulfed him in a tumultuous gentleness, pushing him deeper into his desire. He surrounded her, gripped her with a tender violence. He was the man in the lighthouse, crouched in his deepest, wildest pleasure, innocent and hungry. She had searched with her tongue, her mouth, her hands until she found him, and he wanted no escape. They rode the crest of a gathering wave, spending themselves under the blinding heat of ecstasy until the wave brought them both tumbling through light and space, leaving them throbbing and complete on the shore.

He lay panting beside her on the bed, his eyes closed as

he waited for his heart to settle. Their bodies glowed with perspiration, creating a quiet contrast on the twisted sheets: her long, pale body in perfect line with the smooth, brown hardness of his own. She pressed herself against him and he waited until he could feel her breathing slowing in rhythm with his own, felt her heartbeat against his ribs as it resumed the level tapping of exhaustion. He turned to her and brushed wet strands of hair away from her face as he flowed through those first moments after the experience of sex that is ultimately, finally, an expression of love; fragile, breakable moments when emotions are exposed, laid bare, vulnerable. She looked up at him, her eyes half-closed with the sultry smokiness of satiation. She smiled at him and laid her head against his dampened chest. "You can turn the light off now," she said softly, and the room fell into a darkness laden with the feel and sound of their closeness. She heard him sigh in deep contentment.

"Tell me somethin', ma'am," he said, with a breathless smile to his voice. "Where did you learn all that?"

Though she didn't move, didn't say a word, he could feel an immediate change in her breathing, a quick hesitation in her heartbeat. In those delicate moments after their loving, he could almost hear the tinkling of breaking glass from somewhere within her and he lay bewildered, knowing instantly he had said something wrong. She gently disentangled herself from him, and he imagined he could feel the miniature, wet snappings of invisible silk threads that had bound them so closely only seconds before. He couldn't see her eyes in the dark and wished suddenly that he could. "I'm going to take a quick shower," she said touching his cheek. "You rest for a minute; I'll be right back."

She stood under the spray and let it fall on her chest, raining off her body to the ceramic floor of the shower. She didn't move, standing as still as her trembling muscles would allow. Her lips quivered with a pain she had thought was buried long ago, part of a discarded, unwanted legacy. She imagined herself standing on the beach with the waves slamming into her in equal force with the agony trying to slam out of her. Silent tears rolled down her cheeks and she became acutely aware of their movement. She stared at the marble-tiled shower wall in front of her.

It's not his fault, she kept telling herself, it's not his fault. He had every right to wonder, and God knows I should have expected it. I didn't come to him as a blushing virgin with no past; it's all there, and eventually he was bound to ask. Instinctively, her bruised emotions floundered around in search of someone to blame, and her mother's face appeared on the shower wall.

She saw her youth as a solitary existence where the rearing process was a cluttered room filled with her immaculate, harpish mother, her soft-spoken, weak-minded father, all crowned with the elegant monogram of the Indigo Shipping Company. She was aware of her father as the product of too much old-family in-breeding, heard the sympathetic, tolerant whispers of family and friends during his gradual decline into vacant-eyed madness. Her mother tactfully referred to him as "slightly dotty." Sam knew him as a quiet, harmless idiot, and much to her mother's irritation, Sam loved him dearly.

Sam's mother descended on her with all the pent-up frustrations of opportunities lost because of her marriage. She saw Samantha as the salvation of a respected, dying family line. Henrietta saw new infusion for her own social standing, envisioning herself as the future grandmother of "the lovely and famous Samantha Paget's children."

From the time she was eight years old, Sam had seen Henrietta as a continual, flapping presence in her life, using her family influence to secure local ad contracts where her daughter's picture began to appear with some regularity. By the time she was thirteen, Sam's wide green eyes and winsome expression had begun to arouse the interest of a few small national agencies and Henrietta swung into full battle regalia. The press was on. Desperate for Henrietta's approval, Sam submitted herself willingly to the voracious ambition of her mother. She became a sought-after novelty in New York. Her fresh Southern charm colored every move she made on the fashion runways of New York's top designers, and her oddly disproportionate features came together under the critical camera's eye with a unique blend of "the-girl-next-door" innocence mixed with something exotic, European and knowledgeable. Photographers picked and chose the features about her that best suited their needs: from the nose up, she was a perfect mascara/eye-shadow print; her mouth was ideal for luscious lipstick spreads in slick women's magazines all over the world; her hair, which she stubbornly refused to crop into the shorter bouffant styles, was luxuriantly perfect for major lines of hair-care products. She was a montage of different appeals and looks and her rise to prominence, if not meteoric, was steady and certain.

She waded into the morass of agents and scouts in New York, at first blissfully ignorant of back-office maneuverings and offers, feeling that her looks and abilities were what success would be made of. She employed the best of every lovely woman she had ever admired in her techniques, using those things she knew women appreciated in other women. Agents called her style "indefinable." In reality, it was simply the style of a completely feminine woman—a Southern woman. Sponsors loved it.

Unlike the girls with whom she worked, Sam had been refined and polished by her years in Charleston's best society. Graceful flirtations were second-nature to her, part of her fabric. But she suddenly found herself in a world where poise and simple graciousness had no real place. It was a world where competition was fierce and often ugly, where the best contracts were routinely made flat on one's back. She developed a painful kinship to Charleston during those years, feeling the bitter-sweet understanding of both their bombardments; Sam was a city under siege, being hammered at continually by small but powerful legions of agents; she was in enemy territory, surrounded by women in the business who considered compromise routine and debauchery part of the job; she was alienated in a world that wanted her allegiance, in a world she was capable of conquering—if she was willing to pay the price.

Eventually, the price was paid—over and over again. Eventually, her mother's proddings and pleadings and her own exhaustion with the siege overran her defenses, and Sam began the empty, grinding payment of invisible debts she never understood. But from that first white flag of surrender sent out to the ranks clawing at the fortress, Sam had issued an ultimatum. She had examined her career with cold deliberation, and with the cunning born of intelligence rather than instinct, she selected her own compromises. If surrender to the system was what they wanted, then surrender they would get—but she would pick the times and the men, and there would never be a question of who was using whom. Her career rocketed in direct proportion to the number and quality of white flags raised: she was famous; she was no longer an alien in a land of enemies; she was one of them; she was the best of them. After a while, there was no more staring at herself in disgust on mornings after, no more huddling on the shower floor while she wept in shame, waiting for a cleansing that the stinging spray never seemed to accomplish. There was only a deepening sense of rage that, incredibly, enhanced her image in front of the camera. Her eyes flashed, her movements assumed a new, forceful magnetism. The winsome girl was gone and so was her smile, but the replacement had been increasingly popular. By her nineteenth year, she was one of the highest paid models in the industry.

Her life became a swirling cauldron of grueling hours in front of cameras at locations around the world, an exhausting fog of parties, dinners and social events hosted by the manufacturers whose products bore her face in their ads. She kept moving, kept working, pushing herself to keep from thinking of Charleston and an increasingly persistent feeling that she could only define as homesickness. But there was more to the feeling than that, she knew; there were too many nights when she lay awake in the small hours of morning, remembering a green taffeta dress and a wonderful burning sensation on her lips...

Henrietta glowed with pride and self-satisfaction. She was the star at every club function and tea, praise was heaped on her like mounds of flowers, compliments about her lovely daughter flowed like sweet southern brandy. Even the imperious Eva Rutledge, "the Blitzkrieg" herself, had spoken kindly to her. And every eligible bachelor from the governor's son on up had called Henrietta, hoping to obtain Sam's phone number in New York. Henrietta screened them all carefully with a strict eye to bloodline, and—in spite of Sam's angry objections—Henrietta gave the number to the most acceptable of the eligibles. She was outlandishly pleased with herself. It was all working out just as she had planned.

The day Sam arrived in Charleston with her car packed to the roof with her clothes and belongings, her mother watched in bewildered disappointment as she moved back into her room. "Oh, don't fret so, mother," Sam had said, a cold blissfulness to her voice. "I'm just doing what you wanted me to do—I'm coming back to Charleston to settle down and maybe start a family. You should be pleased."

"Yes, but Samantha, your career..."

"I'm quitting while I'm still ahead," she said, continuing to unload her car while her mother followed her in and out of the house, trying to talk to her. "I'm quitting while I still have a head to think with! Forget about the modeling, mother. I have."

Over the next weeks Henrietta used every wile she could think of to get Sam to explain why she had come back so suddenly, leaving so much behind; but Sam had become a skilled defender against her mother's sneak attacks and Henrietta remained completely mystified and uninformed. She knew only that Samantha was unmoveable when she made up her mind, and there was nothing she could do. She shrugged in exasperation, and quietly began spreading the word that Samantha was taking a well-deserved rest and would be in town indefinitely.

Sam's senses and control came back to her in slow stages as she stood in the shower at Folly Beach. The steady, disinterested flow of water washed away the image of her mother's face on the wall as she pushed her head under the spray and closed her eyes. No, she thought wearily, I can't blame my mother for this. She is, after all, not only a Southern woman, but a Charleston woman, and that fact explains and excuses a world of ills. It wasn't anyone's fault except mine, she decided, for understanding the contest and deciding to win it in accordance with the rules. And on that last morning in New York, staring out her window at a city pouting in a gray spring rain, no one could have understood that she wasn't just quitting her job—she was withdrawing from the game.

She put her hands over her face in a sudden urge to begin weeping, wanting to share her tears with the water pouring onto her face. But she had done that too many times before, had wept in the shower and begged to be cleansed, to be rid of the filth she felt inside. She slowly lowered her hands and turned the spigots, closing off the water and the memories. There was no room for tears in her life with the man in the bedroom, and she decided in that moment to be done with punishing herself for the past. She had understood the cost, had paid it, and now it was over. His clumsy joking compliment about her sexual skill had been just that and nothing more. She had become her own most unforgiving judge and now the case was closed. She had served her time in the land of tears.

When she slipped quietly back into bed beside him, he reached for her and pulled her close, kissing her lightly. "I missed you," he said softly. "Are you okay?" He felt her nod against his chest. "Sam, I didn't mean to hurt your feelings. What I said was supposed to have been..." She pressed her fingers to his lips and leaned up on one elbow, looking at his face against the pillow.

"Joe, I want you to know something," she whispered, because she didn't trust her voice. "The last three years have been long ones, full of experiences and people that have no meaning. As far as I'm concerned, starting now, right here tonight, with both of us knowing that so much has gone on in the past—you are my first man. I believe it with all my heart. But if that's too much of a fantasy for you, then I'll keep that one for myself and give you a reality you can trust with your life: it makes no difference how many men there have been before you—as long as you know that you are the last."

She felt his hands on her face, felt the gentle pressure as he pulled her to him slowly, folding her into him, embracing her with a tenderness new to her. A first embrace. A first kiss that burned her, purged her, and left her clean.

"I'm in love with you, Joe," she whispered, "and there is no emotion in the world beyond that, nothing higher, nothing better, nothing greater that one human being can offer another. It's all there is. I love you. I love you..."

XX

Charlie had never been one to believe in miracles. He had alternately considered himself a pragmatist and a hopeful realist, and his clear sense of what was possible and what was not kept him in solid touch with life through two wars and Eva. He felt horrifyingly disillusioned, therefore, when he realized he was dying; all of the down-to-earth, realistic approaches to his condition did nothing to ease the deep sense of regret. His pragmatism had let him down. He yearned for a miracle.

Lying awake and listening to the late-night mechanical heartbeat of the hospital terminal ward, he smiled with contentment for the first time in months. She's a beautiful girl, he thought. Between the two of them, she and Joe were living proof that maybe, just maybe, miracles do happen.

Unlike most people who came through his door lately, Sam hadn't cast her eyes downward when she saw him. She hadn't tried to pretend that his horrid appearance was anything less than that. She had taken his hand, leveled her wide green eyes on him and told him how sorry she was to know he was so ill. And she meant it, he thought with satisfaction. She truly was sorry! And the way she looked at Joe, ah, yes! This girl is definitely in it for the duration, he thought.

Charlie avoided sleep these days, putting it off as long as he could stand the pain. Then he would get a pain-killer that knocked him out for hours, precious hours that he would never see again, never be able to make up. He scanned his life during his wakefulness, walking up and down the streets of Charleston and re-living events he wished were different, remembering failures and accomplishments with equal intensity. And he began to understand how his life had been so deeply molded by the Rutledge name and fortune, how all his successes had been Rutledge successes, all his accomplishments had been accomplishments in name only. Except for one brilliant, glaring exception, almost everything else he had done in his life could be laid claim to by the intangible ghosts of his ancestors.

Except for Joe. Through him, Charlie had accomplished something in which he could take a unique, separate, even selfish pride. Joe was more his than any natural child could have ever been, because he would have been forced by nature to share a natural child with its mother. Joe was his, because Joe belonged to no one. Charlie laid claim to him, because he was uncharted territory that no one else had wanted—not in Korea, and not in Charleston. He felt a huge surge of warm, deeply personal satisfaction in knowing that this handsome, talented young man had been encouraged and nurtured by him. His fondest and most singular dream was coming true.

And now there was Samantha. Though he knew that Joe didn't recognize it yet, that girl was going to be a Rutledge someday. Oh God! he thought merrily, old Grandpa Paget would roll over in his grave if he knew his precious granddaughter was going to be the mother of a generation of half-breed Korean-Rutledges! He laughed out loud at the thought, and went into a wracking spasm of coughing that brought a nurse running in with a syringe.

He drifted through a thick, drug-soaked fog into the thieving land of sleep, knowing he had seen at least one miracle in his life, and he was deeply, sadly content. He only wished he could live long enough to see their children.

Sitting with the group of three hundred sixty graduating seniors and feeling the heavy, humid sultriness of the air, Joe stared at the crowd of people gathered for the ceremony and realized how easy it was to forget the four years that had been swallowed by The Citadel. All the discipline and all the regimentation was visible now in the posture of each young cadet who sat in identically formal stiffness, waiting to make that short walk across the stage to receive his diploma. The efforts to bring him down, to break him because he was a "fuckin' gook" had all failed. The cadre of upper-classmen who specialized in the hazing of "knobs" who were singled out for special treatment had descended on him like a swarm of low-country mosquitos during his freshman year, determined to see him quit. As he sat serenely and watched the graduation proceedings, he admitted to himself that there had been times when he had wanted to accommodate them, had wanted to punch their obnoxious faces in and walk out. But in the end he had known it was merely the system, a system that quickly culled the half-hearted; it was all part of a ritual, part of the process of turning boys into men. It meant nothing, and compared to his years in Korea, Hell Week was little more than a distraction. He took the worst the cadre had to offer, and then ignored it.

There was a completeness to the day, a solid finishing sensation that made it easy to forget the bitter arguments with Eva when he had accepted the scholarship. The disagreements had left a sour residue in his mind for months, but when he saw her sitting in the throng, the sourness was left far behind. She sat and stared around her at the crowd, at the parade grounds, at the assembled groups of cadets resembling a collection of toy soldiers. She was elegantly dressed and sat with the dignified posture of the woman she had been, but Joe could see even from a distance that the posture was a thin facade, a breakable shield that sometimes cracked and exposed the frightened creature inside. There were moments, he knew, when she had no idea what was happening or why she was there. Sam sat next to her in cool white refinement, reaching over occasionally, squeezing Eva's hand while she pointed out one thing or another. It was an unconscious movement known only to people who are comfortable enough with themselves to automatically extend reassurance to others.

He would remember the moment his name was called and

he walked across the stage to receive his diploma. He had heard the Rutledge name and instantly felt the loss of one person missing from the ceremony—Charlie. And when the diploma was in his hand, when he had saluted and walked away, he felt a clear sense of disappointment, knowing that the one person who should have witnessed this moment was seeing his last days of life from speechless incapacity in a hospital room. Joe had done everything he could to keep his spirits from falling while he watched his roommates accept their diplomas, and when the ceremony was over they gathered together for the last time as a unit and hugged each other. Morelli held him the longest, actual tears shining on the surface of his dark eyes. They congratulated each other and wished each other well in their military careers.

He left The Citadel for the last time, with thoughts of his military contract, his future, and Charlie, all tumbling around in his mind. When he reached Rutledge Hall he asked Sam to wait for him—he had one last thing to do before he was truly finished with college. "Charlie?" she asked, and he nodded. She smiled, touching his cheek, and left the car.

He stood in the doorway of the hospital room and watched Charlie for a long time, his heart twisting in painful contortions. Charlie was literally melting away before his eyes. The disease was stripping the man of everything—his body tissues, his strength, his life, and now it was taking his pride, too. The man was a pitiful, shriveled shadow of what he had once been, and Charlie knew it. The cancer was not allowing him the peace of a deranged mind to accompany his degenerating body; he was aware and understood all of it. Charlie opened his eyes slowly, feeling the presence of someone in the room. His eyes rotated gradually in their sockets from within his sunken, grayish face. It was the face of winter, devoid of the flesh of youth, naked as a leafless tree, leaving only his unnaturally bright eyes and the now-grotesquely prominent hump in his nose. The rest of his features seemed to have vanished along with his body. He had been reduced to skin draped over bone. The robust figure of a six-foot man was gone; he weighed less than ninety pounds.

The odor in the room was stronger than ever, the undefined odor of impending death, and when he closed the door Joe felt encapsulated in a sterile atmosphere deliberately designed to receive the dead. He straightened his shoulders and moved to the bed. Charlie lay motionless, unable to move or speak. "Hey sandbagger!" Joe said cheerfully. "I hope Nurse Goodbody was worth it—you missed a hell of a ceremony."

The absence of motion from Charlie's body made his eyes seem more alive than ever and every emotion he felt was transmitted through his eyes. They glowed with a translucent brightness as he stared up at Joe in his full dress uniform. Joe sat by the bed and took Charlie's skeletal hands in his while he told Charlie of the ceremony. His voice was soft and expressive and he left out none of the small details; it rose and fell with inflection, making even the most mundane details take on a life and substance for Charlie, who listened with the rapt fixation of a child.

"...and Reuben comes up to me after the ceremony and gives me the once-over, you know, the way he does when he's playing the part of snooty butler. He pretends to pick a piece of lint from my coat sleeve, brushes my chest like he's smoothing wrinkles, he's got that pinched look of his and I'm about ready to crack up! But I stand there at attention and let him go through his routine and finally he clasps his hands behind him, rocks back on his heels and says, 'Hmph! Not bad, I suppose—for a kid who used to shit bananas in my bedroom.'"

He showed Charlie the diploma. "It's official, Charlie. Now that you've seen the diploma, it's official. I am a rip-roarin, ass-kickin', no-shit-Sherlock second louie in the U.S. Army." He laid the diploma reverently on the sheet next to Charlie's hands.

"Thank you, Charlie," he said smiling. "And you're welcome."

There was a responding pressure from Charlie's hands and a moistness in his eyes as Joe continued to talk. "I spoke to Ray Jasper again a couple of days ago, Charlie. He says everything has been lined up as far as the business is concerned." And for the next half hour Joe described his conversations with various officers of companies owned by the Rutledge family. All of them had been with the Rutledge companies for years; their loyalty to the family and their unflinching sense of integrity had enabled the holdings to expand and flourish, and Joe assured Charlie that everything would be in good hands until he fulfilled his military obligation.

"And you don't need to worry about Eva," he said. "Reuben and I have had some long discussions about her and Reuben understands that we're counting on him—you and me—to take care of her." He fell silent while Charlie stared. "So..." he said, smiling broadly again. "What do you think of Sam? I understand she's been here to see you several times. Isn't she somethin'? You can't help but be crazy about her—I sure am." He spoke of Sam for a few moments, becoming animated again with descriptions of their blossoming relationship. Then he grew sombre, staring at the thin blue hands in his. "Hey Charlie," he said softly, "this thing with you gettin' sick isn't gonna negate your responsibility to me, you know." He could see the bright gleam of a question in the man's eyes. "You still have a job to do, old man. You're the only person I've ever been able to turn to for advice and you can't quit just because you've got everybody convinced you're dying."

Though Joe was smiling, Charlie could see his strugglings and he squeezed his hand in a signal for him to continue. "You know me better than most anyone, Charlie, and I think you know what I'm thinking now. It's this military thing—my contract. You know as well as I do that after you're gone, if I push it I can get my contract canceled under the "only surviving son" stipulation, family hardship and all that. You know I could do that, Charlie—and you also know I'm not going to. I know you figure that's not what I suffered through four years at The Citadel for, but there's more to it now. You've heard the news reports about Vietnam, you know what a mess that's turning into and that the chances of me ending up over there are pretty great. I should be jumping outa my skin trying to get out of my contract while I've got the chance, right? So tell me…" His voice took on a faint note of urgency. "Why am I still going? It's not an undying sense of loyalty to the military, or even to the country. It goes deeper than that, Charlie. It's Vietnam. It's the war. I feel like…I feel like I'm being pulled, drawn to Vietnam like a hound on a scent and I don't know why. I've got all the reasons in the world to want to stay here—the business, Eva's condition, and now Sam—but I know I'm going. Why is that, Charlie? Why…?"

He searched the deflated features of Charlie's face, trying to hear him speak through his eyes. There was nothing to be found, except his own reflection in the shiny pools, and Joe sighed, lowering his head.

"I don't suppose there's ever an answer for a question like that, is there?" He looked up, forcing a smile. "I just wanted to share that with you, to let you know I'm not running out on my responsibilities here. What I'm doing is something I can't control. It's bigger than me, bigger than the Rutledge empire. It's something I have to do, and I have no idea why."

He felt clumsy and inarticulate trying to explain something that still had no shape or form in his mind. He knew only that it existed, that it was huge and that he had no choice but to answer it. He cleared his throat and stood, walked to the window and stared down at the traffic on Calhoun Street. "Hey Charlie," he said. "I wanted to thank you for everything you've done for me. I want to thank you for finding me in that jail and for not beating the hell outa me when I broke your nose." He turned from the window and walked back to the bed, taking Charlie's hands again. "I want to thank you for bringing me here and giving me a home. I know it would have been an easy thing for you to have adopted a kid here in the States, and the fact that you wanted me badly enough to go through the hassles you went through to get me here and keep me makes me feel real special. I want you to know that I'm damn proud to be your son."

Charlie's eyes became an open, readable script of love and anguish as his lips trembled in an effort to speak. Joe leaned closer to him and shared the hurt, shared the unmasked feeling of hopelessness and unvoiced love.

"Charlie," he whispered, his voice deep with emotion. "Charlie, this is the last time I'll be coming to see you. It breaks my heart to see you this way, dying an inch at a time, and I feel like a ghoul standing here day after day and watching it happen. I can't stand it—this requisite mourning at your bedside, with you knowing there's nothing you can do about it." Charlie closed his eyes once and made a feeble attempt to nod his head. "I want to remember you the way you were, Charlie; I want to see you in uniform, striding toward me across the compound in Sok-Cho, scooping me up in your arms and calling me 'GI Joe'; I want to remember you dancing at a party with Eva, moving her around the floor like the Southern belle she wishes she could have been. I don't want to take the memory of you here in this bed with me the rest of my life. I want to remember the man you really are."

Tears rolled silently down the empty canyons of Charlie's cheeks and he closed his eyes. Joe leaned closer and slipped his arms under the wasted shoulders; pulling Charlie close to him, he held him tightly and rocked him for a long time. When he finally placed him gently back on the pillow, Joe gazed into the eyes that had seen him as a son for twelve short years. He wiped away the tears on the man's cheeks, then placed the diploma in his trembling hands, squeezing them tightly one last time and smiling.

"GI Joe loves you, Captain Charlie."

XXI

August insisted on reducing Charleston to a sweating, exhausted world of drooping trees and gardens that dripped with moisture like miniature rain forests, while residents of the Battery vanished into the hibernation of their impeccably restored homes; air-conditioning was one gift from the twentieth century that Charleston accepted with open, grateful arms.

Along with the stifling heat, Joe felt the shapeless urgency of time slipping away from him. He had two weeks left before reporting to Fort Benning, Georgia, to begin his military tour and he tried to push himself past the constriction he felt inside. He swept himself deeper into the fathoms of unexplored feelings with Sam like a pioneer, feeling the steamy exhilaration of discovery.

On a gray morning that gave him the distinct impression of being inside a baking kiln, he threaded the Jaguar across the few short blocks to Murray Boulevard and flew up the steps to her door. He found her in the kitchen, mumbling to herself in exasperation as she went through the unfamiliar motions of making a cold lunch. She greeted him with a distracted kiss and returned to her sufferings, making no effort to disguise how clumsy she felt in a kitchen. "It's going to be horrid," she muttered, "...should've waited another hour till Louise got here...now what did I do with the mustard...?"

He stood in the doorway and watched her, smiling at the youthfulness that radiated from her like a heat wave. Her hair was pulled back and tied with a ribbon, her crisp white blouse and tailored slacks accentuating the her slender lines. "What's all this?" he finally asked.

"We're taking our lunch with us today, just like a couple of disgusting tourists," she said, her eyes bright with a private enjoyment. "I have something to show you."

He nudged the car into the sparse traffic of the early August morning and drove across the Cooper River Bridge heading north on Highway 17 while she prattled on about everything she saw. "I love this bridge," she said when they reached the summit high above the Cooper River. "Especially from the Mount Pleasant side coming back; it always reminds me of a causeway into the sky—it looks like it goes straight up and stops while the cars keep on going." He laughed when she told him one of her favorite experiences was getting caught in a traffic jam at the top of the bridge, because it was the only time she could stop and enjoy the view. She sat with her legs curled under her, her eyes shining with an infectious good humor that made him forget his impending separation from her. She avoided talking about anything that would remind him of the Army, concentrating on the simple, mind-numbing details of their journey.

In the month since Charlie's death, Sam had been a peaceful, consuming vacuum of caring, a continual cushion of understanding and distraction. During the brutal wash of emotions at the cemetery, Sam had stood quietly to one side and allowed him to simply feel, to fall headlong into the grief as the coffin was lowered into the ground. She stood nearby while he listened to the painful, penetrating strains of "Taps" being sounded in Charlie's honor, and he wondered where he had heard the tune before. Though "Taps" had sounded every evening at The Citadel, he was hearing it now as a song of deepest mourning, a chant of grieving...

The remembrance came to him with the sudden shock of the twenty-one gun salute. The old woman at the camp! The sound of the bugle had been equal accompaniment to the keening he could hear in his memory: a song of celebration and sadness, of loving and loss, of something finished but never forgotten.

Hurtling up the highway, he rested himself in her voice and allowed her to blend her voice with the steady hum of the car. Charleston disappeared behind them and they entered a wider world where they were no longer owners and residents. They entered the South Carolina that belonged to everyone, and though he always enjoyed the free-wheeling airiness of vast expanses of pine forests and long, open stretches of road, he always felt that he was sharing this part of the world with everybody, that none of it was truly his. Not like Charleston. In the intermittent beach-front towns along the way, the quaint old shops crouched in weary indifference, bearing the look of washed-out fatigue that spoke of long, tourist-ravaged summers.

"What exactly is this thing you're going to show me?" he asked. "A museum or something?" She shook her head and smiled. "It's a garden," she said, and changed the subject.

They drove for several miles in silence while she stared out the window. His hand was resting on the gear-shift knob, and when the warmth of her hand covered his in a gentle gesture of familiarity, he turned to look at her. Her eyes were soft but serious, and though she was smiling slightly, he could tell something was troubling her. "Why haven't you told me about your brother?" she asked quietly.

The rush began at his head, swept to his feet and back again and he stared at the road. She tightened her grip on his hand, feeling an instant fleeing, a momentary withdrawal from her.

"Before you shut me out, Joe," she said anxiously, "let me explain something. I haven't been sneaking around asking questions behind your back. Charlie told me about your brother—he offered the information, I wasn't prying. I've waited all this time, hoping you would mention him to me yourself, but—I suppose I get impatient and insecure at times and go charging into something because I just have to know…"

"What did Charlie tell you?" he asked, his voice oddly strained.

"He told me that you believe your brother is still alive,

that you are determined to find him someday. He said it's an obsession with you. He said he was telling me about it because he knew if anything was going to be an obstacle in the way of your loving me completely it would be your love for your lost brother, and he wanted me to understand what I was dealing with. He told me about the nightmares."

He realized with some surprise that in all the nights he had spent with her, he had never had a nightmare. He was surprised because the nightmares had increased in the last year, becoming more vivid. Except when he was with her.

"Joe," she said with a soft urgency, "I know that part of what Charlie said was true. I know you've opened yourself up to me, shared things with me you've never shared with anyone before. I know you give me a very large, precious part of yourself you've never given to anyone, and I love you for that. In fact, I love you so much for the things you do give me, I suppose it makes it twice as hard when I realize there's something you're holding back. There's a barrier, a boundary beyond which I haven't been allowed to pass; you take me just so far into your heart and then you quietly stop and hold me back. And the odd thing is, I have no idea what it is I'm missing. I have no idea what lies beyond that boundary, but I instinctively feel that it belongs to me, and it has something to do with your brother..." She searched his profile, waiting for the tell-tale twitching of a small muscle in his cheek that would tell her she'd gone far enough. It was a silent moment full of unexpressed strain. "Hey look," she said, squeezing his hand and smiling, "I'm not even sure what it is I'm trying to say. I shouldn't have brought it up. Let's make a deal: I promise to see to it you have a wonderful day, if..."

He looked at her when she hesitated, and raised his eyebrows. "If what?"

"If you promise that some day you'll let me share your brother with you."

He reached an arm across her shoulders and pulled her to him. He sighed deeply and let his breath out slowly, rubbing her upper arm in a soothing gesture. He kissed her forehead, but never promised anything.

In no time, her leisurely chatter resumed again and their earlier tension diffused like the light above the thick gray clouds. A half-hearted mist of rain began to dampen the windshield and he shook his head. "Wonderful day for a picnic," he said. She told him to stop fretting and keep driving.

"The turn-off is on your left up here," she said, her eyes scanning the trees that bordered the highway. "You'll know it when you reach it. There's a huge statue at the entrance of two stallions in battle."

He could feel the power of the statue before he saw it clearly—two giant, golden stallions engaged in a ferocious battle, one horse still bearing his naked rider on his back, with a second rider lying on the ground under the two enraged animals, staring in horror at the giant hooves above him. The frozen figures seemed to move as he approached them, and he imagined he could see the flashing of bared teeth, hear the thudding of hooves against flesh.

"Careful," she said, "you'll miss the turn-off."

He blinked and slammed his foot on the brake, swinging sharply onto the narrow road beside the statue. He drove past it through the gates, hardly able to steer the car. The statue had served its purpose. It had reached out and touched that one-in-a-thousand person who could feel the work, as well as see it.

The road beyond the gates twisted languidly through the fringes of a pine forest, but he scarcely saw the trees, the image of the golden horses still thundering across his senses. Sam watched him closely, a slow smile of understanding on her face. She remembered the feeling well: Brookgreen Gardens had received her, too.

He pulled the car into a parking lot and they stepped out into a light misting drizzle that barely moistened their faces. "Looks like we weren't the only ones who wanted to walk in a garden in the rain," he said, glancing at the other cars in the lot. "Tourists," she sniffed, taking his arm.

"It's a statuary garden," she finally told him as they headed for the footpath that led deep into the immaculate landscaping. "It used to be one of the grand old Southern estates. The main house is gone now and the grounds have been donated by the former owners, specially designed as a showcase for the most beautiful collection of sculpture in the world."

He was only half-listening; from the moment he stepped onto the brick pathway he was captured, taken prisoner immediately, willingly.

Giant live oaks spread themselves in gracious welcome, hundreds of years old and still flourishing in serene, timeless elegance. Flowering shrubs and finely-manicured grass lay in carefully-placed patchworks throughout the garden, barely interrupting the banks and walls of ivy and the intricate network of hedges. He stopped in the main courtyard and stared around him, reaching out to the spirit he felt within the misty world of green. The voice of the garden whispered to him in the fountains and sang to him through the birds peering at him from the trees. The rain had created a delicate pale mist that rose among the trees and down the pathways, enhancing the illusion of other-worldliness in which the entire garden was cloaked. Spanish moss hung in moist, feathery tendrils from the branches of the oaks, swaying gently in a breeze. Standing in charmed surprise he could hear the voice of the garden whisper, "Welcome!"

Sam didn't touch him, didn't speak as they strolled the branching pathways. He was keenly aware of her presence without truly feeling it, knowing she was there, wanting her there, and not touching her. She walked with her hands clasped behind her; he walked with his hands in his pockets, his mouth slightly open, submitting himself humbly to the garden.

They stepped through a small gateway into acres of rolling grass, and he caught his breath. Before him was a gigantic white statue of the winged horse Pegasus. The white marble gleamed softly in the rain, set against a backdrop of delicate swirling fog. There was muscle and heartbeat to the movement in the statue, a distant, powerful life of its own, and Joe had the wondrous sensation of very nearly witnessing the huge wings beating into gusting flight; he felt a poignant sense of envy toward the rider on the animal's back, ready and willing to take his place.

She touched his arm for the first time and gently directed him away from Pegasus, back through the pathways among the trees. They moved around a meticulous archway of ivy and he stopped still, joining the statues in their moment of suspension as he stared at the sculpture looming in front of him: on a pedestal in the center of a reflecting pond, fashioned in fine white Georgia granite, was the statue of a man—a nearly completed man. The head, arms and torso of the stone man were completed, and he held a hammer and chisel in his hands, twisting sideways, bending over the remaining solid block of granite, preparing to finish fashioning his own body.

Joe slowly withdrew his hands from his pockets, feeling an odd rhythm begin inside his chest. He moved in slow steps around the circular pond, examining the work, stroking it with his senses, greeting it with his mind. He had an almost frantic urge to walk out into the pond and caress the thing with his hands, to absorb it with mind and body. It was he! And he was the stone man. It was the thing he had felt within himself from his earliest day, an emerging, hammering, scraping thing, this consuming need to create himself.

"It's called 'Man Carving His Own Destiny'," she said and he was astonished by the sound of another human voice. "Yes," he answered softly. "Yes, it is." He turned to her suddenly, a jolting awareness rising in him.

"This is what you brought me here to see, isn't it." He stared into her face, into the clear green eyes that held nothing from him and he knew it was true. She faced him calmly, her hands behind her back, saying nothing. "This one statue..." he said in a growing sense of wonder. He turned back to the stone man in the pond, allowing the tentative glow of a smile for her, for the garden, for the man in the pond that was himself. And she had known.

She had suffered a brief moment of fear when she saw the intensity in his eyes as he stared at her, afraid she had gone too far in expressing her knowledge of him. Was there a chance, she wondered, that she had misjudged the relationship, that she had forced an intrusion she had no right to make? For this was exposure, a soul-baring unveiling. The sunless chamber in his heart, the place of bitterness and angry secrets, the place of trusts destroyed, was suddenly thrown open to the light; and though she knew nothing of the chamber, she knew of the man, of his need to trust. She was offering herself in the only way she knew how: by showing him a mirror image of himself. She stood still, waiting in open humility for him to react, ready to accept whatever he chose to grant her.

It was deliberate; he knew it now, and he marveled at the strange new warmth rising inside. He could feel her brief uncertainty, knew that it stemmed more from her protectiveness of him than out of fear for her own emotions; there was no insolence here, no imperious demand that he approach her now and admit to exposure. She had no desire to see him lay any spiritual sword at her feet. She wanted him only to know that she knew him this well, that she was ready for all that was inside him, and that she would never betray what she knew.

"I don't know what it is," she said softly, "this thing that separates me from you. But I feel somehow it involves your brother, and whether he's alive or dead he's a living presence to me, and I'll do whatever it takes to join him, to be a part of whatever you feel for him. I don't want to compete with him for your love, Joe. If the only place you have for me in your heart is a place I have to share with your brother, then I'll share it; but please, please don't let him stand between us."

Her hair glistened with rain and her face was strangely radiant against the cold white stone. He heard all that she said, had felt it gain painful access to his heart. He was helpless and huge in the face of her understanding, her ability to align herself with a force she had never seen, unafraid of the power that she sensed could possibly destroy her. He had no words, no explanations or excuses for his inability to open himself and receive all that she offered, and, he had no way of telling her, begging her, to please always be patient. Someday the search would be over, someday he would find his brother and he'd

225

have all the answers for her. Please wait for me, Sam! he pleaded with his eyes. Please wait...!

He raised his hands to her, inviting her to join him, to come inside, to stay. He held her close while they stood alone in the rain among the statues of a whispering garden, with an unfinished man of stone looking on.

VIETNAM

XXII

"I'm hit! I'm hit!"

A lightening storm of RPG rounds burst from nowhere, and in those first few seconds of explosion nothing was the same anymore. The entire platoon burst into scrambling fragments, tumbling, diving over each other into the dirt, burrowing, pushing themselves flatter against the ground. The screams began with the first ear-splitting blast. "I'm hit, Captain! Oh God help meeee!..." The explosions tore the air, ripped and shredded the jungle, clawing at their nerves while the fear choked off all thought. One of the men rolled to his back, firing his weapon straight into the air while he screeched at an unseen enemy: "Motherfuckers! You motherfuckers!"

During that first second, when he heard the point man scream in pain, that first second when a lightning bolt threw him off the trail and into the jungle, Joe lay for a brief instant and tried to determine where the rounds were coming from; in that small second, he heard the gut-throbbing terror of all the world close in on the platoon. "Shoot, goddamn it, SHOOT!" he yelled. "Throw some lead at those fuckers! DO SOMETHING!"

That first paralyzing moment passed, and he could see men rolling quickly to their stomachs, firing in the direction of the attack; men lying on their backs, firing wildly over their heads.

"Captain, I'm hit bad! Oh God oh God, someone help me..."

Joe turned from the man's screams and began running

through the heavy jungle, crouched and tense, every nerve pounding. He was a shadow in the green, running with barely a sound as he circled the enemy ambush team. He could hear the chatter of the AK-47's between the explosions and he ran faster, cursing under his breath as more shouts of pain followed the blasts.

He saw the drab-brown uniforms through the bushes. Six of them. He dropped to the ground and low-crawled like a determined snake until he could see them all clearly. And with a familiar sinking sensation, he realized that the screams from the point man had stopped. No time! he thought, there was no goddamn time! He snugged the AR-15 against his shoulder and took cold, careful aim. He watched as each NVA uniform erupted in splashes of red, and their bodies fell in the twisted, awkward tangles of death. It was over in a matter of seconds.

Joe Rutledge believed the silence following a firefight was a silence unlike any other. He had once been mystified by it, often wondering what the difference was, finally realizing it was the stunning silence of lives lost, the sound of no life where there had been life; it was constricting silence, filled with the feel of fear. He lowered his weapon and pressed his forehead to the ground and listened.

Corporal Riggs came running through the brush behind him and dropped next to Joe, his eyes wide and burning with the gray light of fear. Joe saw him, but didn't lift his head. "Are you all right, Captain?" Riggs asked breathlessly, glancing wildly at the bodies of the NVA. "We took four casualties, sir, all dead. No wounded." Joe nodded and sighed, feeling a heavy, disgusted weariness settle over him.

"Have Shepherd get on the horn and get a couple of choppers out here," he ordered quietly.

"Sergeant Shepherd is dead, sir. He was one of the four."

"Okay Riggs," he said, his voice straining through the gravel of regret. "You know what to do. Get on the horn. Let's get the hell outa here."

"Yes sir." Riggs turned to leave, then stopped. "Sir, you've been hit," he said. Joe turned to look at him, and felt the sudden searing pain blast up his spine. "Shit!" he mumbled, wincing in pain. "How bad?"

While Riggs tugged at the back of his shirt, Joe wondered vaguely when he could have been hit. He hadn't felt a thing.

"Shrapnel, sir. Your lower back is torn up pretty bad."

"That's all I fuckin' need," he said, laying his head back on his weapon.

The deep green of the jungle expanded as the chopper lifted smoothly above the triple-canopy mass. The jungle was a place of secrets, of swift silent death or shrieking prolonged agony, a protector of enemies, an exposer of amateurs, a victimizer of fear and a victim of destruction. It was a world Joe had come to trust with the fine-tuned wariness of a respected adversary. In the jungle there were blissfully few questions of "why," and entirely new dimensions of "how." He felt the pain gnawing at his back as the chopper rumbled swiftly away and he wondered how long he would be away this time—knowing in grounded certainty that he would be back.

There were times in those first few days on the hospital ship when he felt disoriented, removed from all that was real, placed in a floating world of suspended life. The ship rode in stately anchorage off the coast of South Vietnam, and Joe would limp slowly along her railings, gazing at the heavy green hump on the horizon. The ship was the last vantage point from which most of her patients would ever view Vietnam; they would go home from here, or to Tokyo for more extensive care. Some of them would die here, but not many. And some would wander the railings, a few misplaced denizens of the jungle who paced in quiet discontent and waited to heal. He remembered voices during those first days, soothing, distant voices heard through an unpleasant fog after surgery:

"You're a lucky man," (a doctor's voice). "None of the shrapnel made it to your spine; most of the slivers were removed. You still have a few buried in the deep tissues close to the spine, but given time, they won't cause any more problems; it would have done a lot more damage had we tried to remove them..."

"You'll be here for while," (a nurse's voice), "...running more tests...let you know when you can leave...get some rest."

And he submerged into the thick blanket of drug-induced slumber. He was up soon enough, prowling the decks and becoming a nemesis of the nurses as they routinely hunted him down to give him his medication. He submitted good-naturedly to their bullying, went along dutifully and disappeared again when they were gone. The railings beckoned him; the jungle planet rising thick and deceptively silent, haunted him.

There was too much time here for dwelling in memories, and it took several days before he gave himself over to the vacancy in his thoughts, wondering with distant surprise what had happened to the last two-and-a-half years. He counted back quickly and realized it had been six months since his second arrival in Vietnam. He absently scratched his cheek as he stared at the sea snakes in the water, wondering how such huge gulps of time could slip away from him unnoticed. The snakes flowed and twisted, their long mottled bodies threading through the water like supple needles embroidering the cloth of the sea, their oddly flattened tails propelling them through the liquid fabric with the grace of master-weavers. He watched their soothing movements and tried to assemble the fragments of time that had so capriciously slipped away from him, realizing that his whole life had passed in just this way—in giant leaps across space that left only sparks of remembered moments behind. This time, the comet's trail began with the heavy heat of a late August day in Georgia...

XXIII

When pursuing the course of one's life, Joe knew, a person will always choose the path of least resistance first. On the day he entered Fort Benning, Georgia, he suspected that the theory applied to him as much as it would to anyone. His early life in Korea had been a prelude to Charleston, a world where only the keenly adaptable would survive socially. His years at The Citadel had been a conduit to this day as he stood at the gates of Fort Benning. And on it went, each phase of his life being a mere staging for the next; he had submitted himself enthusiastically to the Fates.

He was a soldier now, and though he felt a large sense of accomplishment, he understood that he had chosen the least resistant course for himself. He believed that he had an unfair advantage: he had been a part of soldiering and war long before most of his fellow officers had learned how to write their own names. One of his earliest memories of safety and strength had been within the fenced barriers of a military compound. He had learned of discipline and unity from soldiers in Korea, both American and South Korean. At the hands of enemy soldiers he had learned a great deal about the human capacity for suffering, and the cheapening and degradation of life. Many of his future choices in behavior were shaped by the lessons he learned from men who were soldiers.

As he gazed up at the statue guarding the entrance to Infantry Hall, he knew, he had chosen the most logical course

JOE PORCELLI

for himself and that he couldn't view his choice as having been courageous or difficult; his whole life had simply been channeled to this. He stared at the bronze statue of a soldier, weapon in hand, raising his arm in a gesture of "follow me" and he knew he was where he belonged. "Follow Me"—the watch-words of leadership. He had come to the right place.

It wasn't until the weeks at Fort Benning were finished and he was on his way to Fort Bragg and Special Forces training that he became aware that the lessons at Benning had been, for him, an intense process of review. Concepts of military morality and leadership responsibilities, lessons of duty and protocol, were reinforcements of things he already believed and lived by. Much of what he learned, he already felt by nature.

His one real discovery at Benning had been the thrill of parachuting. The last three weeks of jump training had been a wild fling into an expanded part of himself, an exploration of new depths and heights during those first delirious falls through a borderless sky, and he knew that he would never know the same limits, the same boundaries within himself again. He was no longer earthbound, no longer servant to the sovereign of gravity.

Armed with his commission, he entered his training at the Special Warfare Center at Fort Bragg, North Carolina, primed and ready for the completion of the mold. With one overriding cry pounding in his ears— "You do NOT want to be captured"—his training in "Death By Stealth" began. The war in Vietnam had produced a whole new spectrum of tactics to be learned by the American solder, new techniques of fighting that had never been encountered in any other war, and only a select few would earn the privilege of learning the finer points of this intensified warfare. Psychological and covert operations, sabotage, guerrilla warfare, small arms, escape and evasion, demolition; a saturation training that took every mental and physical skill to complete. In the closed, tightly-knit society of the Special Forces, basic skills were sharpened, enlarged, polished and perfected. He felt at times like a street brawler who had survived for years with crude, unrefined slugging matches and was now a skilled fighter of the ring, combining his strength with his wit.

"The accomplishment of your mission is paramount," he was told. "You will do whatever it takes to complete the mission. If you are ever forced to choose between the welfare of your men or the accomplishment of the mission, the mission must come first—at the expense of your own life, if necessary." Though he had accepted his life in the military with quiet enthusiasm and the assurance of knowing he was doing the right thing, his pride upon completing the twelve-week Special Forces training was more intense than he would have guessed. He knew that he would finish and he believed that he would even graduate with honors; he had never questioned it. But shining like a prominent star in a field of other stars would be that one moment at the graduation ceremony where he wore, for the first time, the Green Beret.

When he received his orders for Vietnam there wasn't a momentary fluttering of surprise. He had known when he entered his Special Forces training that ninety percent of the men who graduated were sent to Vietnam, and when he was told to fill out his requests for a duty station—a form laughingly referred to as "The Dream Sheet"—he had put down his three requests with only a dim, tentative hope that he would be granted his wish. In the three slots allotted, he had written "Korea—Korea—Korea."

In those last weeks before leaving for Vietnam, he told Sam about the Dream Sheet as they sat on the beach. They sat huddled together under a heavy blanket, watching the cold waves of a winter ocean dash onto the beach and hurry away again. When he told her of his wish to be stationed in Korea, she had tilted her head slightly, as if trying to see the words from another angle.

"Do you believe in providence?" she asked. "I'm not talking about God or the mystics or anything like that; I know how you feel about God. I mean a set order to things, an elemental force of the cosmos that dictates a logical pattern to everything that happens. Sort of 'a time and place for everything' syndrome. Do you believe in such a thing?"

235

"I suppose so," he shrugged. "Are you talking about fate? I can tell you a lot about fate."

"No...Yes...I don't know what you'd call it," she said, mildly frustrated. "Something like fate, but bigger. Something not so random." He shrugged again and nodded, having no better explanation himself for the forces that had so freely mauled his life in the past. "Well, I think your 'Dream Sheet' fell into a crack in that cosmos," she said firmly. "For some reason, it's not time for you to go to Korea. Ever since you told me about your orders for Vietnam I've been feeling it— this churning out there, this..." she gestured under the blanket in frustrated circles, "...this huge boiling thing. Haven't you felt it? And whatever it is doesn't want to wait for you to go to Korea to look for your brother. It's out there now and I feel it pulling you away from me and I don't think I can fight it because you've given it your consent. Is any of this making sense? Of course it is, because if I've felt it then I know you have. That's why you weren't surprised when you got your orders."

He didn't try to disagree with her. There was a frightening comfort in her ability to share his feelings of fate and "the powers that be." And though he was usually merely patronizing when she spoke of such things, there was a part of him that listened because there was a part of him that believed.

They spent those last weeks in quiet, uninhibited passion—for each other, for life. They scoured Charleston together, frequenting old restaurants and shops that had long ago become passé; they sat through movies they didn't want to see, just for the joy of holding hands like youngsters in the dark; they spent hours wandering the wintry beach finding tiny treasures deposited by a lonesome sea. They talked and laughed and touched, feeling the heavy expressions of "goodbye" in the atmosphere around them. The ocean tossed and groaned and wept against the shore, offering its meager bribes to keep him from going away; the house lay quiet and wordless as though wondering if she had finally done something inappropriate; and Charleston pretended not to notice, pretended not to care while still trying with petulant coyness to attract his attention. Only at night, during the cold rains of winter, would she turn her face away and softly weep. They made love on those nights of rain and tears, surrounding themselves with the hungry, desperate passion of young animals who feel threatened as a species, satisfying an ancient, unignorable need to proliferate. They refused any physical boundaries, denied any reticence or weariness, exhausting themselves and demanding more. It was the only good-bye they would ever express.

When the day arrived and he stepped aboard the airplane, there had been no tears—they had all been absorbed by the tossing sea, by the sombre beach, and a desolate Charleston.

He stepped from the plane in Vietnam as a consortium of men in one man, a conglomerate of his past as a Korean child, a Charleston adolescent, and an adult soldier, hearing all of the voices speaking to him at once. But with that first blast of incredible heat when he walked out of the plane, all the voices rose in one shout of gasping surprise. He closed his eyes to try and define the pungent odor, an overwhelming scent that reached deep into him and found a home. It was the jungle—a relentless cycle of moisture and heat causing the tangled masses of foliage to reek with decay and new life. It was rotting and alive, birth and death springing from the dank jungle floor; it was a world tumbling over itself in its urgency to live, rising and sinking again in a pattern that never seemed to catch up with itself.

The jungle watched him during those first weeks with the mistrust that was a natural part of her. She waited for the first signs of fear in those nights in the jet-black darkness when he discovered there were no sounds, no insects, nothing. She waited for that first ambush hiding within the folds of her heavy green dress, waited for him to scream at her, scream at God, scream at himself in frustration and fear when he saw the bodies of dead comrades lying everywhere. They all did, she knew. All Americans were afraid of her, piteously unprepared for the terror of fighting a war tailored to the jungle by an enemy that had lived within her all his life. She watched Joe, and she waited for those first signs of panic.

When the panic never came and the fear transformed itself into determined pursuit of the job he had been sent to do, the jungle smiled in surprise. She began to show him some of her secrets, tentatively exposing herself to him, allowing herself the pleasure of his reverence. Within the thick canopy of jungle, Joe Rutledge understood the dimension of feeling that a priest would have inside a cathedral. He felt the jungle's timeless clamor for life, felt her refusal to die in the midst of bombs, shelling, napalm and defoliants. Within her foliage, she was stained glass filtering sunshine, and he was a worshipper with an uplifted face.

With his first wounding, when he felt the sharp, blasting pain of shrapnel slamming into his leg, he had stared at the jungle in surprise while she gazed at him through the mist of a steady rainfall. They turned their faces from each other, he trying to hide his anger and betrayal under his furious return of fire, she trying to hide her shame in a curtain of rain.

He was carried into the field hospital at Danang, covered with mud and soaked with blood—his own and that of some of his men. And as he succumbed to the anesthetic prior to surgery on his leg, he thought again of Vietnam, of the fighting, the separation from home and sanity, the dozens of soft-scented letters from Sam, the blood, the welcome packages, the heat, the mud, the leaches—images colliding furiously with each other as his mind gave way to nothingness.

"...what that means in laymen's terms, Lieutenant, is you have a sliver of metal buried deep under your kneecap. The damage in and around your knee is extensive enough that we're sending you to Walter Reed for more surgery and recuperation..."

Lifting away from Danang toward Saigon and a MedEvac flight to the States, Joe stared down at the jungle from above as she spread open green arms and gazed silently at a departing, wounded worshipper.

XXIV

"Aha! There you are! I figured I'd find you out here, Captain."

He turned and smiled at the nurse descending on him. She was young and plain, the kind of girl he had always felt remotely sorry for in school, with her mouse-colored hair done up severely under a nurse's cap, heavy Coke-bottle glasses resting authoritatively on a nose that was a bit too wide for her face. She was the kind of girl that would always arouse something other than passion in a man, the kind of girl men enjoyed being with because she was simple and uncomplicated and non-threatening. She was everyone's sister back home.

"Shame on you," she said, her hands burrowed into the pockets of her white smock. "You missed your medication—again—two hours ago, and you're probably wearing yourself out walking around so much."

"I was on my way home, honest," he grinned.

"Shame on you anyway," she said, trying not to smile. "I'll walk with you, just to make certain you find your way back. You can't miss your medication again today, Captain. Seriously, you need to be more mindful of...stop that now!"

He was pantomiming her words as she spoke, leaning closer and closer to her ear. She batted at him, finally releasing a grin that lit up her freckled face as she took his arm. "Okay, hot-shot, let's go tuck you in."

"Thought you'd never offer!"

"Oh, stop that."

"Can't help it—you bring out the tiger in me. Every time

239

I see you I want to feast on your earlobes..."

He laughed and squeezed her arm as he limped along beside her. They talked of the ship, of the war, of home. She asked where he got his Southern accent— "In South Ko-rea, honey,"—and he asked if all her sisters were as pretty as she— "Of course not!" She asked him about his girlfriend— "I hear she's beautiful, a professional model or something. One of the nurses told me. Lucky man!"—and he asked her about her boyfriend—"I hear he's tough. Eats gooks for breakfast."—She blushed and assured him she didn't have a boyfriend, then changed the subject by asking him about his first wound, how it happened, where he had been sent for treatment. He told her of Walter Reed, of his subsequent two-month Civil Affairs school at Fort Gordon, Georgia. And since she seemed to be in the mood to listen, he told her of Panama.

He stared out over the railings while he talked, absently tracing the outlines of the green hump on the horizon. His mind flowed smoothly backward, sometimes rushing beyond his voice as he talked with a girl that smelled of warm kitchens, telling her of his days in "paradise"...

Remembering Panama was a vast remembering of a land full of voices; they were everywhere in the tiny, goose-neck country that played referee between the world's two great oceans. Panama was the bridge for looters, pirates and migrating civilizations between South and Central America, and all of them left a voice behind in their passing. It was rich, protective, hostile, an irresistible challenge, and Joe suspected that had it not been for the priceless Canal, Panama would have been a continual battleground between two continents. Instead, all the major countries of the world descended on the dog-legged strip of land, insisting on protecting it to insure their own uninhibited trade. Its vulnerable location, which in the past had been the country's downfall, was suddenly its only salvation. In the infant years of the twentieth century, Panama was finally released from its prison of plunder.

Covered with a thick, unyielding jungle, Panama had taken on new importance to the American military while the war in Vietnam raged on the other side of the world. It became a perfect location for the intensive training of soldiers in jungle warfare. From the moment of his assignment with the Jungle Operations committee of the 8th Special Forces Group in Panama, Joe listened closely to the voices in the jungle, in the rivers, on the beaches, infusing the spirit and depth of the jungle into every trainee assigned to him. The voices became lessons of survival, of escape and evasion in a world few of them understood.

He remembered other voices too: young voices, strong and living; members of the cadre who assisted in the training process; men who, with Joe, had learned to listen to the jungle. They were all Special Forces qualified, all highly professional soldiers who took their jobs seriously. They formed a collective lens of experience and skill, focused through the apertures of their youth and natural self-assurance.

In the waning days of October, Joe was called in to Colonel Fenton's office at Fort Gulik. He approached the meeting with an odd sense of apprehension; with an instinct developed early in his experience with the military, Joe knew that something unusual was in the works.

Colonel Fenton, the commander of the 8th, was a character created for every military poster in America: tall, heavily-built with no fat; short-cropped hair that was showing more gray than blond; deep craggy features and blue eyes that were amiable and angry at the same time. Had it not been for his active life in Panama, he would have been one of those men beginning to show the first traces of a paunch around his middle, the first discernible slackness in the flesh of his face. But because of the rigors of military life and the frenzy of Vietnam, Colonel Fenton was maintaining the last vestiges of his youth: the hard stomach and tight, sunburned skin would remain, along with his all-American good looks, only until peace melted his youth away.

He sat behind his desk chewing amiably on the end of an unlit cigar and glared at the recently promoted Captain Rutledge. "I'll get right to the point, Joe," he said out of one side of his mouth. "I've received a request through the 5th

Group in Nha Trang for a small team to operate with the 101st Airborne Division. I've selected you as the team leader." The cigar worked back and forth nervously as the colonel watched Joe's reactions.

"Colonel," he finally said, "Vietnam wasn't exactly part of my plans when my tour was up here. I know you realize I've already served one tour there."

"What exactly were your plans?"

"Korea, sir."

The fidgeting cigar stopped in mid-flight across his mouth, then abruptly continued as his eyes narrowed slightly. "Joe, we're in the middle of a goddamn war; there's no need for any Special Forces people in Korea and probably won't be in the near future. The chances of you getting stationed over there are practically zero. In fact, the nearest SF Group to Korea is in Japan."

"I realize that, Colonel."

"Then you won't mind volunteering for this team."

"Colonel, there've got to be any number of qualified people in Vietnam who could make up a team; there's the 5th out of Nha Trang, there's the Rangers, there's..."

"It's not an A-team, Joe; it's a scaled-down version, a very special unit designed for some sort of reconnaissance work."

"Even so, Colonel..."

"Look, Joe." He finally removed the cigar from his mouth and sighed. "This is a special request from a very good friend of mine, a classmate from West Point. He's asked me to pick the best I have, and you're it. He knows about you already, knows of your medals and commendations and he's anxious to work with you."

"What about the others? Who did you have in mind?"

"They've already volunteered," he said, thrusting the cigar between his teeth again and grinning. "All members of your cadre, all Vietnam vets, as you know." Joe stared in surprise, leaning forward with the first glowings of interest beginning to surface. "My cadre?"

"Yup. All seven of 'em. First Sergeant Fuente—he'll be your second in command—let's see," he scanned a list on the desk in front of him, "Oh yes, Sergeant Mark Mathews, Sergeant Raymond Erskine, Sergeant Patrick Andros, Sergeant Louis Orlando, Sergeant Jack Kralik and Sergeant Anthony Rangonni. As far as I'm concerned, the cream of the crop."

"I'll be damned," Joe said softly. "When would we leave?"

Colonel Fenton stood, straightening his massive shoulders.

"You'll be out of here within the week. After two weeks leave in the States, you'll report to Nha Trang, then on to the 101st Airborne at Camp Evans where Colonel Leonard Hansen will be expecting you. He's the 506th Brigade Commander there, one of the best men you'll ever have the privilege of working with—and a damn good friend."

The day before he left Panama, Joe stood for the last time on the cliffs at old Fort San Lorenzo and stared out to the Caribbean, absorbing himself in the last of the voices. He wondered how others had felt when leaving here, knowing that everyone who leaves Panama takes something of the country with them. Whether material goods or emotional goods, no one ever left Panama empty-handed. He closed his eyes and felt the oldness of the place, the utterly uncounted years and lives swirling in an invisible, sighing wind all around him. And he knew he would be leaving Panama with the music of the Indians in his veins, and the cruel, boisterous laughter of an English pirate echoing in his memory...

The room aboard the ship was beginning to shift, to detach from itself, parts of it raising up, other parts sliding away out of his focus. Sounds were distorted, arriving and receding on strange tides of perception, first becoming rushing waves full of the muted sounds of the ship, then becoming distant silence, the hollow silence of tunnels and caves. He lay on his stomach and let his arms fall over the edges of the hospital bed while he examined the altering going on inside him. This was the only enjoyable part of the injections that burned like fire and left a hard, painful knot on his buttocks: this first stage of drifting, of weightlessness before the heavy fog of sleep closed in, these few moments of quiet derangement were almost worth the sore butt and the forced sleep. Almost. He was never truly comfortable with being so totally helpless during those deep unconscious moments of sleep. He had lived in the jungle too long, lived on the ragged edge of danger for too many months.

He resigned himself slowly to the drug, giving in gradually to a skirmish he was destined to lose. The faint remains of conscious thought struggled to maintain a petulant lucidness, refusing to concede victory to the medication just long enough to remember the raucous laughter of the young men of his team. He lay still and listened, smiling to himself, closing his eyes against the whirling room as he heard their voices approaching through the fog...

XXV

There was a new life-form generated in the jungles of Vietnam, a throbbing, teeming new genesis of military camps that, by their very atmosphere, were different from all other camps in the world. Though they were patterned upon standard guidelines and operated as close to set procedures as circumstance would allow, the compounds of Vietnam were creations unto themselves, a race of military offspring that were set apart like bastard children from their parent bases. They were establishments designed for order in a disorderly, violent country, and they had quickly adapted themselves to their terrain. They sprawled on bulldozed acres of jungle, blatantly built up and powerfully equipped, or they crouched on hastily-cleared knolls on exposed hilltops, bristling with fierce armament. They were hives of activity that could be, at times, deceptively serene; or they could turn into sudden swarming acres of dust, equipment, vehicles, shouting voices and seeming chaos accompanied by the continual thudding drone of helicopters lifting swiftly away toward battle, or swooping in with the bodies of those who didn't survive. Dust rose everywhere at the slightest footfall except during the rainy season. And they all smelled the same: of canvas, fuel and sweat.

But the true separation in this species of military camp, the one distinguishable birthmark that identified it, were the men: one was never certain if the men were responsible for the camp's existence, or if the camp spawned the men. The mark was in the way they walked—determined, invisibly burdened;

245

and in their laugher—tight, hard, frequent. But the camps were reflected most deeply in their eyes. All the horrors of the war, all the death and terror appeared first in their eyes; they were coals from just inside a cave, shadowed and opaque with fear suppressed or fear exposed. The mark never left their eyes, even if they were lucky enough to be sent home. The soldiers of Vietnam would become refugees in their own towns, among their own families; men who had left too much of their lives behind like scattered litter in the jungle.

When his chopper settled carefully within the sprawling limits of Camp Evans, Joe had the same unmistakable feeling of a returning refugee, the vague, insistent sensation of a man returning to old haunts in search of whatever he had left behind. The rest of the team had arrived days before, and when he joined them at a barracks set aside for them, he was swept quietly over with a feeling of having found what he had missed.

"Goddamn, Cap, we thought maybe you'd gone AWOL!" Orlando said, as he grabbed Joe's hand in a fierce hand-shake. They all greeted him with the delight of men anticipating the resumption of delayed camaraderie, in a renewal of the unique bonds of soldiers. This too was a legacy of a military camp in Vietnam: the sometimes frantic closeness of men preparing to face the jungle and the war together.

"I can see you guys aren't wasting any time fitting in here—you look like shit already," he said with a grin. Clad only in the drab green trousers of the Army, shirtless and barefoot, they were a direct contrast to the starched and polished soldiers they had been in Panama.

"How 'bout this, Cap?" Fuente said, gesturing at the room. "Welcome to 'More-Than-Shitty,' Vietnam!"

It was the generic building designed to accommodate up to a platoon of men, a rectangular building topped by a tin roof held down by sandbags. The barracks was sandbagged half way up the entire exterior, finished off with screens running the length of both sides. It was open to the sounds and smells of the camp, insuring its occupants a connection with the life going on around them. There were two small rooms at the front of the building, and Fuente put Joe's duffle bag in one. "Your own quarters," he explained. "More-Than-Shitty goes first class all the way, Cap."

It took only moments to rid himself of his uniform, pulling on a black T-shirt and fatigue pants. He stretched out on one of the numerous bunks and someone tossed him a beer while he listened to the amiable chatter. "Tell me," he said, "why 'More-Than-Shitty?' I mean, other than the dirt, the smell, the mosquitos, the lousy beds and the heat, this place ain't so bad."

"We named it after my hometown, Cap," Andros replied, his heavy Southern drawl rolling through the room like molasses. "Morgan City, Louisiana. The meanest, toughest, ass-kickin'est town in America. Also the ugliest, dirtiest armpit of a town in America. Cap, I ain't kiddin', they got cockroaches down there the size of…"

"Oh shit, here we go," Rangonni said, rolling his eyes.

"I'm serious, son," Andros said, his eyes widening. "One night—this ain't no shit now—one night my brother and I're comin' home from Thibodaux through the bayou, n'up in the road ahead we see somthin' looks like it has to be a traffic accident. We get closer'n our headlights shine on it—and I'll be damned, turns out to be two goddamn cockroaches rapin' a Volkswagen!" They all burst out laughing while Andros maintained his wide-eyed innocence, and Rangonni shook his head, looking suddenly serious.

"That's nothin', man." His thick New Jersey brogue was a sharp contrast to the smooth-as-syrup southern Andros. "Where I come from, the fleas'd make your cockroaches look like pissants. I mean, every Joisey City flea owns three dogs apiece!"

And the game was on; one of those inane, soothing pastimes they had developed together in Panama, a good-natured game of one-upmanship. "Hey, Mat," Kralik coaxed, "shall we tell 'em about Detroit?"

"Detroit!" Erskine hooted, "Dee-troyt, Dee-troyt, lemme see—isn't that where God took a dump on the seventh day?"

"What d'you know about it, flat-foot?" Kralik retorted.

"What the hell would a New Yorker know about God's country?"

"That's right," Mathews said, nodding with mock wisdom. "If you're gonna talk about God's country, you'd better talk to Orlando. Anyone coming from the City of Angels has got to know a lot about God, right Orlando?"

"Sheeit," Orlando said, lounging back with his hands behind his head. "All we do in Los Angeles is fuck." The room disintegrated into laughter while Orlando stared dreamily at the ceiling. Fuente opened another beer, looking at Joe.

"So what did you think of Colonel Hansen?" he asked, the faint traces of his Cuban heritage still clinging in wisps to his words. Joe pursed his lips and examined the beer can. "He seems like a real straight guy. Gives me the impression of someone we can trust," he replied, then smiled. "Doesn't quite fit the typical image of a brigade commander, does he?"

They all shook their heads, recalling how the colonel's slight build, short-cropped hair and sunburned face made him look almost boyish. Were it not for the deepening creases at the corners of his eyes, one would have guessed him to be a young college student instead of the commander of a brigade in Vietnam, a man in his mid-forties. "Well, he might not fit the image," Fuente said, "but I can tell you, he ain't no slouch."

Mathews leaned up on one elbow, dangling one long leg over the edge of his bunk. "Now that you've talked to the colonel, can you give us any idea what this is all about?"

Joe leaned over and snatched another beer from the huge canvas water bag someone had filled with ice. "It looks like," he said between swallows, "the 101st is getting their balls kicked in up here and they haven't been able to figure out what they're dealing with. Regular recon missions haven't turned up shit, so what Hansen has in mind is a special 'sneaky-Pete' team, long-range reconnaissance workout in Apache territory."

The men glanced at each other, then looked at Joe. "You mean we dragged our butts all the way from Panama for recon work?" Rangonni asked, bewildered. "Shit, they got plenty of idiots right here they could get for that. Why us, Cap?"

"Because it isn't just straight recon work," Joe replied. "What Hansen has in mind is a unit operating independently, with the ability to damage enemy supply routes, disrupt communications and commit sabotage, as well as carry out ambush and rescue missions. He wanted a team that's qualified and experienced with all of it, and he says he wanted the best. So he contacted Colonel Fenton. The rest is history."

The silence was filled with an indefinable, low-grade electric pulse, a quiet charge that seemed transmitted by the smoke of several cigarettes in the room. Though they said nothing, Joe could see in every man's eyes the acceptance of the gauntlet thrown down by Hansen. There would be other moments like this: inexpressible and full of the emotions known only to soldiers. But stepping away from it in his mind, examining the room, the camp, the country, Joe knew there would be no moments of any greater closeness than what they were feeling right then. All the work they had done together in Panama, all the time spent exploring the rowdy nightlife in Colon, the days and nights in the jungle on training missions—all those unregistered moments focused now in the barracks at Camp Evans as they silently accepted a challenge together.

The sun cooled its blaze beyond the western fringes of the camp and someone switched on a radio filling the room with the nerve-numbing rhythms of The Rolling Stones, The Mamas and the Papas and Buffalo Springfield. They spent the rest of the evening drinking beer and singing along with the voices from another world in which they suddenly felt themselves out of step, oddly unsynchronized. There was no thought then of disrupted lives, interrupted futures, of possible death. On that one night in "More-Than Shitty," Vietnam, *they* were the future. And if it is ever possible for young men at war to be happy, they were that night.

In the weeks and months that followed, they counted time not in terms of the number of missions but in terms of missions completed; not in terms of leaving the base, but in terms of returning. Their lives became a fusion of day and night, jungle and weapons, rain and heat. They moved farther into each other, feeling the heat and hearing the rapid breathing, reading body signs and listening with their eyes when danger prevented speech. By their instinctive solitude as individuals they knew the ability to function alone; through their intense understanding of each other, they worked as one mind and kept each other alive.

During those months Joe watched the country, watched its places and its people, listened to them and learned from them. He was a part of an alien structure, a man in an American uniform, and he felt the painful collision of two worlds within him as he stood and watched the lines of refugees moving from one bombed location to another. He felt their fear, felt their sorrow. Their lives were his. They all stared at him with his own eyes, looking to the tall American GI with hope and mistrust—hope for salvation but not trusting him to provide it. He was at once removed from them by his good fortune, and joined to them by his heritage.

In his mind he matched the enemy with the jungle, placing them together in a union that made them both more understandable, less mysterious. The Viet Cong—or the gooks, or "Charlie" or the NVA, whatever name and face the enemy assumed—became a script written in the fine, legible hand of nature. Plunging deeper into the reservoirs of instinct, Joe would squat on a hillside for hours and watch the jungle while remembering his encounters with "Charlie," remembering his moves and his reasons. He waited and listened, finally discovering Charlie's greatest asset: his patience. Joe sat as a studious pupil before a tutor who was unaware of the lessons he taught. And then he waited for the night.

When there was no sound, no life, no movement, when even insects stopped their music, Joe would stretch forth a spiritual antennae to feel the darkness, to touch it, and to speak to the enemy hiding patiently not far away, an enemy waiting for the American to give up and move.

"*I know you're there, Charlie,*" he would whisper with his mind.

"*I know you're there too, Joe. I'm waiting for you.*"

"You'll be waiting a long time, Charlie."
*"No I won't. You'll give up—you Americans always lose
patience and give up. That's when you'll die."*
*"You don't know me, Charlie. My patience has no limits. You
never figured on me. I'll live, because you taught me how."*
"I taught you?"
"I learned from the best."
The hours would creep by with no movement, no sound
from either man. They could feel each other sweat, feel the
insistent pain from lack of movement in each others' legs.
There would be no sleep because a sleeping man changes his
breathing pattern. Nothing. Total stillness. And Charlie would
begin to wonder...
"I know you're there, Joe."
Nothing.
You are there, Joe, I know it."
Nothing.
"You're there—aren't you Joe?"
Now it begins.
"Where are you, Joe?"
Nothing.
"Joe...?"
Charlie would strain his neck just a fraction of an inch to
peer through the dense foliage, and the wait would be over. A
short burst of fire from Joe's weapon, and it was finished.
There was no victory here. With all of his training, all his
understanding of the war and what his purpose was, Joe was
never able to feel anything beyond an odd vacancy when he
was forced to speak to Charlie in order to destroy him. There
was no triumph; only a sickening sense of loss.
The men of his team sensed the difference in him, this
bewildering attraction to the jungle and all things in her. They
admired and trusted his knowledge of the enemy without fully
understanding it. There was a vibration in the air around him,
a diaphanous sheath of energy that drew them to him as their
leader and inspired their loyalty while separating him from
them as surely as his Oriental blood. Through mission after
mission they followed him without question, knowing only

that he communicated with the jungle in ways they couldn't fathom, but knew were real.

On the day the team linked up with an exhausted, frightened patrol that had lost their commanding officer in a firefight, they were all in good spirits. Dirty, tired and hungry for their first hot meal in three weeks, the team had received orders to bring the patrol to a safer location for pick-up by choppers, and as they moved out through the heavy growth, they felt the relief of knowing the "ride home" was only a few hours away.

He supposed later that it had been his anxiousness to get back after a long, fatigue-ridden mission; he supposed it was the breaking of one of his own rules—never, NEVER get complacent—that prevented him from sensing the ambush in the trail ahead. And when he heard the first barrage of RPG rounds tearing the air around them, when he heard it explode and heard the point man scream, he blamed himself. When the second round blasted the trail behind him, throwing him into the bushes as everyone scrambled for cover, he had felt only anger at himself. His only clear, conscious thought had been of a young man's scream somewhere up ahead: "I'm hit! I'm hit! I'm hit...!"

XXVI

She pushed through his door just as he finished dressing. She stood still for a moment and stared, her face brightening, her eyes growing wider behind the thick glasses. He grinned at her as she laid a clipboard and pen on the stiffly-made bed. "Good morning, freckles," he said jovially. "How do I look?"

"Well, well!" she said, folding her arms and examining him closely. 'I've never seen you in clothes before. Come to think of it, I've seen more of your butt than face! You look great, Captain. How are you feeling?"

"My butt thanks you, my back thanks you, I'm feeling fine. A little stiff maybe, but fine. I missed my evening bee sting last night and wondered where you were."

"Not my shift. I worked three weeks of evening shifts— ever since you got here—and my rotation was last night. I just came in this morning to have you fill out a couple of forms before you leave."

"Gonna miss me when I'm gone?"

"Ha! The only exercise I've had since I landed on this bucket has been chasing you down for your medication. I'm going to do myself a favor and personally throw you off this tub! I'm surprised they let you stay this long; wounds like yours belong in Tokyo, at least. You must have done some fast talking to keep them from shipping you out of here after the first couple of days."

"I knew you'd miss me. Give me a good-bye nibble on that earlobe?"

"Now stop that!"
"Heartless wench."

Lifting away from the deck into a searing blue sky, he watched as the hospital ship *Hope* became a small white sliver in the water. He would wonder at times what became of the nurse with freckles and the smell of supper-time kitchens around her, a girl from back home who patched up broken soldiers.

But on that day, as his chopper bolted between sky and water toward the emerald field on the horizon, his thoughts were flung beyond the field into the dusty reaches of Camp Evans and the men of More-Than-Shitty. The long, nervous days of pacing the rails while his body healed were over. The green horizon loomed larger. He was coming back...

"I saved them for you," Fuente said, as he handed Joe the small stack of letters. "I knew you'd be back sometime this week and I didn't want to chance having them lost in the fucked up military mail shuffle. Oh, and there's a package in your room, just got here yesterday."

"Thanks, Top," he said, unbuttoning his shirt and looking at the letters in his hand.

"Get yourself settled, Cap, and take it easy for a few minutes."

"I think I'll do that, and we'll talk about my meeting with Hansen when everyone gets back from lunch."

Fuente nodded and turned to leave, then stopped and looked at him. "By the way," he said with a smile. "Welcome back, sheethaid. You're not gonna get yourself fragged every time you want a little R and R, now are you?"

"I might. Lots of good-lookin' nurses on the boat."

Fuente closed the door behind him and Joe stretched out on his bunk, feeling the stiffness in his back against the friendly sag of the cot. The first letter was postmarked over three weeks before. He counted the envelopes. One for every day of the three weeks he had been on the ship. He smiled and slit open the first one, taking his place in the generations of soldiers who hungrily devoured news from home. When he pulled the letter out, a yellowed, papery flower petal fluttered to the floor. He picked it up carefully and smelled it. Gardenia.

April 29, 1969
Dear Joe,

It probably won't have any fragrance at all by the time you receive it, but I wanted you to have a tiny part of Charleston's vanishing spring. This one came from the bush in Reuben's garden. He says there's a story about his garden you'll have to tell me someday...

May 1, 1969
Dear Joe,

Well, I've really done it now! I've irrevocably incurred the wrath of God and my mother, both angers being one and the same. I am now the proud owner of my cousin's tour business, "Low Country Carriage Tours," which in itself is not so bad where my mother is concerned (it's tacky but tolerable). However, I have sealed my doom in her eyes by going to work at the company as a tour guide on one of the horse-drawn carriages, hauling (God help me!) tourists all over Old Charleston. My mother nearly turned to a pillar of salt when I told her. She looked at me as though I were the city of Sodom itself! You can just hear her, can't you? "...no young lady with any BREEDING would be caught DEAD driving around behind a HORSE, catering to a bunch of TOURISTS and making a SPECTACLE of herself!" Of course, it didn't end there. She reaches into her arsenal and throws my career at me, my agent, my social standing— "It's not as if you need the MONEY, for God's sake!"—and on it goes...

Joe laughed out loud at her description of Henrietta's discomfort. He knew she had left out the worst of the arguing, had failed to mention the strained silences, the low-key sniping, the doors slammed in anger. What he didn't know, what Sam had avoided telling him, was that the arguments had cost Henrietta dearly. Her objections over the carriage company had been mere forerunners to something much deeper, something she was at a loss to understand, and even more impossible for her to accept—Samantha's love for Joe.

In the very beginning, in those early teenage years when she realized that her daughter was infatuated with Charlie Rutledge's boy, she had been tolerant, even a bit amused. After all, she reasoned, he was such a darlin' thing with his coal-black hair and eyes and his pugnacious ability to become so popular with his peers in such a short time. He was a novelty, an interesting conversation piece. It was a bit disconcerting, however, when her daughter seemed to take no interest in anyone else. And when Samantha's career began to take shape so early, Henrietta was more than mildly relieved at having her preoccupied and out of reach. Not that the Rutledge boy seemed to have taken any interest in her, thank the lord! It seemed to be a one-way attraction, and Henrietta believed it would end with the blooming of her daughter's career.

Henrietta hadn't yet recovered from the shock of having Samantha abandon her work when she arrived on the doorstep late one night with the Rutledge boy—my GOODNESS, he's a MAN now!—and invited him in for coffee. It was a worse nightmare than she could ever have imagined in those early days. All of her tactful suggestions, all of her skillful maneuvering learned over a lifetime was laughingly brushed aside at best, or openly ignored at worst. The girl was hopelessly in love. Henrietta began to quietly panic when she saw the feeling mirrored in the young man's eyes.

There had been no reprieve for Henrietta when he was swept away to Vietnam. Though she knew she should loathe herself for her desire to have the war rid her of a devastation she didn't know how to deal with, her loathing eventually evaporated when she saw the look on Samantha's face the day she found out that Joe had been wounded. Henrietta knew that she had to try and fight this thing. It simply wasn't going away on its own.

"Samantha, honey, I'm a little confused," she began one day when the girl seemed to be in jubilant spirits. "You have to help your mother understand a thing or two." Her voice was honey-smooth with the warmth of Southern motherhood. "Try as I might, I can't seem to understand your refusal to at least talk to Artie. He's been a marvelous agent all these years, and I think you owe him the courtesy of at least..."

"No, mom."

"Now honey, don't cut me off before you hear me out, I just want to know why you..."

"We've been through this a dozen times, mother, and there's nothing more to say on the subject. I spoke to Artie before I left New York. He knows it's finished and that's it, so let's don't bring it up anymore, okay? You just end up angry."

Henrietta wrung her hands and furrowed her brow, appearing on the verge of tears. "I DON'T understand this, I simply DON'T! A wonderful career, all the possibilities in the world. Why, you could have right now at this very minute every eligible young man in the country calling on you, you could be making arrangements for a lovely future with someone who..."

"Someone who what, mother?" she sighed, rolling her eyes in exasperation. Henrietta was venturing into untried territory, never before having openly challenged the girl on her relationship with Joe. She proceeded with feline caution.

"Well," she gestured absently, "someone who is...someone Charleston respects and who...oh, you know what I'm trying to say! Don't force me to founder around so!"

Sam put her hands on Henrietta's shoulders and seated her on the sofa. She looked her mother directly in the eye, a habit Henrietta found disconcerting and unladylike. "Mom, listen to me," Sam said softly, her eyes shining, her face warm with a strange smile. She pulled a heavily postmarked envelope from her handbag and held it up in front of her mother. "This man right here is the only future I'm interested in. He's the beginning of everything for me. There's nothing beyond this one man—no career, no spotlight, and certainly no other men. This is it, mom, this is really it! I'm in love with him! And I want you to be excited for me, I want you to be pleased that I'm so happy."

The words, spoken so easily and openly that way— "I love him"—were like the falling of heavy stones in a stream for Henrietta and she began to vibrate with a building desperation.

"How can you love him, Samantha? How? You've got nothing to compare the feeling with. You haven't even spoken to another man since you got back from New York. How can you be so sure? What is it you SEE in him?"

Sam shrugged good-naturedly. "You can't deny he's a handsome man, mom. Intelligent, slender, beautiful smile. Come on now, mom," she chided, tugging at her mother's sleeve, "even you can't ignore how handsome he is in his uniform."

"Samantha, PLEASE..." Henrietta pleaded, "you KNOW what I mean! What-is-it-you-see-in-this-boy?"

"All right, mother," Sam said putting the letter away. "I'll tell you why I love him, but I warn you, you'll be disappointed. You see, I know what you're up to. I know you're hoping I'll admit to some shallow infatuation you can pick apart and disregard as foolish. You're hoping I'll give you all the ammunition you need to blow him right out of the water. Well, it's too late for that, mother. There's no hope of ever finding anything surface about what I feel for him. I love him for everything he is, from the inside out. I've discovered that he's a complex study of counterparts. For everything good in him there is an equal and opposite being somewhere inside. For all of his generosity, I've discovered he's only generous with those things in him that are easily given. There's a part of him that I can't have, and I love that part of him, too. For all of his kindness, I sense a deep, cold unkindness in him, a brutality, and I love the darkness in him. For all of his self-assurance, all his confidence and fearlessness, there are times when I sense something young and small and bewildered in him, and I love him for that. I love him for his vulnerability, for his rock-hard assurance. I love him for his manliness and his childishness. I love him because he makes me feel safe when I'm with him, and because he finds safety in me. I love him because he makes me feel like a woman without forcing me to give up my girlhood. I love him for all he gives me, and even more so for all he can't. Because eventually I'll have it all, and there's nothing you or he or God can do to erase that. I've deliberately bound myself to all that he is. I've absorbed all that is weak in me with all that's strong in him, and I've insisted he do the same with me. To leave him now would be tearing away flesh and blood and bone and soul and I would most certainly die."

Henrietta sat and listened with the expression of someone being continually struck in the face. Her eyes were wide, her mouth slightly open, a look of intense pain etched in her entire posture. She was breathing in short shallow patterns.

Sam looked at her levelly. "I love him, mother. And when he gets home, I'm going to marry him and give him a whole house full of fat babies."

Henrietta was suddenly jolted from her terrorized trance and her face turned harsh, vulpine. "What do you mean?" she snapped, her lips curling in disdain. "What do you mean you're going to have his babies? How can you even THINK such a thing! My God, Samantha, just imagine what your damn KIDS would look like!"

Henrietta saw the look, saw the raising of a drawbridge and the aiming of every cannon. Her words had been a death knell, a loud, coarse pealing from the belfry of her own prejudice, and there was nothing she could do but make a stand on the boggy ground from which she was born. Her hands were trembling and tiny muscles in her cheeks were twitching. So it was done. She had said it and meant every word, painful as it had been, and she battled desperately for control in the face of knowing she had just made a fatal tactical error.

Sam stood slowly, her eyes narrowed and strangely bright. "I'll forgive you for that one, mother. I'll forgive you because I know you can't help it; you can't do anything about the place and time you were raised. You can't change the generations that molded you into an insufferable snob and a petty little bigot. I'll forgive you because in your own way, you are stupidly honest. You haven't added hypocrisy to your world of sins. You spoke your mind, you had your say, and I know where we both stand."

Her mother stood on shaky legs and faced her daughter, wanting somehow to retrieve what she could feel slipping away, yet not daring to retreat. Sam's voice became a tight, solid whisper.

"I'll forgive you this time, mother. But don't ever bring this up again. Don't ever again challenge me about Joe. Because there's nothing in this house, in this town, in this world that is as important to me as him. He's mine. I'm going to marry him. And I don't ever want you to make me choose between him and you. It's too late for that. In my mind, the decision was made a long time ago."

Joe looked up from the stack of letters when he heard the men returning from lunch. He hurried through several more letters where she explained how Eva was faring: "...not very well, I'm afraid. She sits for days at a time in Charlie's study, talking to herself as if he were there. She's terribly thin...Reuben has to practically force her to go outdoors at least once a week for a short walk or a drive. You'd love it, he's such a marvelous bully!...Eva asked me the other day how you were doing in school..." She included bits and pieces of news from Shady Mae: "...Ginny's going to college this fall, can you believe it! The first girl EVER in their family to go to college. Shady's so proud when she talks about her it looks like her whole body is rising like bread dough...she misses you...Reuben misses you...everyone talks about you..."

Fuente knocked on his door as he was opening one of the last letters, and Joe told him he'd be out in a minute. Someone switched on the radio and he could hear the strains of "Wichita Lineman" slipping through the wall.

May 7, 1969

Dear Joe,

I didn't go in to work today. I've been sitting by my window realizing how much like other women I must be right now. I don't suppose my heartsickness, my fear and helplessness at knowing you're hurt again is any different than what millions of other women have gone through at a time like this. It's just that I feel so uncommon, so isolated from everyone and everything, I can't imagine anyone ever having felt this way before. I try to convince myself that it's just selfish fear, a fear of losing you, because I think I could conquer that. There's more here, something I had to tell you about because—selfishly again—it'll make ME feel better.

I knew you were wounded long before Reuben heard it from the Department of the Army. The night before, I was having trouble falling asleep. I paced my room, went for a walk along the seawall across the street, watched TV. I tried not to think about you, tried not to let my mind wander into all the horrible things that are possible where you are. I lay in bed and bludgeoned myself into sleeping. I woke up sometime later trying to scream, covered with sweat. I sat up in bed, gasping for air, thinking I could hear lightning striking somewhere. I thought at first it must be storming but it was clear and beautiful outside, not a cloud in the sky. In that moment, I KNEW something was wrong. I knew you had been hurt. Later on, after Reuben told me, I sat and calculated the times and realized you must have been wounded that night. I felt it happen, Joe! I heard it happening! It's difficult now to even begin expressing what this knowledge does to me, how strangely, dangerously sweet it is. There is a part of me that insists it's a horrible burden, the ability to feel you across the miles. And yet there's another greater part of me quietly persuading me that this's all part of it, all a part of my deliberate consumption of you. It's rather a joke on me by our famous "powers that be," an extra added responsibility for you I hadn't expected, but am grateful for. I just wish I knew how to handle the fear...

But in all this, I also understand you're not in danger of losing your life (not at this moment, anyway), that along with the burden of knowing when you're hurt, comes the blessing of knowing when you're alive, when you're going to be all right. I suppose I'll also discover how much "mother-henning" you can handle when I ask you to please be careful. That isn't for you, understand, it's for me—something I need to do, like whistling past a cemetery in the dark. A useless, comforting gesture. Please, be mindful of yourself, be mindful of me, and remember there's a very real extension of yourself that feels the pain, suffers the nightmares, shares the darkness with you. Protect us. Try to imagine how much I love you, then keep us alive until this bad dream is over. Sending Love and Laugher,
Sam

There had been another moment like this one, he knew; as he tucked the letters carefully into his footlocker he tried to remember when he had felt this way. His mind rapidly collated years with memories—childhood, Korea, Sok-Cho. And there it was, separated from the files and tagged with a large red question mark: the old soothsayer. He remembered the incense-shrouded hut, the look on her face as she spoke. He remembered his fear while facing her and his bewilderment after. He wondered then, as he did now, what it had all meant.

He remembered the feeling of being in the presence of something he didn't understand, mixed with the feeling of macabre trust. As mystified as he had been, he knew now he had believed her. Something about her own conviction about an unseen dimension and her belief in her ability to see into it had made him believe what she said with a groundless certainty. As he stood and slipped into a T-shirt before joining his men, he allowed Sam's letter to assume an equal position with the abilities of the fortune teller: unexplained, mysterious, but ultimately true.

"Well, would y'all look at this!" Andros yelled happily above the music when Joe finally emerged. "If it ain't the walkin' wounded himself. Hey you assholes, show some respect! 'Ten'hut!'"

"Fuck that," Orlando said with a grin, grabbing Joe's hand. They crowded around him in excited, relieved welcome, exchanging light-hearted banter about his wounds, about his absence, about his return. "This place's been like a fuckin' kindergarten since you left," Mathews said. "Except for a couple of advisory stints with the goddamn ARVNs we've been sittin' on our asses for nearly three weeks."

"Well," Joe smiled, settling onto one of the bunks, "were you able to teach 'em anything, Mat?"

"Shit. You know how it is with them, Cap. All they want is to crawl into a hooch somewhere and let us stupid Americans do all the work. Same old shit." Everyone grumbled in agreement. The South Vietnamese Army regulars weren't highly regarded by American GI's. Their indolent attitudes and lack of performance in the heat of battle were continual irritations to the American units required to work with them, and Joe could sense with some amusement that his men had tolerated their assignments with the ARVNs the way a baby-sitter tolerates an exasperating child.

For the next thirty minutes they all took turns giving their versions of events during Joe's absence, asking him questions about the hospital ship, exchanging jokes about the nurses, complaining about their boredom. "You'd better enjoy your vacation while you can," Joe said. "I have a feeling, after talking with Hansen, that things are gonna get hot real soon."

They gathered close to each other in their minds, like men around a campfire planning their futures. There was no more barracks, no bustling camp, no other sound except Joe's quiet voice. He was the catalyst, the sealing force of the unit; they pulled to him and to each other in relief like fragmented divisions of a wheel.

Colonel Hansen had greeted him warmly when he arrived, shaking his hands with the firm grip of welcome. "It's good to have you back, Joe. I'm glad you're all right," he said, the wrinkles around his blue eyes deepening as he smiled. Colonel Leonard Hansen was a man of economy—few words, few movements, every motion and thought geared for action and results. There was a tightness to the man, a wiry precision that made him appear much taller than his actual five foot seven inches. His office reflected his personality and figure— small, lean and consummately orderly. His lack of encumbrance, physically and emotionally, left him open and available to his career, to the men with whom he worked. Joe had come to appreciate him as a man of uncomplicated power; he was, in Joe's mind, part of the upper strata of military commanders.

"Firebase Airborne was overrun last week," Hansen told him, typically avoiding superfluous details. He lit the first of a habitual chain of cigarettes and looked at Joe from across the desk. His eyes, which had a perpetual look of good humor, were hard and serious. "A sapper unit suicide mission. All twenty-nine that made it through the perimeter were killed, but not before fifty-four of our men were killed." He paused for a moment to allow the impact of what he was saying take shape in Joe's mind, closing his right eye against the smoke trailing from the cigarette. In addition, Hansen had explained, there had been a fierce battle in the Iron Triangle portion of the Ashau Valley involving three companies from Firebase Eagle's Nest, and a chilling discovery had been made.

"It wasn't until the fight was over and mop-up teams moved in that they figured out who and what they had been up against," Hansen said. "They counted 114 NVA regulars killed—all of them from the 29th NVA Regiment."

Joe's eyes widened slightly and he leaned forward. The name itself was synonymous with one of the worst periods of the Vietnam war—the 1968 Tet Offensive. The 29th NVA Regiment was the most seasoned, battle-hardened unit in the North Vietnamese Army. Since the Tet Offensive they had taken refuge in Laos where they were free to lick their wounds and regroup, waiting for the right time to strike out again.

"But that's not all," Hansen continued. "In that same skirmish in the Ashau, they killed nine Chinese Communist advisors."

"We've known all along the NVAs have used Chi-Coms, Colonel." Hansen shook his head, stubbing out the cigarette. "Never this far south before, and never so many in one battle. This is a first. Intelligence reports confirm large amounts of troop movement and activity just across the Laotian border, somewhere behind Hill 934 and Hill 936. And now a successful attempt to overrun a firebase, along with the discovery of so many Chi-Coms operating farther south than ever before—something goddamn big is brewing around the Ashau Valley, Joe."

Though he had become tuned long ago to the mood and spirit of military briefings, Joe felt an oddly removed sensation with the colonel's last words, a suspension of reality that allowed him to hear across space and distances. The words had sounded somewhere inside him with the deep resonance of a clarion's horn—the Ashau Valley. It was a challenge issued. A beckoning voice. He was being summoned.

"We know they're out there in huge numbers," Hansen began again, "but so far we haven't been able to figure out how they're being supplied. We're bombing the piss out of the Ho Chi Minh Trail, and though they continue to repair and use it, the line is too disrupted to be depended on for supplies. Every other route has been covered. We've reconned the Song Bo river, which has its headwaters in the southern mountain range near the valley, but turned up absolutely nothing. Other than a steady stream of trail-runners with fifty-pound sacks of rice tied to their backs, which wouldn't be enough to supply the type of force we're talking about, we've found no other continual conduit. And yet, we know they're receiving massive amounts of supplies."

For the next two hours they poured over maps and intelligence reports like tailors looking for flaws in a new bolt of cloth. They brought up possibilities only to eliminate them one by one. The ashtray filled and emptied twice and Hansen finally sat back, rubbing his eyes. "Go get some rest, Joe. We're just running ourselves in circles right now. We'll go over this again tomorrow."

By the time Joe finished explaining the situation to his men, the sun was low in the sky and the relief of a late afternoon breeze pushed through the screens. They sat quietly, absorbing all they had just learned.

"So what now, Cap?" Kralik asked, scratching his blond head.

"We don't know yet," Joe answered. "I'll know more tomorrow after I meet with Hansen again. Right now we don't even know where to begin."

"Well, I sure as hell know a good place to begin," Orlando said, pulling on his boots. "Let's go to An-Lo and hoist a few at Mama Phu's, celebrate the capn's return to More-Than-Shitty."

"Goddamn, Orlando," Rangonni moaned, "you might as well buy stock in that place. You must own it by now, all the money you've spent at that flea bag joint. Can't you think of anything better to do?" Orlando bent close to Rangonni's ear and grinned. "Mama Phu has two new girls," he coaxed in a loud whisper. "Get a jeep," Rangonni said, jumping to his feet and reaching for a shirt.

XXVII

By the time they made the ten-minute drive to the outskirts of An-Lo, they were well on the way to forgetting the serious atmosphere of their earlier briefing. They laughed readily, their faces finally resembling the faces of young men. As they approached the rice paddies outside the village, Mat leaned toward Joe. "Hard to believe such a peaceful place can exist right in the middle of a fuckin' war, ain't it?"

It was a scene so perfect in its timelessness, so appropriate and right that it would have been difficult to imagine life any other way for the people of An-Lo. But as they sped along the road between the flooded, fertile blocks of land, Joe knew he could take none of it for granted. He could never look at the rice fields and languid village and believe that this was unbreakable. Only a few months before, the village had been cowering under persistent shelling from stubborn, invisible cells of Viet Cong until Joe and the team had searched them out and destroyed them. And though the village was tranquil now, there were no guarantees of permanence. There were no "happily-ever-afters" in Vietnam.

The sunset spilled across the water like liquid fire, trembling gently with the movements of softly chattering villagers bent to their work. Three lumbering water buffalos, graceful in their awkwardness, were silhouetted against the sky, perfect charred shapes burned into the sunset. There was no measure of time here, no calendar to mark the passing of generations in the rice paddies. The people of An-Lo merely assumed the vacancies left by their ancestors, stepping dutifully onto the stage of ancient lifestyles. They were understudies to time-honored, unchanged traditions they would retrieve and perpetuate, no matter how many times they were interrupted by the war.

In the center of the paddies, constructed on a rise of dry land, a small pagoda rose seemingly out of the golden water, standing in serene guardianship of a people that would not be protected, and whenever Joe saw it he was reminded of the transiency of peace. Through the fearsome shelling that erupted on their discovery of the last of the Viet Cong mortar teams, Joe and his men had taken refuge in the pagoda. And though the V.C. knew it, not a shell landed close enough to do any damage. The sanctity of the edifice was honored by the enemy as an extension of their centuries-old pattern of living. The pagoda remained unscathed, a silent reminder that wars and warriors arrive and pass, but ancestry and devotion live forever.

Orlando slowed the jeep to move around a small group of villagers returning to An-Lo from the rice paddies: two young children and two women, one young, one old, both balancing heavy loads at the ends of long poles extended across one shoulder. They were shuffling quickly along in the odd gait learned early in their lives, a rhythm perfectly synchronized to the up-and-down shifting of the weight on their shoulder. When the jeep passed, the children waved and yelled and the old woman grinned widely, revealing a mouthful of teeth blackened by years of chewing the mildly euphoric betel nut. The men smiled and waved back and Orlando whistled and craned his neck to stare at the younger woman, almost running them off the road into a rice paddy.

"Orlando, you sheethaid!" Fuente yelled. "Keep your eyes on the road! She's probably married to a V.C. Commander."

Their laughter drifted out across the paddies to a listening pagoda in the sunset, the sentry of ages who had heard the laughter—and the screams and the tears—of soldiers before. And this laughter too, the pagoda knew, would pass away.

The village of An-Lo was beyond disillusionment. Though on the surface she appeared as fragile as a flower, easy to bloom, easy to crush, deep within the homes of her five hundred residents her heart was strong and slow to die. An-Lo was located astride the Song Bo river, with a road running through the middle and a bridge at its center. An-Lo loved the bridge while fearing its importance, knowing that the only reason she had been destroyed in the past was because of the strategic location of the bridge to the movements of troops and supplies from the south. Conversely, the bridge was now its protection, the only reason for a battalion of South Vietnamese soldiers to be stationed permanently on her outskirts.

Nguyen Phu Xuan was a part of the oddly discordant heartbeat of An-Lo. She had seen her share of days as a refugee, and with the tenacity born of war-torn Oriental womanhood she had consistently found her way back to the bitter-sweet sanctuary of An-Lo. There was no way of determining her age; the skin of her face was barely wrinkled but strangely stiffened and set. She moved with a quickness that could have been sprightly youth or the panic of approaching old age. Her hair bore no traces of gray, but sprouted in thin, wild sprigs that defied combing, giving her a perpetually startled appearance. She was tiny and stern and slightly deranged, and the American GI's avoided incurring her wrath when patronizing her house of business. She had proudly placed her entire name on the outside of the deserted school house, and through the sleight-of-hand known only to the wily Vietnamese, she had opened the one and only bar in An-Lo. In their habitual aversion to unpronounceable names, the Americans knew her only as "Mama Phu."

There was always momentary silence when someone new pushed through the screen door while everyone glanced around quickly to see who it was, but by the time all eight of them had entered and crossed to the bar, the noise in the room had assumed its former volume. All ten tables were taken up by soldiers, both from Camp Evans and the ARVN camp, and the smoke from dozens of cigarettes created a murky yellow haze in the light of two bare light bulbs in the ceiling. A radio blared from the shelf behind the rough-hewn bar, and men's voices filled the space between music and smoke. They pushed up to the bar and each ordered a beer, taking turns at teasing Mama Phu. She stood barely head and shoulders above the bar while standing on an empty ammunition crate to operate the ancient cash register, banging it soundly with a miniature fist to make the cash drawer regurgitate its contents. When she spotted Orlando she flew to his end of the bar, dragging the crate with her.

"You!" she screeched, dropping the crate and climbing aboard, leaning over the bar and poking her finger into his chest. "You! You numba fuckin ten, GI, you numba fuckin ten! You no souvenir me piasta last time you here! No mo girl fo you, numba fuckin ten!"

In the simple, no-frills world of Mama Phu, everything was trimmed to the basics, especially her judgments of soldiers. To her, a GI who was "numba one" was okay by her, and a "numba fuckin ten GI" was the lowest of the low. And there was nothing in between. Orlando had taken an impish pleasure in deliberately arousing her ire and from the beginning there had been open warfare between the two. She flew into a sputtering rage every time she saw him; he adored her.

"Now wait a minute, Mama Phu," Orlando pleaded, assuming his best innocent look. "My credit's good here, you don't need to get so riled, I was gonna pay you."

She shook her head rapidly, her stiff hair flailing in the smoky light. "You no good GI, you no souvenir me, you no get girl, numba fuckin ten!" She pounded his chest relentlessly, her eyes shining with anger. There were sporadic hoots of laughter and shouts of encouragement from the men at the tables, almost everyone at one time or another having fallen under the repudiating finger of Mama Phu. Orlando reached into his pocket and pulled out a handful of MPC's.

"See, Mama-san? I was going to pay you this time, honest!" Her hand darted forward like a slender viper and snatched a twenty-dollar MPC from the bundle. "Hey, wait a minute! It was supposed to be only five!"

She jumped down from the crate and began scooting to the cash register, glaring at him over her shoulder. "Interest!" she said, and slugged the cash register.

Mat leaned on the bar next to Joe, shaking his head and smiling. "Boy, is Orlando gonna be pissed when he finds out both new girls have been commandeered by Van Treung," he said, jerking his head toward the corner.

Colonel Van Treung, commander of the ARVN battalion, sat at a corner table, each arm draped across the shoulders of two young girls. He was laughing, alternately drinking one of several beers and fondling the girls, both of whom were showering professional affection on him. They giggled at his jokes and nipped at his ears, taking turns at furtive, feather-like brushings of the front of his trousers. Joe stared for a moment, feeling a slow, rising irritation as he watched the man. He turned back to the bar, guzzling the rest of his beer and signaling Mama Phu for another.

"Useless fucker," Joe muttered, and Mat nodded.

"Ah, Captain Rutledge!" Van Trueng suddenly called from his corner. "I thought that was you. Come and join me in a toast!" The man's English was nearly perfect, bearing the faint traces of a French accent, and Joe could feel his irritation deepen. He tried to ignore him, sipping on his beer and staring straight ahead. "Come now, Captain," Van Treung urged, his words slightly slurred with the beers. "Come and join me in a toast to...to our great American benefactors. A toast to the generous country that has come to the rescue of its weak sister."

The crowd of men nearby became gradually quiet and Joe could feel Mat tensing imperceptibly beside him. Joe sighed, realizing his petulance was about to be the cause of a small scene. He took his beer and seated himself at Van Treung's table while the noisy chatter began again.

The beer had loosened Van Treung's perpetually rigid posture and he lounged between the girls in the supple hardness possible only to a slender, wiry man. His features were smooth and even under short dark hair, and he smiled now with the slightly drunken awkwardness of a man who is unaccustomed to smiling.

"A toast," he said, raising his can of beer, "A toast to Big Brother!" he grinned. Joe glared at him calmly, raising his beer slowly.

"To America," Joe replied quietly.

"Oh, forgive me!" Van Treung said in mock apologetic horror. "It was not my wish to offend. Very well then," he said, weaving slightly. "To America."

Though he knew he had never been an intolerant person, Joe discovered with some surprise that he was becoming furiously angry with the arrogant man across the table. He believed he had seen it all, had lived through the gambit of human flailings in war and in peace and there had been few questions that had no answers. But sitting before him now was the embodiment of a syndrome he was at a loss to explain, and he leaned forward, looking closely at the smiling colonel. "Tell me something, Colonel," he said, allowing a smile to form that didn't extend to his eyes. "Why is it that the weak sister seems to be having such a good time, while Uncle Sam fights her fucking war for her?"

He spoke quietly, his voice never carrying beyond the table, but his voice had the impact of a cold blast of air. Joe was mildly surprised to see the instant change in Van Trueng's face, the sudden light in the fogged eyes, a quick firming of his slack jawline. He smiled stiffly, remaining calm. "And what is it you think we ought to be doing, Captain?" His speech was noticeably smoother, more articulate.

"I'll tell you what I think you ought to be doing," Joe said, rising to the bait of an argument. "I think you people should be taking the responsibility for your own goddamn war. I see American boys out there getting their asses shot while you and your men sit here and take it easy, screwing the local girls and drinking black-market American beer. I see Americans fighting your war, YOUR war, Colonel, and the lack of interest and ineptitude of your military does nothing but disgust me. We're only supposed to help guide this jack-ass of a war. Instead, we've ended up carrying the sonofabitch on our backs. Now you tell me, Colonel, do you still want to know what you ought to be doing?"

He could feel the cold, level surface of his own anger like the cutting edge of a poised sword, could feel the dangerous push through the neutral territory of bland good manners and into the darkness beyond. He could see the same journey being made in the eyes of the Colonel, the same voyage to the brink of violence, and he waited for their paths to converge.

But the confluence never occurred, the clash of emotional metal being only momentary. The light of certain battle in the Colonel's eyes began to fade, suffocated by a look of muted sadness, profound resignation. He sighed deeply and smiled.

"Let me tell you something, Captain. You—like every other American involved in this war—have sadly missed the point. You have mistakenly assumed that our attitude as soldiers is one of unconcerned cowardice. You have erroneously translated our indifference as ineptitude and you couldn't be further from the truth. However, I hold you only mildly responsible for your lack of perception. There is much you do not understand about my people."

Van Treung's voice was clear, with a soft sincerity that poured like cooling water over hot steel. He removed his arms from around the girls and sent them for more beer while he leaned forward, bracing his elbows on the table. "You must forgive us, Captain, if we seem to take the war lightly. That is because we DO take the war lightly. We have to, or we would all perish. You see, all of us who are alive today have known nothing but war since the day we were born. It has been a part of every waking hour of every day of our lives. It is nothing new, it was here yesterday and it will be here tomorrow. You— you Americans—you come here to a country you know nothing about to fight a war side by side with us for maybe a year. And when you have done your heroic deeds, killed your share of the enemy, served your allotted time, you get back on an airplane and within ten short hours you are home where it is safe, where there is always food and a promise of tomorrow.

"But we who are born here must remain here long after the last of your kind is gone. We remain here with the battles, the uncertainties, the continual death. Nothing ever changes for us, Captain. Our lives are filled with the hopelessness of it and there is no escape. You must forgive our lack of enthusiasm when we are reluctant to learn new and better ways to annihilate each other. Please understand us when we do not rush excitedly into another battle. Because to die in a glorious firefight is not glorious to us, Captain. It is simply death."

The girls returned with the beer amid loud appreciation from the soldiers nearby. They placed the cans of beer on the table and took their positions at Van Treung's side.

"You see, Captain," he said, his voice rising slightly in an effort to lighten the atmosphere. "When life becomes as cheap as it is in Vietnam, it becomes at the same moment very, very dear. We try not to waste it."

There had been only a few moments in his life, Joe realized, when he had felt so completely upbraided. He stared inwardly at himself, amazed at his blindness in a world to which he was so closely akin. They sat together, two soldiers embroiled in a tradition as old as the earth, neither guessing at the depth of the other, and Joe felt a distinct sense of guilt for not having sensed the bond earlier. But he also realized that to try to apologize for his earlier harshness would have been a loss of face for himself that would have cheapened the impact of what he had learned. And he had truly meant the things he had said; the fact that he had misjudged the motives of an entire people was, to him, another matter of conscience he would deal with on his own. He sat still, waiting for the proper moment to gracefully leave the table.

"Come now, Captain," Van Treung said gaily. "Please do me the large favor of relieving me of one of my lovely companions." He pushed one of the girls toward him and she slipped into a chair beside him, smiling that odd smile of innocent evil, the guileless smile of a seductress. "I find myself feeling less than adequate tonight and I know you will be generous and share the evening with this young lady whom I promised to lavishly entertain. But as you can see," he said, standing and pulling the other girl with him, bracing himself heavily against her, "I will have all I can do to redeem myself with only one."

The girl steered the weaving Van Treung through the back door toward one of the small huts behind the bar, and Joe turned to look at the girl next to him. She smiled and pulled closer, twining her arm through his and glancing at the back door, raising her eyebrows in a question. He shook his head and reached for his beer. She nodded and cuddled closer, tracing the edges of his ear with a slender finger.

"Goddamn! Would you look at that!" Orlando exclaimed. Kralik, Erskine and Fuente all turned to see the girl caressing Joe's cheek.

"Well, I'll be damned," Fuente said, smiling.

"YOU'LL be damned? Shit, he's got my girl! Hey, Cap!" Orlando yelled in pretended offense. "You plannin on warmin the saddle for me or what?"

"Yeah, Cap!" Erskine yelled, "Take her out back and show her your wounds!"

"Better not show her the one in front, though," Orlando chimed.

"Don't worry, honey," Andros called to the girl, "I hear he still has a twelve inch stub!"

The girl smiled, enjoying the attention, and though she didn't speak a word of English, she began to communicate perfectly with the interpretive body language she had learned in her craft.

Joe had hoped to become just drunk enough to escape the situation with a minimal amount of grace, and every time she tugged on his arm, motioning toward the back door, he ordered another beer. She was beautiful and willing, and the beer, rather than numbing him, was sensitizing him to her every touch. But there was a small warp in the scene, an odd misplacement he couldn't identify, a buzzing, waspish memory. Between the bantering, her alluring persuasions and four more beers, he finally looked at her, his head swimming, and smiled. Taking the girl by the arm, he got to his feet. When he tried to move, he realized how many beers he must have had and he leaned against the girl. Moving carefully, he navigated toward the back door. His men began to clap and cheer, Orlando exercising his most piercing wolf whistle.

"Awright, Cap!" Andros yelled.

When she lit the candle in the hut, Joe quickly tried to adjust his eyes to the dim interior while she moved to him and began expertly unfastening the button on his shirt. There was no furniture except a battered mattress lying on the floor and an empty ammunition crate that served as a chair. The candlelight undulated against bare mud walls and a dirt floor, and the dim whining of something in his past began to grow louder. He felt oddly that he had seen this place before.

He watched the yellow light playing on her shiny black hair as she slowly pushed his open shirt down until it slipped off one arm. She looked up at him with practiced sultriness and stepped back, dropping her one-piece dress from her shoulders. She stood naked in front of him, running her hands over her body and smiling. Her ivory skin absorbed the light from the candle and exuded a glow of its own, soft and tawny. Her hands traveled over tiny breasts and narrow hips, down the length of slender thighs and back again, where her fingers rested against a pubis plucked free of every hair. She was a soft image of polished gold and ivory with a frame of long black hair that swept the length of her back, and he could feel a familiar awakening in his groin as he turned away to lay his shirt on the floor. He felt a gentle touch on his lower back as she carefully traced the ugly red welts from the shrapnel, and when he turned around he could see the faint, sincere flicker of concern in her eyes. She backed away and knelt on the filthy mattress, staring at him with her own eyes now, the eyes of a young girl that knew little of vampishness or seduction, and yet by their very innocence were a greater lure than all the rest. In that moment it was easy to believe she knew nothing of war, nothing of survival, that she was just exactly what she appeared to be—a young girl ready to give herself to her first man.

The steady hum in his head became louder and louder as he stared at her, becoming the klaxon of a memory bursting through the fog of a long-forgotten sea. When she smiled and held out her hand to him, the memory rushed through the mist toward him, crashing into him, tumbling him over and over in painful waves. Sitting before him on a sleeping mat in a one-room hut lit by a solitary candle, was a girl named Sook. The Vietnamese girl was gone, her image replaced with the image of another victim of war who had used her only possession in order to survive. He was suddenly heartsick with longing and remembrance, feeling the full impact of his own position in the vision. He was one more American G.I. towering above a girl who was ultimately helpless in his hands, trusting him to simply take what he wanted in exchange for a pittance. His was the liquor he had smelled on the exhausted girl in Sok-Cho; his were the hands that had left bruises on her soft skin. He felt the fragility of the line between his past and present, felt an insistent stab of guilt at being able to cross so easily from one side to the other while the girl on the mattress remained trapped in one dimension that would never change. She was the girl who limped home with a roll of toilet tissue under her arm and this was her pain, her hopelessness and he felt her arms around him once more while she wept and rocked him to sleep. She had followed him all these years, drifting silently through the backwaters of his soul, suddenly gaining embodiment in the form and circumstance of this girl, reminding him of who he was and chastising him for ever having forgotten.

Her eyes mirrored her bewilderment as she stared up at him, waiting for him to remove his pants. She had never known a GI to hesitate before, usually having to employ her skills toward quite the opposite reaction. And when he slowly put his shirt back on, fastening the buttons while he gazed at her, she became truly mystified. He reached into his pocket and withdrew a twenty-dollar MPC, holding it out to her and smiling. She looked up at him for the first time with the tracings of hurt etched in her eyes, realizing he had no intentions of taking her, and a sense of pride as warped and bent as her whole life insisted that she not accept payment for a service she hadn't rendered. She was much too accustomed to paying the full price for all she received; there were no bargains for her, no discounts and this new gesture of kindness was alien. She lowered her eyes and shook her head, reaching for her dress to cover herself.

He knelt on one knee in front of her, putting his fingers under her chin and raising her face. She was puzzled and uncertain, stripped of her flimsy costume and left with only herself. Her eyes were wide and innocent and he smiled at her, taking her hand. He placed the bill in her palm and gently closed her fingers around it.

"Pretend it's a seashell," he whispered to the girl in his memory. *"A gift from a pelican."*

When he pushed through the back door and entered the bar again, he was greeted with the disbelieving expressions of his men. Orlando shoved a beer into his hands. "Jesus, Cap, I wasn't in THAT big a hurry. What's she got out there, a three-minute egg timer? Go tell her you still got two minutes on the meter!"

Joe stood calmly at the bar, shouldering the ribaldry and good-natured stabs at his virility until Mat moved in next to him. "I don't know about you, Cap, but I've had about all this bullshit I need for one night. How 'bout it? You ready to blow this place?"

He looked at Mat and smiled, finally feeling the full affects of all the beer and the weariness of his first night off the hospital ship. "Yup," he said, and belched contentedly.

Amid loud protests from Orlando, they all left together, climbing into the jeep and heading for Camp Evans. A quarter moon grinned down on a jeep sprouting a tangle of arms and legs as it bounced along between the plate-glass rice paddies. The pagoda listened in pragmatic silence as the sounds of men's jubilant, slightly drunken voices floated over the water, joining together in a slurred, gusty song: "Out in the West Texas town of El Paso, I fell in love with a Mexican girl..."

Later that night, unable to sleep, with the restlessness of being too drunk and too tired, Joe wandered to one of the sandbag berms that faced the perimeter of the camp. He sat on the bags and rubbed his eyes, feeling the odd clarity of thought that sometimes comes in the wake of exhaustion, when he heard someone approaching. "Can't sleep?" Fuente asked.

"Not yet. Pull up a chair."

They sat together and stared out at the silent perimeter, feeling the anomaly of emotions that was Vietnam, the peace above a vicious undertow of violence. Fuente lit a cigarette, the match light flickering briefly against his hard, brown face. At first they talked of things they both knew and understood: of the Army, of life as soldiers. They spoke of their divergent backgrounds, of the fates that had placed them in America and brought them together in Panama and now Vietnam.

"Fifteen years old," Fuente said, his dark eyes riveted somewhere in his past. "Fifteen years old when I arrived, sweeping out hotels and bars in the Cuban section of Miami, doing anything I could to make money. Uneducated, broke and hungry, I lied about my age and joined the Army when I was seventeen because I'd heard they were offering citizenship to any aliens who served two years." He took another drag on the cigarette and smiled. "Back then it wasn't easy being Cuban in the U.S. Army. Jesus, the heads I've had to bust just to prove brown was beautiful!"

They laughed about the fights they had been in— "racially oriented altercations" Joe called them—and of how quickly they had both been recognized, each in his own world, for their ability to exchange violence for violence.

"You know, Cap," Fuente said quietly, "the Army has been good to me. It's the only way of life I know and I can't complain. I'm a damn good soldier and I know it. When I got the opportunity for Special Forces training, I jumped on it, then busted my ass working as part of the cadre in Panama." He looked at Joe and smiled, his slender, craggy features barely visible in the darkness. "I've always wanted to work with a team like this one. This, for me, is an opportunity of a lifetime. And to be able to work with this particular group, well...that just makes it that much better."

They sat silently and listened to the sounds of the sleeping camp, feeling the unique, unspoken bond formed by the consortium of their lives—an emotion created by their shared soldierhood, by the camp, by the darkness, by the war.

"I don't know how I did it," Fuente said, flicking his

cigarette into the dirt, "but I managed to find a pretty little Cuban girl that wanted to marry me. She gave me two sons and a daughter...well, here, I have some pictures in here somewhere..." He rummaged in his wallet until he found the photos. He squinted at them in the pale moonlight, finally pulling one from the stack, almost shyly admitting that this was his wife. Turning it into the dim light, Joe could see it was the photo of a pet dog, a mongrel of some sort.

"My god she's ugly!"

Fuente jerked his head around, glaring at him. When he saw it was the wrong picture, he snatched it away amid gales of laugher. It took a bit of coaxing, but Fuente finally relented and showed him the rest of the photos. "That's a fine family you have there, Top. You have every right to be proud."

Replacing the photos and rising, Fuente stretched and scratched himself. "Goddamn," he yawned, "I gotta piss like a racehorse. We musta drunk enough beer to float a battleship..."

He had turned and was headed toward the latrines when Joe suddenly stood, his rapid movement causing him to sway on unstable legs.

"That's it!" he shouted, and Fuente turned quickly. "Top, that's it!" His eyes were wide with excitement, his head clearing rapidly. "The battleship—that's what made me see it! It's the river, Top. The gooks are using the river to run supplies." He slapped his hand against his forehead and closed his eyes. "Why didn't I think of it before, it's so perfect! It's the goddamn river—and I know how they're doing it. All I need is proof."

XXVIII

Hansen sat on the edge of his bunk, blinking his eyes to focus on Joe and Fuente while his hand automatically searched the side table for his cigarettes. "Rutledge, goddamn it," he mumbled sleepily, "we've had aerial recons of the river almost continually for weeks now and we've never uncovered a thing."

"Colonel, those recons are flown during the day, and the gooks aren't going to move on that river in daylight. No one's ever done a night recon on the river."

Hansen rubbed his eyes and nodded. "So what's on your mind?"

The three of them huddled over a diagram of the river while Joe outlined his plan.

"I want to split the team into three segments: Fuente, Kralik and Andros I'll have on the river—here," he said, pointing to a location twenty miles upstream from An-Lo. "And Rangonni, Erskine, Orlando I'll put—here—ten miles downstream from the first group. Mathews and I will run a backup daylight recon in a Loach, give the river a thorough going over." He explained camouflage and equipment, emphasizing the need for Star-Lite scopes for the night teams. He explained a few more technicalities while Hansen listened with one eye closed. When Joe was finished, Hansen stubbed out the cigarette.

"All right," he said. "Go for it."

The reconnaissance of the Song Bo began the following night.

For three deep, soundless nights they sat in heavy growth next to the river, listening, watching, scanning the slow, languid flow of the water. For three nights nothing moved on the river or on the heavily booby-trapped trails on either side. Dressed in mottled jungle fatigues, they blended into the jungle, their faces shaded in green and black, mottled green bandannas tied over their hair. They were no longer men, no longer separate organisms that walked and breathed on their own. They were absorbed into the life of night-green along the river, vanishing as completely as if they had been erased. They didn't move. They didn't speak. They were the jungle.

During the day the river was haunted by the steady, rumbling buzz of a light observation helicopter that foraged from one side to the other. The Loach hummed up and down the river over and over again while the pilot chewed a wad of gum and grinned behind dark aviator glasses.

"There ain't nothin' down there, Cap'n, I'm tellin ya," the pilot yelled over the churn of the rotors. "You're wastin' your time."

Joe pointed to the opposite bank and motioned him to keep flying, and the pilot grinned and shook his head. Crazy fuckers, he thought. All them Green Beanies are nutso.

Deep into the late hours of the fourth night with still no sound, no movement on the water, Andros put his face close to Fuente's ear and barely whispered, "Looks like the Cap'n had a wild fly up his ass on this one," when Kralik carefully gripped his arm in a painful vice. Andros froze, his eyes slowly following Kralik's gaze to the large tangle of bushes on the bank barely ten feet away directly in front of them. They watched with widening eyes as the heavy clump, the size of a small house, moved slowly, steadily away from the bank. There was no sound, no movement other than the mass itself pushing gently out into the sluggish current. It wasn't uncommon to see small bushes floating down the river, or tree branches covered with leaves. The river was languid and shallow, collecting its share of the jungle's litter, and at first they thought this might be a larger version of a dislodged snag of tree branches. But there was something different about the way it looked, the way it floated.

"Jesus Christ!" Kralik whispered. "The river flows the OTHER way! It's moving upstream!"

At that instant, as the mass reached the center of the river, they heard the sputtering of a small gasoline engine as it struggled to come to life. It stammered once, stammered again and kicked in, chattering in a regular rhythm as the floating section of the river bank moved steadily upstream.

They stared at each other, eyes wide and grinning with excitement. The river had given up her secret.

The following morning saw the Loach take to the river with new insistence, a voracious curiosity that kept it moving gradually up the banks, at times almost nosing into the heavy foliage. They flew until they ran low on fuel, refueled and returned, buzzing incessantly back to the river. For hours they searched up and down, side to side, while the pilot chewed, grinned and shook his head.

"Hey, wait a minute," Joe called, turning to Mat who sat in the seat behind him. "That bamboo clump over there—does it look different to you?" Mat looked closely and nodded. "Looks like it's been cut out in the center. Wasn't that way yesterday. Can you see anything in there?"

"Move in closer," Joe yelled to the pilot, and the Loach swung toward the bamboo thicket next to the bank.

With the sudden rising of a sixth sense from deep inside, Joe could hear the sound of the chopper fading away as they approached the thicket. Every sense, every instinct flared to raging life within the silence and he could hear a sudden inward shout from the enemy in the thicket—*I have you now, Joe...!*

"Not too close!" Joe screamed, pointing at the thicket, which instantly erupted into flaming life with gunfire from within. He could hear the rapid thudding of rounds slamming into the fuselage of the chopper as the pilot frantically tried to swing away. The Plexiglas bubble surrounding them spider-webbed with the impact of bullets, and the pilot's head jerked backward, his sunglasses flying off his face as a bullet struck him in the throat. The chopper dropped like a swatted insect into the water, catching one skid on a sandbar, tilting sideways while the rotors churned the water like an eggbeater until the sandbar dragged them to a stop. Bullets pounded the exposed side of the chopper as Joe slipped quickly into the water, pulling the dead pilot with him. Mat followed and jerked the dog tags from the pilot's neck as Joe wedged the body tightly in the water against the chopper. Machine gun fire from the thicket grew more insistent as the rounds began searching the water around the chopper. The two men dived beneath the surface and disappeared.

Fifty yards downstream, on the opposite side of the river, two heads slowly appeared above the water, peering from beneath the overhanging bank as the gunfire grew more intense. Hugging the bank, they moved silently downstream, keeping only far enough above water to see where they were going. The river drew them on, while the gunfire receded further and further into the distance. They swam silently a few yards apart, keeping close watch on the banks as they moved, submerging when they were forced to move away from the protection of the foliage. For seven miles they swam, alternately submerging and surfacing until they reached the bridge at An-Lo where they climbed out under the weapons of the surprised sentries.

As quickly as Joe's report was made, they were back in a Huey and headed for the river again. Sitting next to the door gunner, they watched as the chopper moved in on the bamboo thicket like a bird of prey, hovering above the water while the M-60 machine gun poured out its retribution, raking the thicket with an unrelenting fury. The explosion from within the bamboo caused the big Huey to rock sideways with its force. A giant, rolling ball of flame burst from the thicket, forming a small, heavy mushroom cloud in the air.

"Goddamn!" Mathews yelled, "looks like they were haulin diesel!"

After searching the riverbanks for the body of the dead pilot and finding nothing, the Huey moved to the downed Loach and hovered while they dropped bundles of C-4 plastic explosives onto it, fulfilling orders requiring that no equipment be left behind after a mission, especially aircraft. The Huey moved away and hovered for a moment while the C-4 was detonated, bursting the little machine into a thousand pieces. They swept back down the river, checking one last time for the body of the pilot. The search was futile—the body was never found.

Joe sat and watched the expression on Colonel Hansen's face later that day when he finished explaining the plan he had devised for the supply boats on the Song Bo. Hansen stared at him behind a blue shield of cigarette smoke, saying nothing as the impact of the idea played like sun dappling across his face. "It's a daring plan," he finally said, leaning forward through the haze. "It borders on suicidal."

Joe smiled and stood. "That's why it'll work—Charlie'll never be expecting it."

The arrangements were made and equipment assembled, beginning with three RB-6's requisitioned from the Navy—inflatable rubber rafts—and ending with eight Viet Cong black-pajama outfits, complete with cone hats. Orlando stood in the barracks and stared at the small collection of equipment and weaponry, his hands on his hips, shaking his head. "And what crazy sonofabitch pulled this idea out of his ass?" he asked, trying to mask his obvious relish of the plan. Joe shrugged and pretended innocence. "Beats me, Orlando. Hansen's staff, I guess."

"Hansen's staff, I guess," he mimicked with a grin. "Sheeit."

The sleepless jungle looked up in the pre-dawn darkness the following morning, listening to the sound of helicopters rumbling above the treetops, three of them, huge lumbering Chinooks that dropped low in three separate locations a few miles apart. She smiled in the darkness with this new game, another version of "the shell and the pea." Only one of the choppers contained the eight men and their equipment, disgorging them into the steamy darkness. The enemy hiding along the river might have been confused, but the jungle knew, and she watched with wide, darkened eyes as the eight men disappeared toward the river.

They worked quickly in the short time before dawn, inflating the rubber boats and camouflaging them with branches from the jungle. Tying them securely to the bank, they loaded the weapons: three M-79 grenade launchers, two 90 mm rocket launchers with canister rounds and, in the last boat, an M-60 machine gun with two thousand rounds of ammunition. A radio was placed in each boat just as the sky was beginning to turn a barely discernible blue with the first light of day. They slipped into the foliage next to the river, their faces camouflaged under the cone hats, feeling the odd looseness in the black pajamas as they settled in to begin the long wait for nightfall.

The river was a creature of two dimensions, changing her face with the rising and setting of the sun. The river hummed to itself during the day like a wide, quietly senile old woman who has seen too much in her long life. She meandered in one time-worn pattern day after day, mumbling softly to herself in contented oblivion. During the monsoon season, she complained in bilious gulps as she overflowed her banks and washed away anything flimsy enough to be uprooted. Her ailment soon ended, however, and she receded into her banks to resume her perpetual gurgling.

At night, the senility evaporated with the fading light, replaced by a calm deadliness, a serene, deliberate mask of the macabre. All sound ceased, the quiet murmuring becoming a muted vacuum of silence as the river cloaked itself with the ink of night. Any movement was malevolent, and sound was an almost certain danger. The river erected blockades of sinister shadows at its banks and posted sentries of misshapen masses of foliage in the current that seemed to vanish when approached. Once darkness fell, the river loved no creature and the men in the three camouflaged rafts could feel the animosity as they pushed silently away from the bank.

Crouched low in the first boat, unseen behind the covering of bushes, Joe knelt at the front and swept a Star-Lite scope slowly from side to side, examining the sinister stream. Jackie Kralik knelt at the back, using an oar to guide the raft in the slow current. Mathews sat in the middle, a rocket launcher lying across his lap. Fuente, Rangonni and Orlando manned the second boat, while Andros and Erskine knelt in the third with the machine gun between them. They moved down the river at fifteen yard intervals while the river slinked into itself, engulfing itself in a silence so profound that even the sound of an oar breaking the surface became a relief to the senses, a small reassurance that not every sound had been sucked into the black hole that was the river.

Through the magic of the scope, Joe saw for the first time the incredible amount of life existing along the river at night, life that moved and shifted, darted and slithered, but made no sound: tree snakes, frogs, and the sudden, surprising glow of a small pair of eyes in the water next to the bank—a rat, he thought, as he saw the slick, shiny body disappear under a clump of foliage. The water a short distance ahead began to stir and he swept the scope in the direction of the disturbance, his heart racing. A snake coursed smoothly through the water, cutting a fine, distinct path.

He loved the river, even in its silent antagonism. The river was a spark to an ancient fuel within him and the others. They sensed the danger and drew from it like an energy field, passing it between them in an unstated acknowledgment of the mission, its perils and its eventual satisfactions. Joe looked around at Kralik, who smiled and issued a thumbs up at Mathews, whose eyes were bright with anticipation. To a man, they were feeling the same thing: the indescribably heady excitement of a well-planned, daring escapade in which danger was at its peak. They floated for nearly six miles before hearing a sound, six long miles of darkness broken only intermittently by a moon sliding between heavy clouds, a moon made for Halloweens and hauntings. When the sound first reached them, it took several moments to shake the ringing deafness of silence from their ears to hear it clearly: the distant, muffled sound of an outboard motor.

The river suddenly tensed, feeling the helplessness of knowing that powers were operating on the surface that wouldn't be denied, knowing that all the silence and malevolence were nothing when measured against the will of the men in the rafts. Mathews rolled onto his back, holding the 90 mm across his chest; in the second boat Rangonni did the same. Andros and Erskine crouched lower, their eyes bright in their smudged faces. When he first saw it rounding the bend, Joe smiled—a predator's smile, cat-like and satisfied. This was it!

A giant mass of foliage nudged its way around the bend, moving carefully, deliberately upstream toward them. Considering the amount of foliage, he judged the craft to be close to thirty feet long. He lowered the scope and picked up his oar, running his hand along the AK-47. He shifted himself in the boat, bracing himself on his knees as he put his oar in the water, making a mental inventory of their weapons: the standard Communist issue AK's, five hand grenades each, a smoke grenade each, a Smith and Wesson .357 magnum sidearm, and one of his personal favorites, a K-bar knife tucked into a sheath, hilt down, on a shoulder strap. They were ready. It was about to begin.

Reaching for the handset on the radio, Joe squeezed once, sending the "all set?" signal. He received an affirmative pair of clicks, took a deep breath, and stood up in the boat.

They were only fifty feet from the supply boat when someone on deck finally spotted something moving in the water. When the VC at the rail saw the cone hat, black pajamas and waving arm, he lowered the weapon he had aimed directly at Joe's head, looking suspiciously at him as he floated closer. Several others gathered at the railing, two of them shirtless with twisted bandannas tied around their heads. There were five of them, including a man at the tiller, and they were all heavily armed, staring over the side at the strange apparition in the water. Joe continued to smile, waving congenially. When they were close enough, he knelt and put the oar in the water, turning the raft broadside to the supply boat as if he were preparing to stop.

"Now, Mat," he said quietly.

Mat sat up, hoisted the rocket launcher to his shoulder and fired, all in one smooth movement. An explosion of light, fire and tiny nail-size pieces of metal slammed into the side of the supply boat, killing every man at the rail instantly. The sound of the explosion, which was unearthly in its volume only seconds before, suddenly vanished, sucked into the great, silent void of the river. The deck of the supply boat smoldered quietly, the shattered remains of its crew lying everywhere. There was a small movement from the man at the tiller and Joe turned in time to see him slip off the side into the water. "I'll get 'im, Cap!" Kralik said, and dived into the water, surfacing a few moments later a short distance away. "Sumbitch's dead, Cap."

When they boarded the supply boat and stared down into the hold, Fuente whistled softly, gazing around in disbelief. "Madre de Dios!" he whispered, "I've never seen anything like this! The whole goddamn boat is loaded to the gills." Drums of diesel fuel, bags of rice, assorted medicine, dried fish, five-gallon cans of Nuoc Mam, the foul-smelling sauce the Vietnamese used on everything, all kinds of dried and canned foodstuffs. And then came the real surprise: over five hundred American-made M-16 rifles with boxes and boxes of ammunition, crate after crate of TNT, picks, shovels, entrenching tools.

"Well, I'll be damned!" Joe said between clenched teeth. "Here's the fuckin' leach repellent I've been waiting for ever since I got to this place. Motherfuckers were gettin MY leach repellent!"

All of it was new. All of it was American-made.

"Sink the sonofabitch," Joe said, "and let's get outa here."

Using picks, they broke holes in the bottom of the boat and watched until it settled to the bottom of the river, its deck barely visible above the water line.

They were a part of the river again as they resumed their journey downstream. As though they had undergone some special rite of initiation into the violence lying in the silence, they could feel a melding of sensations, a mixing of the deadliness of the river with their own adrenaline-spurred realization of success. It had worked! And except for the fact that they were unable to take anyone alive, it had been a total success. The river had worked unconsciously in their favor, providing cover and darkness, while Joe's Oriental features enabled them to get close enough to do what had to be done. Their hearts raced with a curious anxiety, a mixture of excitement and fear, every instinct telling them to be wary of the simplicity of the success, yet every emotion shouting exultantly: "We did it! We did it! It works!" Every sense sharpened, becoming even more acutely aware of the darkness, of the voiceless river. Sweat soaked the black fabric of their outfits, mosquitos buzzed, bit and went ignored in the wild electricity streaming between the three rafts.

The second supply boat, hugging the right side of the river as it slid upstream, was a virtual re-run of the first: the signaled greeting, the gentle turn broadside, the ear-splitting explosion from the rocket launcher. And again everyone aboard was killed in the initial blast, leaving behind a boat heavily laden with American-made goods that soon lay foundering on the bottom of the river. There was a ringing sensation in Joe's head, a steady, distant clanging that became louder as they moved away from the second boat. Their eyes were all wide with a shared instinct of something too near perfection, something too smooth, though they tried desperately to cling to the exhilaration of success. They were gripped by the persistent belief in the cleverness of the river, a feeling that they were being toyed with, lured in, set up. They crouched lower, their eyes darting along the banks.

With only a partial consent from Joe's consciousness, something deep within him joined with the soundless river, sharing silence for silence, blending, merging, until he was one again with his surroundings, listening to the river through the ears of first life. And he smiled.

"I'm coming for you, Charlie."

"You're out in the open now, Joe. I feel you on the river, I know you're there. This time you're mine!"

"You'd better be sure it's me, Charlie."

"It's you."

Silence.

"Joe...?"

The rocket launcher erupted and another explosion

ripped the silence, smashing into the supply boat and the men on its deck, ending his inner conversation with a muffled, distant scream that was sucked into the silence along with the blast.

"Jesus H. Christ!" Rangonni exclaimed as he kicked open the hold, revealing yet another overload of cargo. "No wonder we can't seem to win this war—Charlie's got half our goddamn supplies!"

Fuente sighed and looked at Joe while the others took a quick inventory. "You see that gook over there, the one by the railing?" Joe nodded, glancing at the dead man. "He's one of Van Trueng's men."

Joe's head flew up and he stared at Fuente, his eyes hardening. "Van Treung! Of course! I should've thought of it before; he had to be in on this." He walked over and lifted the dead man's head by his hair, staring into open, sightless eyes. He dropped the head. "Van Treung, that sonofabitch. He's the conduit to the river, using the battalion to funnel the supplies...goddamn. That fuckin' traitor. He's not only screwing over the Americans, he's betraying his own people."

"Cap'n, look out!" A man hiding behind a stack of crates had suddenly risen from within the hold, aiming his weapon at Joe when Orlando screamed. The man whirled toward Orlando, firing wildly. Orlando's head jerked and he stumbled backward over the railing. Six AKs blasted into the hold, smashing the man into a twitching pulp as Joe dived over the side after Orlando.

He pulled Orlando's limp form into the first raft while the others hurriedly sank the supply boat. Orlando's head and face were covered with blood, but there was still a faint, erratic heartbeat. Crouching low in the rafts, breathing heavily with the shock of having one of their own wounded, they drifted on downstream with the ominous, sharp-edged feeling of exposure—sudden and violent. The wild rush of winning was shrouded now in the prospect of death, and the river was no longer a co-conspirator, if it ever had been. They were alone again, sealed on the river by a purpose, feeling the gnawing anxiety to be done with it.

Fuente and Kralik worked swiftly to stanch the bleeding from Orlando's head, their hands moving rapidly with practiced skill, trembling slightly from the huge jolts of adrenaline pounding through their bodies. "It's hard to tell for sure in the dark, Cap," Fuente said softly, "but it looks like just a graze, a deep flesh wound two—maybe three—inches long. He's still unconscious, but the bleeding's stopped."

Though their pick-up site was only two miles down river and a short hike inland, it seemed like all the distance in the world as the boats moved at a snail's pace on the dark water. They used their oars as rapidly as they could without creating any noise, each keeping a tight, silent wish within himself, a wish not to encounter any more supply boats. In a nearly direct violation of a principle they had been taught over and over again, the mission was no longer paramount, and they each hoped desperately not to have to put their loyalty to the service in the balance against their devotion to a friend.

They reached the exit point and pulled the boats out of the water, deflated and buried them, breathing a collective sigh of relief. "Hey, sheethaid," Fuente whispered to Orlando as he re-bound the bandage on his head. "That's a hell of a way to get outa humpin' all this goddamn gear back to the chopper." Kralik and Erskine braced Orlando between them, wrapping each of his arms around their necks, dragging him through the dense jungle that was beginning to see the first light of dawn. Orlando began to regain consciousness in stages, clumsily attempting to use his feet as he dimly realized they were headed back.

No one spoke. They moved steadily, quickly on, cone hats dangling from the backs of their necks, all of them bristling with weaponry. They followed Joe resolutely through the jungle, tracing his steps with the assurance of trust and habit. When they finally stopped to give Orlando a rest, Kralik walked ahead a short distance and crouched in the dew-soaked foliage to watch the trail. Fuente checked Orlando's bandage, now bright red with slow, steady bleeding. Orlando opened his eyes and Fuente put his finger to his lips in a "hush" signal. Orlando nodded weakly and closed his eyes.

"Cap'n," Kralik whispered tensely, "there's a couple of gooks up here." Moving quickly up the trail, Joe could see three of them. He followed as closely as he dared, his heart racing with the possibility of taking a prisoner. One of them glanced over his shoulder. When he saw Joe, he reached for his weapon. Instinctively, Joe swung the AK up, pulling the trigger. The rounds slammed into the VC's body, throwing him into the bushes next to the trail while the other two made a wild dash for several deserted huts just beyond the trail.

Leaving Erskine with Orlando, the rest of the men fanned out around the village, a hamlet so small it hadn't appeared on any of the maps Joe had studied of the area. Fuente joined him in the bushes and together they crawled to the edge of the village. A half dozen seemingly deserted huts occupied a clearing that was being quickly reclaimed by the jungle. On the surface the area appeared to have been vacant for a long time. But when Fuente wrinkled his nose, Joe knew he was smelling the same thing: the odors of a lived-in hut, a pungent mixture of decaying vegetables and human waste. "They're in there," Fuente whispered. "I can smell 'em."

Two of the huts suddenly erupted with explosions of light as the VC began pouring out a barrage of fire. They lowered their heads and moved back while Joe reached for the radio. In moments there was the scream of mortars being lobbed into the village, and with a confirming command of "Fire for effect," he directed in a pounding barrage of artillery fire directly on top of the village. The earth rumbled and shook with the blasts, shivering like an animal being stabbed. Joe and Fuente bombarded the huts with round after round from the grenade launchers; bamboo and sticks flew everywhere, the sky rained dirt and fire and there was no relief. The huts burned and crumbled, smashed to the earth. The air was thick with the smell of cordite, dry and choking with smoke from burning huts and dust. And from somewhere within the destruction, Joe thought he heard a scream, a high-pitched scream of pain and dying. He didn't believe it would be one of the Viet Congs—they almost always died silently. He convinced himself he hadn't heard it, that his mind was too weary, his senses dulled by lack of sleep.

In the midst of the whine of mortars and the steady thud of grenade launchers, Andros' machine gun rattled to life and strafed the burning huts with hungry persistence. There was no silent communication now, no attempt to hear voices in the green. The sound of destruction fed itself, nurtured itself in their minds and there was no letting up until they saw movement from one of the burning huts: two Viet Congs came staggering forward, their hands in the air, yelling "Chiu hoi, chiu hoi!" Ordering a cease fire Joe left the two dazed prisoners with Fuente and began moving through the decimated village, certain now he had heard the scream. If the VC's were alive, then someone else...

It was the boy he saw first, sitting in the heavy pall of smoke and staring at him with eyes that locked onto him and held him fast. He sat motionless next to the body of a young woman whose chest was an ugly mass of blood. Her delicate features were spattered with the blood from her chest; her hair lay in splayed tangles in a puddle of reeking waste water thrown from inside one of the huts. In the crook of one arm lay a baby of perhaps six months. The boy watched Joe approach slowly through the smoke, his weapon held in one hand, his face still smudged with camouflage. He was an image from within a nightmare set against a backdrop of fire and destruction, but the child never moved, never let his eyes waver from the vision as Joe knelt in front of him, gazing into the magnet of the boy's eyes.

It was recognition, simple and profound, a remembrance and horrible greeting. There was no sense of reversal, no feeling of looking back through the eyes of the man he was now. He was the boy, the boy was he, and there was no guilt; only a giant, consuming hatred, finding new life, new expression in younger eyes. The boy clenched his mother's fingers and said nothing. He was beyond pain, beyond sorrow, flung with violence into a land somewhere in the outer territories of emotion, a vast plain of mistrust, a land for the misbegotten where Joe had been exiled as a child. In the boy's eyes, Joe could see the very essence of hatred, and he realized how much of it he had kept with him all these years, how much of it was finding harbor and kindred reflection in the eyes of this child.

Through a great distance, he heard the moans from a wounded Viet Cong who lay a few feet away, heard the unmistakable sounds of near-death. He groaned incoherently, his eyes becoming rapidly opaque as his life oozed away from him. Looking at the VC, then back to the boy, Joe reached out and took the unresisting hand, guiding him to the dying man. Placing the heavy weapon in the boy's hands, Joe knelt and gently directed his finger to the trigger, supporting the barrel of the gun while the boy stood quietly, a look of cold, indifferent understanding on his face. The boy squeezed the trigger, sending a short burst of rounds thudding into the Viet Cong who twitched and jerked, then moved no more.

They stood together and stared at the body, and Joe could feel the mammoth crash of his past with this boy's present, the two forces joining in a rush of released hatred. The boy finally turned to him, dropping the weapon without looking at it. He returned to his mother and sat next to the baby, wrapping his arms around his knees and staring straight ahead.

In the returning mist of his senses, Joe could hear a distant, familiar rumbling. With some difficulty, he realized Fuente had summoned the choppers, and while the mop-up teams went to work in and around the village, Joe picked up the two children and placed them aboard one of the waiting Hueys. The boy sat close to the doorway, the baby gripped firmly in his protective arms as the machine lifted away. Joe watched until the chopper was a small speck in the distance, seeing not the vanishing aircraft but the deep, black penetration of the eyes of an orphan that stared at him with an understanding too complete.

XXIX

"Operation Sampan, I'm sure," Hansen said, "will go on record as one of the most successful operations launched in Vietnam."

The briefing room in the Tactical Operations Center was alive with the electricity of accomplishment the morning after the mission. Colonel Hansen was glowing with the iridescence of success. "The members of Captain Rutledge's team have all been recommended for a Bronze Star in recognition of their efforts on the Song Bo. And I'm pleased to report that Sergeant Louis Orlando, the only casualty of the operation, is doing well on the Hospital Ship Repose and is due to be transferred to Japan for further treatment. Congratulations on a job well done, Captain."

Even more far-reaching than the discovery of the supply boats was the capture of the two prisoners at the village, and Joe knew that much of Hansen's barely-concealed jubilation was a direct result of information obtained from them over the course of the night. The TOC began to cloud with cigarette smoke as Hansen turned to the maps on the wall behind him, detailing recent intelligence reports and outlining a plan of action.

He confirmed the existence of huge masses of troops behind Hills 934 and 936 at the Laotian border, confirmed the amounts of supplies being routed to them over the Ho Chi Minh Trail and, until yesterday, the Song Bo river. "And with the capture of a wounded Chi-Com advisor, the fact that we're up against the 29th NVA Regiment has been confirmed."

Joe heard only scattered bits of the remainder of the

296

briefing, feeling oddly unfocused and nervous, his left leg bouncing up and down slightly in a quick, distracted rhythm that would have been translated into the drumming of fingers on a desk. He stared at the map on the wall without seeing it, listened to the Colonel's voice without hearing it. His mind kept turning away, kept staring up into a departing helicopter that contained two fragments of bitter light that were the eyes of the boy—the boy in Vietnam and the boy in Korea.

"...with this in mind," the Colonel was saying, "I've decided to move my C.P. out to Firebase Eagle's Nest to be closer to the action. We're not going to give the enemy an opportunity to prepare. This time, gentlemen, we're taking the fight to him. We're meeting the dragon head on." The colonel turned and looked directly at Joe. "I need to send you and your team on ahead to Eagle's Nest. Things are heating up fast out there, and I'll need the latest intelligence reports. You'll leave at first light for the Ashau Valley. As for Colonel Van Treung and his illicit activities, Intelligence will handle it immediately."

They were the first completely solid words Joe had heard since returning from the river: the Ashau Valley. Something churning slowly inside him pulled the words in, rolled them around and examined them and flung them against his senses. The Ashau Valley: the clarion's call.

He pushed away from the back-slapping and congratulations when the meeting was over, feeling an almost irritable need to be with his own men who waited for him at More-Than-Shitty. With Orlando's wounding there was a bonding that had taken place—a gossamer thread of steel that welded them to each other in mutual fallibility. He felt the instinct to huddle with them in sad-eyed closeness, to gather with them against the unseen forces of fragile mortality. They were refugees like him, having suffered the stunning realization of breakable life, having stepped briefly into the jaws of ravenous death and out again, leaving a part of themselves behind. They were truly one now, more so than ever before. He was anxious to be among his own.

He briefed them on what would be taking place and saw

the faint, expected flicker that was something akin to disappointment. They were anxious to be a part of the gargantuan thing taking place in the Ashau Valley, yet there had been little time to adjust to their new perception of the war. They knew of death, had seen more of it than most, but had managed to remain insulated and serenely aloof as long as it didn't involve the unit. It was different now. They ached with their own mortality.

"Goddamn, Cap," Erskine said, smiling slightly, "they sure intend to get their money's worth out of us, don't they?"

It would be all that was ever said about their abrupt departure to Eagle's Nest, their only expression of a need to adjust.

"Erskine, round up a couple of coolers of beer," Joe said, taking off his shirt, "and while you're at it, round up a cooler for the rest of us, too." Everyone tried to chuckle, tried to dispel the cold, heavy pall of foreboding. "I don't know about you guys, but I'm gonna spend the rest of the day and most of the night wrapped around a beer. Tomorrow the shit hits the fan."

The sun climbed high and dust from the bustling camp filtered in through the screens, passing through the rays of sunlight in the room like a transient storm. They lay on their bunks and listened to the radio, writing letters or just thinking, remembering, coming to grips. They talked quietly among themselves and Joe watched them as they spoke, seeing their differences and similarities, watching them interplay with each other like sun with shadow, rain with earth. What he saw in their eyes was not a lack of fear: it was simply a refusal to let the fear matter.

Erskine sat next to the radio, humming to himself and staring at a Playboy magazine while he slugged down one beer after another. When he finally goes home, Joe thought with a grin, he'll be the first to get a paunch on that stocky body. All that muscle will turn to plain old beef when he gets married and settles into the real world. Not like Rangonni, Orlando and Mat, who would stay thin and wiry for years, who would retain their dark good looks well into middle age. Andros lay stretched on his bunk, his head thrown back and his mouth open, snoring peacefully in exhaustion. His feet didn't reach the end of the bunk, and Joe realized with mild surprise that none of the men except himself and Mat were over five foot ten.

"Hey, Cap," Fuente said, looking up from his absent game of solitaire, "you got some mail in there. Read any of it yet?" Joe shook his head and took another swallow from the can. "I'm saving the best for last."

Tossing the magazine aside, Erskine clasped his hands in front of him and stared at the hard brown knot they made as he braced his elbows on his knees. "What's gonna happen," he said to no one, to everyone, "when we hit the Ashau? When we do what we need to do, flush out whatever we're supposed to flush out?" His voice was quiet, intense, not with anger, but with searching. "What's gonna happen when we secure whatever ground we're supposed to help secure out there and then we move on to the next Ashau Valley, and the next, while Charlie moves back in and reclaims what we took away from him and then abandoned, and the whole goddamn process starts all over again?" He looked up at Joe, his blue eyes calm and level, but openly bewildered. Though no one spoke, all eyes moved to look at Joe in unstated certainty—certain that if the truth wasn't to be found with him, then neither would be the lies. "What the hell's the point, Cap? If what Hansen is saying is true and it's the 29th NVA we're going up against out there, we're in for one hell of a blood bath, and for what? For a few acres of real estate that we never wanted and don't intend to hang onto once the battle is over? Assuming, of course, that we win this time. I don't get it...what's the point...?"

The words refracted again and again within the invisible glow, glancing off the light and searing Joe's mind as he recalled thinking the same thing only hours before—What's the point?—while the enemy has spent years slipping and sliding through the jungle, appearing for only seconds while he blasts the head off of the man standing next to you, then disappearing again as completely as if he never existed. What's the point?—when the soldiers actually fighting the war were kept from whatever knowledge in the upper echelons of the military that fueled this goddamn war; when the soldiers obeyed orders they would ultimately obey, no matter how defeating and frustrating, as they watched the very best of young American manhood being swallowed into a black hole, never to emerge again, like watching a wound that refused to stop bleeding while the heartbeat of a nation began to throb spastically—What's the point? Joe looked from one young face to the next, feeling the answer—and its weight—before he spoke.

"The Ashau Valley," Joe began, spacing his words deliberately to accommodate both the beers and his pounding emotions, "will be where we find out what being an American soldier really means. Up to now in this war, it's been easy for us to sit here and take pot-shots at everything: at the enemy, at our own leadership, at this goddamn country. Up to now we've been able to posture and strut and bitch about the fact that you can't fight these little bastards because they're cowards that won't come out and meet a challenge head on, when deep inside we know that if they win the war by their sneaky tactics—dodging and weaving, setting their ambushes and blowing the hell out of us—even if they manage to win the war that way, we can kick and scream and shake a fist at heaven and yell, "No fair! No fair!" and it won't matter—they still win, and they know it. They can do this kind of shit forever and there isn't a whole hell of a lot we'd be able to do about it, except try to win the war on their terms, which could take generations. And they know it!

"But somewhere behind the western hills of the Ashau Valley, Charlie has decided to call our bluff. For the first time in the war, the enemy has pulled together as much armament and troop strength as he has been able to gather in one place, and he's issuing us a challenge: just this once, we'll fight the war on American terms, matching strength for strength, and let's just see who wins. So we've never been sure if Charlie could hold up in our kind of battle, out in the open, toe-to-toe? Well, let's find out. So we've never been certain if clear-cut battle lines were more effective than guerrilla warfare? Well, let's find out. The horn has sounded, boys, and this time we know the rules. Did we always think of this war as being THEIR war? Well, it may be their war, but by God, this is OUR fight; it's what we've waited for—one honest moment in this whole "cluster-fuck"—and we can't afford to lose. It's not just American military procedures that will be put to the test in this one; it's the concept of the American man himself. For the first time in this war, Charlie is going to stand his ground. We asked for it. Now we'll have the chance to find out if we meant it."

There was a hum to the air in the room, an almost audible transmission of thought and feeling when Joe finished. No one spoke; no one was afraid; everyone understood. And in those brief seconds, Joe knew that he had merely voiced what they had all known, what they had all felt. He had given it form and meaning, but they had all known the truth from the beginning, from their first footfall on the lush green heart of the jungle. And if the coming battle would be a measuring stick of their worthiness as soldiers, as men, as Americans, then by silent agreement, they were ready. They gave no thought to the idea that anything in the Ashau Valley would change the course the war had taken—it was too old and too vicious for change. Instead, in those first gleaming moments after Joe spoke, their only thought was: this will be it! After this one, win or lose, we will have won. Because we meant it.

The day rolled quietly into evening, and the dust settled, giving way to the hordes of mosquitos that explored the screen. The music got louder because the camp got quieter and because the buzz from the beer made it hard to hear. They began to laugh more easily, began to exchange stories and jokes about home, girls and sex. They were on foot in spiritual territory made unique by their unity, by their youth, by the war, and the beer was making it easier to cross that special border into a land of darker shadows and brighter suns; a land of no illusions where life is dearer because death is so close.

"All good Italians love a toast," Rangonni slurred, standing on uncertain legs. No one had bothered to put on the lights, seeming to find comfort in the faint light from the compound itself. Rangonni weaved slightly in the semi-darkness, holding his beer can aloft. "A toast! To Orlando. The best goddamn man with a blade I ever saw, the horniest sonofabitch I ever knew, a hell of a soldier. And my best fuckin' friend."

"To Orlando!" they all chorused, raising their beers.

"That sheethaid," Fuente said, raising his can the highest.

They placed the empty cans one by one on the floor at the foot of Orlando's bunk, stacking them in a pyramid with Rangonni's can on top.

After a few more toasts—to each other, to the Captain, to the Song Bo, to Charlie, "to fucking Ashau!"—Joe slipped into his room and closed the door. Almost immediately he felt the isolation, the nervousness closing around him like a fist. He grabbed the stack of letters and opened the first without looking at the date, sitting on his bunk with his elbows braced on his knees. His left leg began its rapid strumming.

"Dear Joe," it began, and he rubbed his eyes, feeling the sudden pressure of things common, things of normal life. It was a weight, a heavy, shapeless thing this mundanity, this sweet normalcy. Every soldier he knew yearned for the letters, longed for the trite, simple details; it was assurance that somewhere in the world there was still sanity. But tonight it was an unexplainable burden. "Dear Joe..." He could even hear her voice every time he looked at the words, imagined the greeting like the touch of her hand trying to get his attention: "Joe...dear Joe..." He lay the letters aside, shut off the light and stretched out, believing he must be exhausted and drunk if he was unable to read a letter from Sam. He sat up a few moments later, staring into the darkness. He finally opened the door and went outside into the stifling night to sit on the wooden step of the barracks.

He wasn't sure how long he'd been there before he heard the screen door open behind him. There were only faint sounds now from within the camp, music from distant radios, an occasional burst of laughter. He was sitting with his eyes closed when Mat sat down beside him.

"Know something, Mat?" he said. "If you close your eyes, sometimes on a night like this you can almost imagine you're back in the States sitting on a front porch in summertime." Joe glanced at the man next to him, at the slender face and intense brown eyes, at a slim, hardened hand that held a glowing cigarette. Mat slouched on the stoop with the easy, boneless grace of a man confident of his posture, his long legs stretched in front of him and crossed at the ankles. "Been a long time, hasn't it?" Joe asked. "A long time since we had a chance to just sit and shoot the shit."

"Since Panama, I guess. Where was it...Pina Beach? No, no, it was that day on the Chagres River, waiting for those meatheads to finish their crossing. Yeah, that's right. Seems like yesterday."

"How's your wife, Mat?"

"She's fine," he replied, beaming in obvious pride. "Last letter said she was big as a house, due in two months, can you believe it? Where's the time gone—over seven months since our leave in the States..."

"Well, whatdya think? A boy or a girl?"

"A boy," he said, nodding with assurance. "Mat Junior. Guaranteed."

"Whatdya mean, 'guaranteed?' You may be in for a surprise in a couple of months when you end up with a squallin' little split-tail."

Mat shook his head with confidence. "Nope. I used an old family secret that's worked for generations. Everyone in my family had sons on their first try for years on back, no problem. When you decide to get serious with that girl of yours, I'll give you the secret as a wedding present."

"Oh, bullshit," Joe laughed. "Tell me now—and this better be good."

"Well..." Mat hesitated, scrutinizing him. "Oh, all right. Seein' as how you're my friend, I suppose Grandad Mathews won't mind if I share the secret with an outsider..." Mat looked around in mock conspiracy, glancing over both shoulders, then leaned close to Joe and whispered, "You have to aim it high and to the right."

Against the muted baritone hum of the camp, their laughter rose and filtered away, fragmenting on the sultry air; the loose, easily-aroused laughter as that of young men who had put aside the savagery of war for a few fleeting moments. It wasn't the same laughter of young men at home on a front porch—there was too much of the strained color of hardship in the tone to ever truly resemble the laugher of youth—but it was open and free, unfettered by illusion.

They talked quietly of Mat and home, of the trite, cherished things. "I don't want a hell of a lot outa this life," Mat said. "All I want is to get outa this fuckin' war and go home where I've got a job waitin for me at the GM plant. I wanna come home at five, pat the ol' lady on her chubby little ass, roll around the floor with the kids, kick the dog outa my favorite chair and wait for supper. I've got it all planned and it's already started with this first baby. Simple life, simple ambitions..." He smiled and threw the cigarette stub into the dirt, linking his long fingers around one knee. "What about you, Cap? Got any grandiose dreams for the future?"

Joe shrugged. "It seems like the simple dreams are always the ones that evade me. Seems like something always complicates things for me."

"Maybe that's because you weren't ever meant for that kind of life, Cap. Some of us are born to be happy with a life that's easy to explain, easy to justify. I don't think you're one of those people." Joe laughed with mild self-consciousness and Mat looked at him with cool certainty. "It's true, Cap. You weren't meant for GM plants and metal lunch buckets. Some of us will settle into that and think it's perfect, but you're different. Take this Vietnam thing, for instance. When I got drafted, I decided to be the best soldier I could be; I was gonna do my job, serve my time and go home with a clear conscience. I'm damn good at what I do, but it's just a job to me. With you, it's something close to an obsession. It's all so natural to you. Some of the things I've seen you do, the times you KNEW someone was out there and kept us from getting our asses blown away—my wife has a word for what you got. She calls it 'ju-ju.' And anyone with the ju-ju don't belong in no nine-to-five world."

Joe picked up some pebbles and sat toying with them while Mat spoke, his leg strumming. Mat lit another cigarette and smiled.

"Just look at you," Mat chided. "You can smell it on you like campfire smoke. There's something big brewing out there and you can't even sleep for wanting to know what it is. Me? I'm gonna sleep like a baby and dream about doctor bills—and therein lies the difference in our lives."

The conversation drifted quietly, deliberately away from personalities and destinies, away from the complexities that governed their lives, and they spent the next hour disguising their helplessness by reminiscing. They talked of Panama, of those wild, steamy days when they first met, talked of it as though it had been a lifetime ago when it had been little more than a year ago. They laughed about the fight at a bar in Colon— "God, that was fun, Cap!"—and how between the two of them they had nearly destroyed the bar before escaping on Joe's motorcycle. They talked of diving excursions on the Chagres River— "We had to be fuckin' nuts to dive that river, Mat. Between the sharks, the currents and barracudas, it's a wonder we weren't eaten"—and of treasure hunts in the underwater caves off the northern coast. They talked of girls, of marriage, of friendship.

"You know, Mat, I'm not sure what it is about me, but there's something that's always prevented me from making real close friends. All my life I've been a loner, done things by myself, made my own way. It's like...well, I guess there must be a fear there, a fear of getting close because I don't want to lose it once I have it."

Mat shook his head, his face assuming the same unclouded serenity as before. "There's more to it than that, I think. You have a way of stripping a man of all the bullshit, a way of showing him for what he really is. You push a man to his limits and beyond, physically, but especially mentally and spiritually, and that tends to weed out a lot of would-be friends. You don't leave any room for half-measures, inside or out. It's all or nothing with you, and too many people are accustomed to dealing on the surface alone. It ain't easy being your friend." Joe's leg finally fell silent and he sat motionless, listening to what would have been chastisement from anyone else; the words coming from Mat were a huge, unconscious compliment, an affirmation of unspoken feelings. "It ain't easy being your friend," Mat repeated, "but you're stuck with me."

Joe smiled and tossed the pebbles into the dirt, hearing the faint clacking as they rolled together like marbles. They didn't speak, knowing that words were sometimes the clumsy tools of emotions better left unvoiced, that some friendships, like manhood itself, were simply felt rather than discussed.

It was four in the morning when they heard Fuente rousting the others for breakfast before leaving for Eagle's Nest. "Up, sheethaid," he grumbled as he went from bunk to bunk.

Joe knew he should be tired. He knew he should be feeling the bone-grinding weariness that accompanies pure exhaustion. But as he stood at the LZ and waited for Colonel Hansen, he felt as though he had just slept for hours. His nerves tingled with an unfamiliar tautness, strung across his body in vibrating bands. Everything he saw seemed to be outlined, pressed forward in uncomfortable clarity. He paced for a moment, then looked at his watch. The rest of the men were already loaded aboard two waiting Hueys that sat and churned in patient agitation. Pulling the letter from his rucksack, he made one more attempt to read a few lines.

"Dear Joe," he heard her say, the sound of her voice masking the roar of the helicopters. And without realizing he had done so, he turned to the last page like the reader of a novel who knows the best part is at the end. He listened with his eyes while he felt her hands on his face. "...my love. Wherever you go today, whatever you do, carry this one thought with you and keep it close to your heart. Think of it as the one final truth: no one will ever love you the way I do..."

Her voice faded into the sound of an approaching jeep and he returned the letter to the rucksack like a man in a trance. The words were no different than words she had spoken before, but like everything else he was seeing on that strange, hollow morning, the words burst forth from the page and branded themselves to him with a force that stunned him. "...no one will ever love you the way I do...no one...no one..."

"Couldn't get here any sooner, Joe. Joe?"

Like the volume on a radio suddenly turned up, he heard the colonel's voice and blinked. Hansen looked at him with a critical eye. "You okay, Joe?"

"What? Oh. Yes, Colonel, I'm fine."

While they spoke briefly of the colonel's plans to be at Eagle's Nest within the next three days, Hansen watched him closely, scrutinizing eyes that were oddly bright, a face too rigidly set. When they finished, Joe turned away and began running for the chopper, unable to remember whether he had saluted or not.

The sun had risen somewhere above the jungle, a huge red orb of heat that glanced off treetops and splintered light off whirling rotors as Joe ran with his rucksack gripped in one hand, his AR-15 in the other. He stared at the yawning doorway of the lead chopper where the door gunner was checking his weapon. Fuente sat in the doorway of the second Huey, smiling at some bit of shared humor with someone inside. The sun struck windshields, danced within dust clouds hurled up by the rotors as Fuente turned his head slowly toward Joe. For no reason Joe could define, his legs became heavier as he ran, weighted and sodden, though his gait never changed. The deafening roar of the rotors diminished as he got slowly closer and when he looked again the doorway of his chopper had changed, had become larger, cavernous, swirling with dust and smoke from unseen fires. The door gunner and the mounted weapon were gone as though both had been sucked inside. He could hear the pounding of his heart in his ears in rhythm with the eerily retarded movement of the rotors— "whump...whump..." His eyes widened as he felt himself being pulled forward in the vacuum, hearing the echoing growl from within the cave—a beast that beckoned him, leered at him and called his name.

"Captain Rutledge...hey, Captain, are you all set?" he

heard the pilot yell. Breathing heavily and leaning against his rucksack in the chopper, Joe nodded, closed his eyes and gave a thumbs up to the pilot, feeling the instant response as he was lifted away from the earth in the belly of the beast.

The jungle lay quiet in the sunrise, watching the two powerfully awkward birds rise from the blister on her face that was Camp Evans. She spread her heavy green skirt in lush, smooth ripples from the distant coastline to the mountains bordering Laos, stretching herself in the morning mist. She was a siren breathing her essence toward him, luring him as much against her own will as his. The shadow of the rotored pterodactyl haunted the hills, sweeping up and down the swells in search of a home as the jungle moaned in open seduction. From above her curvaceous shoulders scented with her own unique, pungent perfume, her neck rose above and begged his attention. The foothills grew to maturity in sudden mountain ranges that separated adversaries from each other—tall, jagged spires cloaked with the same eternal emerald, her jewelry in morning dew, her clothing shrouded now in capes of ermine mist, majestic, stately and inherently deadly.

"*Come to me,*" she whispered, "*join me, know me. Forgive me...*"

Joe sat in the doorway, clinging to his weapon and listening. The mountains rising up ahead were the final lure and he felt himself reach inwardly toward them, willing the chopper to move faster, get closer. When they whirled into the valley at the base of the mountains, he felt the rising crescendo of the siren's chorus and gave himself breathlessly over to his capture at the hands of its blatant beauty. Prehistoric in its innocence, the heavy grasses waved below him like rippling satin in mountain breezes, broken by a shimmering bank of platinum that was a stream threading along its sinuous length. It was Vietnam as it would have been from the creation, green and fertile, full of every kind of life, from the gentlest butterfly to the deadliest tiger; from the most delicate flower to the most poisonous snake. It was a heartbreaking paradise. He felt an urgent serenity, knowing that finally he was approaching the source of the vacuum. The Ashau Valley. He had arrived.

When the inordinate ugliness of the knoll appeared, he furrowed his brow in amazement. Swooping in over Firebase Eagle's Nest on the eastern border of the valley, Joe suffered a moment of distasteful shock at seeing the monstrous space of gray where all green had been scraped away to make room for the armaments of war. Dust rose in boiling columns everywhere with the flurry of activity of men and equipment; an entire hilltop had been ravaged and cleared, rising like a steaming sore, its surface alive and crawling with foreign organisms. The fringes erupted with the jutting fingers of weaponry: batteries of .155s, .105s, 4-deuce mortars and 8.1s. Bunkers protruded along the perimeter, emerging as solid pustules fortified with green sandbags and sprouting lethal M-60 tanks crouched in defense of the sore and its life forms, staring in steely threat across the valley to the mountains beyond.

The Hueys settled amid the dust and clamor, disgorging their cargo of seven men who moved together across the compound, attracting the stares of the unkempt denizens of Eagle's Nest. Shirtless, sockless men with boots unlaced and caked with mud moved about the camp with the hard, indifferent expressions of men under defensible siege, battle-weary and toughened by their exposure to death. They stared with cynical eyes at the seven clean and polished newcomers, assured that Eagle's Nest and the Valley would soon have seven new baptisms by fire, conversions by the might and force of the thing lying just beyond the mountains.

The rites of entrance were performed, bunkers were assigned and they settled in to await the arrival of Colonel Hansen. The sun had found murderous haven here, delighting in the lack of green protection over the exposed earth. After pushing his way through the preliminaries of situating his men, Joe threw himself greatfully open to the scouring sunlight, pulling off his shirt and stretching out on top of his bunker, barely noticing the raw, lumpy discomfort of sandbags against his skin. In only moments he was asleep, an exhausted victim of forces out of his reach, beyond his control.

The dream was an omnivore, stalking him from behind

the ridges of consciousness, matching him step for step as he moved through his days, waiting for the right moment, the vulnerable hours when he surrendered to grinding fatigue. The dream had achieved adulthood along with him, emboldened by age and strengthened by his exhaustion. It sprang at him now with all its force, sensing his weakness, rolling forward in savage thirst. He saw his six-year-old hands clinging to the tailgate of the truck, heard the crunching of young bones as his brother disappeared into the snarling cloud, saw the yellow eyes turn to him, narrowed and hungry. He felt the beast open its mouth, heard it scream his name as it reached for the truck, one terrifying howl that was no longer his Korean name; now it was *"Captain Joseph Rutleeeeedge...!"* as it reached one horrible claw toward the truck and grabbed hold with shattering force...

The blast jarred him to the bone and he sat straight up, covered with sweat, barely catching his breath when another explosion from the huge .155 nearby almost rolled him from the sandbags. He stared around him with wide eyes, trying to breathe around the obstruction in his throat that was his thudding heart. He covered his ears with his hands and leaned forward, getting his bearings and adjusting to the incredible roar of the guns. He was too accustomed to stealth and silent maneuvering. But the guns had rescued him from the dream; he moved away from the bunker with the distinct sense of having been saved. When he finally slept again that night within the darkness of the bunker, he wrapped his senses around the voice of the guns, taking refuge behind them, hiding from the animal. He slept for eighteen hours, deeply submerged and drained.

XXX

He spent the next two days staring out across the valley from his vantage point along the perimeter. He molded himself to the shape of it, the feel of it. By the time Colonel Hansen arrived, Joe had memorized every nuance, every change in character; he knew it in sun and shadow, in early-morning fog and the depth of night. The valley felt his scrutiny and preened, showing him all her flamboyance and subtleties, shifting and smiling, inviting him in.

A fine, persistent rain obscured the valley the day after Hansen's arrival. As he approached the waiting choppers, Joe smiled to himself and cast a glance at the mysterious valley. *You can't hide from me*, he told her as he gave the thumbs up and all six choppers lifted away like a startled covey of quail. It was the shell game again, easier to accomplish in the trickery of rain.

The briefing with Hansen had been short and direct. Their target for reconnaissance was a blind knoll at the base of Hill 934, a saddle formation behind the knoll that was hidden from the probing eyes at Eagle's Nest. "I need to know what's out there," Hansen had said, and the mission began with Joe's newly-assigned call sign—"Swifter 1-2"—and instructions to communicate directly with Hansen—"Silver Eagle".

The Hueys went through their elaborate dance around the valley, lowering and taking off again while one of them released its seven-man cargo a mile from Hill 934. The rain seemed to lift with the vanishing of the choppers, the valley parting her curtain in order to watch the maneuverings of this silent group of intruders. The rains of May were vagrant and

311

capricious, first deluge, then trickle, then faint mist evaporating into humid sunlight, returning moments later as a flood. The mountains seemed to pull the rain up into themselves as the team moved through the heavy wet foliage, shielding themselves in the whispering drizzle.

They discovered the communication wires within the first hour. At the bottom of a soggy draw, Joe spotted a collection of fresh footprints, and in only moments he discovered a thin, black, double-strand communication wire running toward the hidden saddle and the second knoll just beyond.

"Negative," Silver Eagle responded to Joe's question, "don't cut them. Follow them. I want to know what's on the other end."

Rangonni shouldered the radio while Kralik adjusted the mottled boonie hat over his unruly hair, squinting up at the incessant rain. Swinging his weapon around he moved up the faint trail, disappearing over a small rise while the others prepared to follow. The loud *crack* of a sniper's rifle rebounded against the filmy air—the gut-twisting, lonely crack that wrenches a man to his soul—and instantly everyone dropped. Mat crouched low and ran up over the rise while the rest of them began laying down a massive field of fire in the direction of that single, terrifying shot.

When he saw Mat half-crawling, half-running down the trail with Kralik draped over his shoulders, Joe felt a violent sense of upheaval, a parting of solid ground within. And through the fissures he heard the siren's wailing song: *"Know me! Join me! Forgive me...!"* Kralik's head was drenched in blood, his face obliterated in a mask of red. Mat carefully laid his limp, unresponsive body on the ground.

"Silver Eagle, this is Swifter 1-2." Joe's voice was level, unbetrayed by the white of his knuckles gripping the handset. "Receiving sniper fire, one casualty, WIA. Need MedEvac bad, over."

"Swifter 1-2, this is Silver Eagle. Roger your transmission, MedEvac on the way. Withdraw casualty to pickup zone Bravo, then resume mission. We're onto something here, over."

"Roger, Silver Eagle. Requesting fire support at these coordinates..."

While Andros and Rangonni worked frantically over Kralik's bleeding head, getting him ready to move back to the first knoll for pick-up, Joe read the coordinates into the handset.

"Fire one Willy-Peter at my command," he said, waited a second, then, "Fire!" The monotone whine of a single white phosphorous round split the gray rain and landed in a small blaze of smoke in the jungle only fifty meters from their location. Joe took a deep breath. "Silver Eagle, you're on line. Right two-five, fire for effect—Fire!"

The distant wrath of an exploding battery of artillery pounded the sky in anger like faraway thunder, and shells wracked the jungle, tortured it, shattered it with the force of a hundred earthquakes, tore it apart in search of one man.

"Cease fire!" he finally shouted into the handset, and while the wretching earth stopped trembling, Rangonni and Andros slipped back toward the knoll, dragging Kralik between them as they ran. "Silver Eagle, this is Swifter 1-2. We're moving out, over."

"Roger your transmission, Swifter. Silver Eagle out."

Lowering the handset slowly, Joe felt himself stepping inwardly toward a spinning morass, felt the light mist of rain as an ethereal veil he was required to part with his hands to move forward. He felt a distinct sense of foreboding, a conscious haunting in the air when he looked over at Mat, who kept guard on the trail next to him.

"Mat, take point."

In those three small words held in that one, tiny, suspended instant, they both felt an entire lifetime flutter through their open fingers. There were no questions, no pleadings or excuses; they both saw it, both knew it was being reflected in a thousand pools of darkness between them. But there were no hesitations in that one instant when they both knew that Mat was going to die.

"Yes, sir," Mat replied calmly, knowing the words were a death knell, knowing that Joe heard it and understood.

Mathews smiled slowly, turned and walked swiftly up the trail.

The *crack* reverberated over and over, one empty roaring sound that bounced a million times against the shores of his soul as he saw Mat fall. Running forward, Joe grabbed him with one hand, threw him over his shoulder and ran back to the others, laying him carefully down next to Fuente.

Mat's eyes were closed in the quiet, expressionless way he had when he was sleeping. His face was calm, bearing no signs of pain. It was as if he had dropped to the ground to take a nap. Except for a small, bloodless hole directly in the center of his chest at the v of his open shirt, the man was sleeping. "Patch him up, Top," Joe said and began thinking of what needed to be done next. After a quick, frantic check, Fuente looked up.

"He's dead, sir."

"Forgive me!" the siren whispered through the tears of rain. *"Forgive me..."*

"Bring him back!" Joe snarled, grabbing Fuente's shirt, snapping the man to his feet. "Bring him back to life! Bring him baack!"

All the laughter, all the plans, the youth and the dreams had been blown away with the insignificant little *crack* of a sniper's rifle. He was trembling with rage and helplessness, the agony that was twin to unforgivable loss, the loss of more than just a life. This was the loss of a concept, a dream reborn and perpetuated in a new generation—in Mat, his young wife, and now their unborn child. "Bring him back!" he screamed. Fuente remained motionless, allowing Joe to vent the first violent waves of pain, never making a move to break the grip on his shirt.

The release happened in quick stages, from roaring, helpless anger to numbed aching understanding. Joe stared at Mat for one last time, then turned away and grabbed his weapon.

The jungle found him. It entered his soul and entwined him with the vines of hatred that went beyond hatred, an instinct so huge, so consuming it crushed everything in its path as it grew. The last vestiges of the civilized man went fleeing in the path of the primal being crashing through the underbrush. Fuente saw it happening, saw the emergence of something dark and unreachable, and there was nothing he could do to stop it. Not a word was spoken. Joe moved away with only one single conscious thought: "I'm gonna kill him."

There was nothing rational in his world any longer. He was the jungle, the jungle was him and there was no separation. He ran up the trail after the sniper with the silent, mindless intent of an animal, and the sniper, sensing something oblivious and fearful behind him, began to run. With the same instinct that senses impending death, the sniper knew the raw fear of becoming the hunted. He was reduced to a small thing with only one alternative: to run and keep running, because the thing on his trail was obsessed. This was fear beyond imagining, the terror of being tracked by the insane. The sniper looked to the jungle for help, dodging into territory no one but the insane would have been willing to follow him into. But the jungle turned her face away, left the sniper on his own to either live or die. Moving frantically, using every skill he had learned over a lifetime of living in the tangled mass, the sniper pushed steadily toward the second knoll, then turned suddenly and ran in another direction, then turned again, running at right angles to himself. Through all that day and into the night he ran, looking over his shoulder, never stopping except for brief seconds. At times he could hear the American close enough to rustle leaves somewhere behind him and the fear would send him flying. Night closed in and he had prayed for the expected hesitation in the American, knowing their inherent fear of the jungle at night. But it didn't happen; the American kept coming and there was no rest.

Through all of the next day and into the next night the sniper ran, zigzagging and crisscrossing his own path. Several times he thought of stopping and ambushing the crazy man, but all thoughts of ambush fled on the instinct of knowing when an animal is too smart to be trapped—or too deranged. When he stopped, the thing behind him stopped. When he ran again, the beast followed. There was no time, no room to breathe—run, run, run. Through the panicked depths of that second night, he no longer cared how much noise he made, how clear his path was to follow. He crashed and stumbled through the bushes, wheezing and choking, running, running...and still the American followed.

Joe found the sniper at sunrise of the third day, squatting on his haunches in a small clearing not far from where the chase had begun at the base of Hill 934. He raised his head when Joe stepped silently out of the bushes. The sniper's eyes were wide with exhaustion, his face haggard with bewilderment and fear. His torn, sweat-stained uniform clung to his thin body like paste, his chest heaved, his mouth opened. He stared at the tall American, astonished at his clear Oriental features above the ripped, rain-soaked American uniform. The sniper stared at his eyes, seeing at last the physical embodiment of insanity that had hunted him down and run him to the ground like a trapped fox. The eyes were human, but not in the terms of human life as he had come to know it.

The sniper held his rifle out in front of him with both hands, then tossed it onto the ground, never taking his eyes off the American. He began to raise his hands in surrender, but something in the American's eyes made him slowly lower his hands to his knees. From within the distortion that crazed fear produces in a man, the sniper saw the American raise his weapon to his shoulder, saw the tiny black opening of the barrel as if in an unbelievable dream. With open mouth and bewildered senses, he heard the solitary blast echo through the clearing, saw the flash of light from the barrel that slammed his head backward, sending his body sprawling into the grass.

Joe walked slowly into the clearing and stood over the body, waiting for the deep, basic satisfaction of avenged death to wash over him. He expected it, needed it, hungered for it. But as he stared at the sniper, at the neat, clean hole between the man's eyes, he knew it wasn't happening. It was too quick, too painless, too honest. His soul raged around inside him looking for an avenue of revenge that was deeper, more complete, more savage. He heard the deep groan from the man in the lighthouse, and he felt himself reach for his knife.

Joe knew his enemy. He knew that the Vietnamese believed they had to be buried with all their parts or their spirits would wander the earth forever looking for the lost part in order to reclaim it and enter into his heaven. The fractures blasted into his soul by Mat's death cried for the price, begged him for it, pushed him to his knees over the body, guided his hands. "A soul for a soul," he heard the primal man hiss as he cut off first one ear and then the other. He stood up, staring at the grizzly prize in the palm of his hand, at last feeling the purging pain wash over him. He felt the tangible calming of the flailing spirit inside him and he turned away, stuffing the ears into a breast pocket.

He stopped short when he saw the two men standing at the edge of the clearing. Fuente and Erskine stood quietly, completing a silent vigil that began two days before. They had stayed far enough behind not to interfere, close enough to offer support if it was needed. They had watched without moving while Joe exacted the final payment.

There wasn't a word spoken on the long walk back to the LZ, but Joe could hear the warring inside him, the battle for his senses and his sanity becoming pitched and intense. He didn't want to hear any of it, kept shaking his head as if trying to rid himself of stinging insects in his ears. But in the end he was a product of horrible logic, of burdensome reality, and the adjusting process began to overrun the slavering, huddled man in the lighthouse. He grudgingly seated himself at a spiritual truce table, ready to listen to reason.

They reached the LZ after a long, speechless trek, and radioed for a chopper to pick them up. Joe moved away and walked slowly back to the place on the knoll where Mat had fallen; he gazed out over a country that had taken so much from him, and from which he himself had taken, over and over again. He saw the drape of green, felt the wind, heard the song of her from the jagged parts of his heart. We're all takers, he thought, all of us rapists and pillagers and wild men. We take and take until we lose everything—even humanity. We're pitiful, wretched scramblers in the offal and wreckage of war; we remember only those things we choose to remember about ourselves, losing the plain and treasured parts of us in the ugliness. Only a rare few ever keep themselves in perspective; only a few are ever that uncluttered. He thought of Mat, of his intelligent simplicity, his lack of malice in a malicious world, and reached into his pocket for the ears. He stared at them, trying to find the satisfaction again, tried to justify their presence in his hand.

And you, he lashed out at himself, you who have seen all this as a child, you who understood better than anyone—here you stand with a payment Mat would never have wanted you to seek. He would have been the first to let the sniper surrender, to give him his life...

He held the ears out over the spot where Mat had fallen and dropped them to earth, feeling a quiet, tangible unburdening. "There," he said, knowing the jungle heard him. "I give you back your soul." And he felt the weeping of rain on his face.

XXXI

There was no sense of ever having returned to Eagle's Nest. The jungle, Mat's death, the sniper and the restoration of sanity and souls continued to cling to him like damaged gauze through that next day. Though he went through the required motions that established understanding and cognizance, he was still deeply removed from reality. He never had to look at the valley again from his haunts along the perimeter, knowing that those vigils had been the offering of himself, the open hand extended over the jungle just as he had been offered to the powers on the rocks of Sok-Cho. The jungle had watched him, had waited for him during those hours and during all the months before, waiting for that one act, that one sure indication that he was ready, that he was finally completely alone. She waited for him to isolate himself, sensed that he would do so, gave him the opportunities, tempted him, drew him forward, finally taking Mat and offering the sniper. Continually, she preyed on his sense of isolation, fed it, prepared it. It was the orphan she wanted, the man truly alone. She had waited and wept, shedding monsoons of tears as the vortex around the valley gained velocity, pulling him faster and faster toward the center, toward the quickening beast behind Hill 936...

"Colonel! Colonel, excuse me, sir..." the RTO said, as he burst through the door into the briefing room. Everyone turned, feeling the urgency in the blatant breach of protocol. "Excuse me, sir, but I just received a transmission from Colonel Kirchow's chopper. They were on a recon of the skirmish at the base of 936, about...here, sir. They've been hit, they're going down." He quickly pointed to a position on the map.

Joe sat stiffly, seeing the room and faces in disjointed segments: Hansen's grip of concern; dark-shadowed eyes that poured over maps; tightly controlled voices that issued orders for saturated fire support around Kirchow's position; desperate efforts to salvage a recon mission turned sour and to save Firebase Airborne's battalion commander. Ten frantic minutes of listening to the transmissions from the downed chopper, hearing the fragments of battle and the near-pleading voices calling for help before the final transmission: "Silver Eagle...!" And then silence.

Joe saw Colonel Hansen's eyes as he lifted away with his team, saw Hansen staring up at the chopper with the pleading of Kirchow's voice still in his ears. "Bring him back," Hansen's eyes insisted. "Bring him out of there..." Joe saw the valley stretch below him, felt the waves in the silken grass, felt the mountains rise ominously above the bloodshed below. He closed his eyes, sorting sounds and feelings from the real and unreal, trying desperately to ignore the merciless suction pulling him to the raging eye of an unseen storm. He opened his eyes and stared at the four men who remained of his fractured unit, and he winced. He wondered if his throbbing head and numbed interior were the forerunners of battle fatigue, shell-shock, whatever the experts wanted to call it. On the surface it was so simple: missions he had trained for, such as the rescue of Kirchow, or the recon where he lost Mat; all of them were basic operations he had performed before. So why this sense of foreboding, this pounding feeling of wrongness as an accompaniment to everything right and necessary? He rubbed his eyes and head, trying to ignore the eyes that he could feel watching him from somewhere below, eyes that glinted in the shadow of the pterodactyl.

Finding the disabled bird wasn't the ultimate challenge on this mission, Joe knew. The difficulty and danger lay in avoiding the jaws of the ambush that held Kirchow and his crew in siege. It took three maddening, protracted hours of careful maneuvering through the jungle above the crash site before the team was close enough to help, and by that time the lonely, sporadic firing from the trapped crew had finally ceased. Sweating, anxious and silent, the men moved as quickly as they could to the decimated craft, feeling in advance the sick frenzy of knowing they were too late.

The chopper sat at an improbable angle on a slope, its tail rotor broken completely off, its fuselage riddled with bullet holes. There was no sound, no movement, no evidence of any outside force. It was as though the chopper had simply fallen from the sky, empty and shattered, a bit of litter from a careless universe.

And then he saw them. Lying side by side, stretched out neatly in a row were five dead American soldiers, and even through seasoned eyes the scene was a shock. The bodies were stripped naked— "Bastards even took their dog tags," Fuente whispered—torn flesh, gaping holes exposing entrails, bloody, naked skin; the seeming victims of some prehistoric thing that had been startled in its gory feeding frenzy and had slinked off through the jungle, snarling to itself. Joe's body became an open, receptive nerve-ending, a scanning, probing sensor that examined the air as they moved the bodies to a safer location. His eyes darted back and forth with practiced absorption while he detonated the explosives placed in the chopper, watching it disintegrate and burn in lonely memorium on the hillside.

He knew that they were out there—a thousand eyes watched him from the hills. He was being examined, his every move keenly observed by an enemy who inexplicably held its fire. Joe's senses roamed the hillside as he reported their situation to Hansen, his eyes flitting to every small movement as he waited for instructions.

"Swifter 1-2, this is Silver Eagle. Proceed to the knoll 200 meters above the crash site and set up an OP. Reinforcements will arrive at first light. We'll retrieve the bodies then."

The roaring feeling of displacement, of glaring error, surrounded him. From 1500 meters below, the battle that Kirchow had been attempting to observe boiled and rumbled, an entire company from Firebase Airborne being held at bay by an entrenched enemy. Between the enemy below and the knoll above, Joe could feel a frontier of hostility. Every instinct, every protective function within him rebelled against pushing up to the knoll. He could feel the eyes watching, waiting for his decision when there was no decision to be made—he knew he would follow orders.

During the two hours of zigzagging their way toward the summit, a merciful intermittent rain hid their movements. But the same rain that provided cover while they reached their location and set up an NDP became a downpour of maddening dimensions during the night, forcing them to stay awake and watchful. In those drenched, sleepless hours before dawn, Joe knew he had never felt so glaringly exposed in any other situation in Vietnam. He felt the enemy all around him, sitting out there, hunched in the rain, waiting. He held his weapon close under his poncho and sat with his back against a tree, feeling himself to be an infinitesimal speck in the cosmos, wondering why he should also feel like the center of some raging, misguided solar system. He stared around him at the four men, knowing with bewildered certainty they were being pulled into the careening orbit along with him. He was beset by a desire to beg some unseen power for clemency for his men, to make someone or something understand that they were merely bystanders, but there was no answer from the jungle, no voice of comfort of condolence. Only wetness, sleeplessness, and the fear of approaching daylight.

When he received the order at six in the morning to move on to the top of Hill 936, Joe dropped the handset and stared at the warming jungle that rose above and below him. Mist from the heavy rain lifted in banks and drifts, filling the air with an aquatic mystery. He gazed down at the short saddle formation they would have to cross to get to 936—a green, swollen land bridge between the knoll and the mountain. The chilling awareness of his vulnerability rode heavily on his shoulders as they moved down the back of the knoll toward the saddle. A persistent stab from his sixth sense probed and warned and signaled, all to no avail. He followed orders and kept moving.

As they emerged two hours later into a clearing on the saddle's upward draw, the furies of hell exploded around them in a solid wall of bullets from somewhere above. A few paces in front of Joe, Rangonni suddenly lurched backward as if having been sucker-punched. He lay on his back, shot in the stomach and writhing in painful contortions, unable to make a sound. The machine guns up ahead poured out their deadly rain; bullets tore at the earth as Joe grabbed Rangonni's collar and dragged him back. Erskine and Andros half-dragged, half-carried him quickly back toward the knoll. The machine gun nests above them raged on in a thick wall of tracer rounds that pounded the earth, seeking, devouring, seeking again. By the time they reached their position at the top of the knoll, the machine guns were silent. Fuente worked on Rangonni with the rigid expression of a man who recognizes impending death, while Joe radioed for fire support, asking where his reinforcements were.

"...reinforcements deployed from Airborne at first light...pinned down by heavy enemy fire...battalion deployed from Eagle's Nest to your location, over."

And if that doesn't work, Joe said to himself as he broke off transmission, if that doesn't work, we're up the creek. With a poncho wrapped around his stomach in a feeble effort to stop his bleeding, Rangonni would be the first to go, Joe thought. From down below he could hear the sounds of an intensifying fight; he could see choppers hovering over the battle site like a swarm of dragon flies. Enemy artillery shells from somewhere behind Hill 936 screamed overhead on their course toward the battle below. Three companies from Airborne thrashed and scrambled, trying desperately to break through.

An hour later, as if in direct answer to his unvoiced fears, he was notified that the battalion from Eagle's Nest was hopelessly pinned down. The four of them watched the frenzy below until Andros suddenly turned and started firing. A wave of NVA soldiers appeared through the bushes, not running, but walking resolutely toward them. Andros' machine gun exploded obediently while the NVAs dropped like scythed wheat. There was no time for dismay, fear, frustration, any of the myriad of emotions they were entitled to; there were only the weapons, blasting in determined defense against a churning surge of humanity; no feeling, no perception except that of the threat before them.

Joe never heard the drone of the plane above him, only dimly remembered hearing someone's voice on his radio. He recalled only one thing clearly from the Forward Air Controller's voice: "Roger, Swifter, hold onto your hair. Here it comes..."

Racing across the sky in groups of four, Navy fighter planes soared over the saddle, swooping in low and dropping napalm bombs as they screamed by. While the enemy's attention was drawn to the fighters, Joe sat and picked them off one by one like ducks in an arcade. When the smell reached him he stopped firing and sat back and coughed, trying to rid his senses of the nauseating stench of burning flesh. Dozens of bodies lay on the saddle below, covered with the searing jelly that would fry them into crisp, charred logs.

"Rangonni?" he asked Erskine, "how's Rangonni?" Erskine shook his head and lifted the poncho liner slightly for Joe to see the wound; the man was quivering in shock, his lower lip was trembling. And as Joe watched, helpless and guilt-ridden, the quivering lip stopped and the opaque eyes closed. Erskine turned away and slammed his fist into the dirt, keeping his back to the others.

Joe grabbed the radio and began directing in artillery fire over the hillside, feeling the shells land with steady, grinding punches. "More," he called, "more!" He needed to feel it, to hear it, needed to smother the painful roar that had found sudden haven in his head: *You can't take them! It's me you want!*...

His spirits rose in nearly-crazed satisfaction when he called in a B-52 strike. Astonished at his own delight in their destructiveness, Joe watched as the giant planes passed over in waves, dropping their loads of bombs like a female fish ejecting a bellyful of eggs. Trees exploded in splinters, geysers of earth and foliage and fire erupted again and again, the jungle twisted and tore and heaved, branches wrenched and split, crashing into the foxholes while the men inside ducked and covered their heads. Chunks of charred and burning bodies splattered like sickening rain over everything; bits and pieces of flesh and bone clung to what remained of the jungle when the bombers were finished. By the time the last of the planes disappeared, the hillside no longer belonged to the jungle; every green thing had been destroyed, leaving a ravaged, naked wetness, brown and broken.

There was silence then, total and painful. The four men on the knoll stared around them at a planet suffering through the process of creation in reverse, where huge acres of mountain had been blasted up and turned inward, reverting to what they had been in the beginning—ugly emptiness with no life.

The sun slipped furtively behind the mountain, washing the hillside in blue shadow that gradually blackened like a bruise. The FAC signaled his exit with a promise to return at first light, and the horror of the day was replaced with the perpetual terrors of the night. The fighting down below, where the bludgeoning of the battalion continued, was diminished now to sporadic firing, persistent, maddening and lonely. Joe sat with his back against a tree which was now little more than a trunk, stripped of its leafy arms. The others leaned against banks of dirt, their heads bent in exhaustion and relief. He watched them and listened, feeling a keen sense of guardianship and knowing that the vigil wasn't over. He looked out into the darkness, imagining a gray howl in the distance and shivering with the youthful fear of believing that the beast of his nightmares had been torn from his mind and given life. The forces were being marshalled out there somewhere, and he could feel the omnivore as their standard bearer.

In the hours after darkness Joe leaned forward and listened, trying to see the jungle with his ears. The entire hillside was moving, he could feel it. One by one, the others moved their heads above the dirt berms and listened. "What the fuck?" Andros whispered, his hands tensing on the machine gun. "What're they doin'?"

"They're coming back for their dead," Joe whispered, and something hungry and jubilant sprang up in him as he reached for the radio. *Now!* he thought, bringing the handset to his face, now while they're not expecting it, while they're out there by the hundreds! But his hand froze around the handset, his voice rushed into an empty vacuum in his throat as a vision of the pagoda in the rice paddies loomed in the darkness. He listened to the movement below, the eerie rustling of clothing and footsteps that covered the hillside as men of violence made one final gesture of respect to each other, and he lowered the handset. There was a consummate reverence on the mountain as men searched through the rubble of exploded bodies, the same inordinate sense of holiness that prevented the shelling of a tiny pagoda, a heartbreaking humanity amid the savagery. A large, thrashing part of him screamed for annihilation, "*Now! While they're vulnerable, now, do it now!*" But he smiled from his spiritual corner, enjoying the victory in this one small skirmish. There would be no sniper in the clearing this time, no ears taken. A part of him raged while the rest of him smiled and listened and braced for the next temptation. "I'm learning," he thought, "I'm learning how my war is fought."

The wordless rustling continued through all the hours of darkness, a continual river of quiet devotion while the NVA worked. There were no voices, only invisible movements, and the initial skin-crawling sensations gave way to watchful acceptance as dawn crept across the sky and made the hillside visible again.

They stared in disbelief. A hillside once covered with hundreds of bodies and bits of bodies was now completely bare. Nothing. The NVA had retrieved them all.

Moments later the FAC returned to his droning position above them and, as if to acknowledge the beginning of a new day, enemy artillery from behind the mountain began pounding the besieged battalion again, renewing the battle with a vengeful ferocity. The choreography began again as Joe watched the frantic battle below and called in fire on positions all over the hillside. Mortars screamed in from Eagle's Nest and slammed the mountainside with no rest, no mercy. The earth below them bucked and heaved and erupted, with no time to heal or settle before the next exploding fist smashed it again. When silence fell, Joe sat rigid and tense, reading the air with his senses. It wasn't the silence of the end or even of rest; it was the silence of savage beginning.

"Roger, Swifter, I have the Jolly Green Giants ready and waiting. Pop smoke." Grabbing the smoke grenade, Joe released it and sent a plume of purple smoke into the air to mark their position. "I see goofy grape, Swifter. Keep your head down, buddy, here it comes."

There was a new and distinctive growl in the sky as the C-130's approached. In a computerized patchwork of destruction, the 50-caliber shells thudded into the earth in precise patterns over the hillside as the planes circled again and again. The rounds were the heavy footfalls of a restless giant that rushed around and slapped bodies into the dirt as it ran, spraying blood and flesh in its path. For a full hour the giant stalked the enemy, growling and thudding and smashing bodies. When the giant wearied of his game, the planes flew away and left only death on the mountain, death and blood and the tint of red in the upturned earth. Nothing moved. There was no sound. "Swifter 1-2, this is Silver Eagle. What's your sit-rep?"

What word was there for this? Joe wondered. What phrase can ever describe what I see down there, a word for the shattered bodies and rivers of blood? It's a slaughtering field. "Silver Eagle—it's a hamburger hill," he replied. And the horror of it, he knew, was that it wasn't over, that the battalion below was under worse siege than before and that help was indefinitely delayed. The smell of death lifted in heavy drafts of air and settled over the four men struggling to retain their equilibrium in a world suddenly feeding on itself, their eyes mirroring their stripped emotions, exposing their fear.

He made feeble attempts to turn his mind away from the helplessness in their faces during those shouting silences. He poured cold water from a canteen into a pouch of LRP rations, knowing that he wasn't hungry but drawing comfort from doing something ordinary, concentrating on the movements like a man staring into the monotony of a campfire on a freezing night. Small, unconscious moments and movements became precious and rare amid the insanity.

He discovered that he hated the silence; it made the yellow-eyed howling so much louder. Guilt became his worst antagonist during those hours as he felt the fear transmitted from his three men; he felt the strangling sensation of unfairness as the whirlwind gathered force out there in the dark, and he clenched his fists against its immutable power. He was the triggering mechanism for all the destruction, he was willing now to accept his role, but he screamed inwardly for the release of his men.

The soft rustling of the night before had become louder this time, the enemy sensing the nearness of the end for whoever held them off the knoll. Their movements were louder and less cautious as they reclaimed their dead, and Joe listened from deep inside him as his men tried to sleep. For the first time since Mat's death, he allowed himself to reach out to an unseen enemy in the jungle, permitted that mental penetration into the bastions of another existence. And the sound that rose to greet him on his entry was horrendous.

There was no longer one voice hiding in the bushes. Now there was a throng of voices, an auditorium full of clamoring, angry cacophony in the darkness: *"They're only four of them...what are we waiting for...kill him now...kill him NOW!...."*

"Wait!" One voice emerged from the din of the others, barely a whisper but heard with the impact of a shout. *"Wait!"* the voice said, *"I know him!"*

Joe blinked his eyes and leaned away from the tree. "What?" he said aloud.

"I know you," the voice said again.

"No, Charlie, that won't work," Joe said. "You can't trick me that way."

"Shhh!" the voice said urgently, *"not so loud—she might turn you into a toad."*

His weapon clattered to the ground as he stood and

braced himself against the tree, his eyes wide, his heart pounding. "What did you say?" he rasped, staring out at the darkness where all sound had stopped. But the link was broken, the delicate conduit vanishing with his first movement and there were no more voices. Only the soft echo of that last receding phrase...

"Hey, Cap'n," Fuente whispered, "who're you talkin to?"

Joe slowly sat back down and picked up his weapon with trembling hands. His eyes scanned the darkness, trying desperately to pierce it while his breathing deepened. "I...I thought I heard someone out there," he finally said.

"There IS someone out there, Cap, hundreds of 'em. You're beat. Why don't you try to catch some sleep. I'll take over the watch."

Joe shook his head and pulled closer into himself, his eyes darkening with frantic anger. *"That won't work!"* he flailed at the force around the mountain. *"That won't fuckin' WORK!"* he screamed within. His mind threw itself from one profanity to the next, twisting and bashing itself in frustration. *"You can't get to me that way, motherfuckers!"* his spirit roared. And quietly, slowly, it began to rain.

When daylight reached a finger into the sodden foxhole it illuminated Joe's haggard, rain-streaked face, shining tentatively into eyes that were red-rimmed and hollow with lack of sleep and something more—a wild, distant fear that had no definition, no name. The hillside was empty again, washed over with rain that created gullies and streamlets in the tortured soil. The four men huddled under ponchos with burning eyes staring from beneath soggy boonie hats. They sat in battle-numbed oblivion, indifferent to the puddles that formed around them until they heard Fuente yell: "Madre de Dios!"

The rain had lifted enough for them to see the largest wave yet of NVAs hurtling across the muddy ground toward them. Andros swung his machine gun, and through a tight, angry understanding, Joe could hear him firing in short, sporadic bursts instead of long sustained strafes. The ammunition was almost gone. And they were about to be overrun.

He felt the spinning scream at the eye of the storm, as the torrent of bodies rushed toward them, a wide, endless field of dirty brown. The beast bared its teeth and salivated and Joe could feel every nerve tightening down for the onslaught.

Three battalions from Firebase Eagle's Nest had thrown their weight against the enemy at the foot of the hill and the NVA had retaliated against their superior firepower with the sheer weight of their numbers. As the braced and terrified men on the knoll watched, the gigantic force coming toward them split in three parts, each flank pouring down either side of the mountain toward the battle below, leaving the central force to penetrate and destroy the infuriatingly persistent little group on the knoll.

Only after Joe had called for support and emptied another clip into the advancing tide, only when he heard the distant approach of the Cobra gunships did he manage to stop firing long enough to see a group of NVA approaching them from the side. Fuente saw them at the same moment, and together they whirled and faced them just as four gunships roared in above the brown mass, pointing their deadly noses downward, mini-guns groaning with the sound of a man straining under a heavy load, spitting rockets into the scattering horde.

"Sonofabitch!" Fuente yelled as he fired at the group surging into their perimeter, his jaws clenched, eyes narrowed and hard. They knelt side by side, Joe and Fuente, firing into the group. They heard the thud of bullets hitting bodies, the *whump* of air leaving men's lungs as the rounds smashed their chests; he saw their frenzied, determined eyes as they came closer, closer, blood spraying everywhere.

And then it was finished, the forces scattered and retreated, the gunships groaning and spitting as they followed the retreat. Joe and Fuente collapsed backward and stared at the sprawled and shattered bodies of the enemy soldiers who had penetrated their tiny defense, nine of them, one lying obscenely over Rangonni's body. Breathing heavily, Joe closed his eyes. When he heard Fuente groan, he looked at him, then moved quickly, feeling a sharp, numbing pain down his left arm.

"How bad are you hit?" Joe asked as he opened Fuente's bloody shirt. Fuente shook his head and smiled. "Not as bad as you, it looks like. Hurts like hell, but it ain't bleedin too bad." There was an ugly hole close to Fuente's shoulder cap and Joe bandaged it as well as he could with a bandanna, oddly unaware of the pain in his own shoulder. Only then did he notice the others, and his heart sank in his chest.

Andros and Erskine lay next to each other in the shapeless positions of sudden death, their weapons still clutched in their hands. Andros' chest was flayed and torn, his face spattered with blood, his blue eyes slightly open. Erskine lay on his side with a small hole in the front of his head that expanded and grew on its course, leaving the back of his head blown open.

"Oh, Jesus," Fuente mumbled as he moved painfully to them, checking them for signs of life. He hung his head and breathed deeply, carefully closing Erskine's eyes. He turned and looked at Joe, his face a mask of grief. "Goddamn it, Cap," he whispered, and turned away.

Joe found his tree, the naked, ravaged tree that had been his pillar for three endless days. Leaning back against it he stared into a sky that was making amends for the rain of the night before, spreading above him now in endless blue. He knew that the anger would come, knew that it would only be a matter of time before his deadened senses would function again and drag him into the throes of rage. The howling cosmos had taken two more innocents, and the anger would find him. But the novocaine of shock still held him in a state of suspension that prevented him from hearing a faint, insistent drumming along his nerves. Tearing his bandanna from his neck and opening his shirt, he examined the small, bloody hole just under his collarbone. Reaching up and behind him, he felt the exit wound on his shoulder blade, a hole the size of a fifty-cent piece. There was no real pain, but he discovered that he was barely able to make a fist with his left hand. Using his teeth, he tore a strip from his bandanna, wrapped it around an empty shell casing, then inserted the plug into the hole in his chest, feeling the spiny fingers of pain as it entered. "Fuente," Joe said quietly, finding it oddly difficult to breathe.

"Yes, sir."

They looked at each other and smiled, transmitting a world of unspoken thought and understanding between them. Fuente's eyes acknowledged Joe's unvoiced question, and his smile gave the answer. He was a soldier, a man who didn't need explanations during war; he knew what Joe had to do, and in those seconds he gave his consent.

"Just wanted to hear your voice, sheethaid," Joe said, and tried to smile. "Just you and me now, amigo." And he reached for the radio.

...the bedroom in Charleston was suddenly stifling, burning with a heat that wasn't heat but was a cold so suffocating that Sam threw off her covers in her sleep. She moaned once, trying to awaken herself from a dream of someone chasing her, someone with no face, no hair, no name...closer, he's getting closer and I can't run any faster...closer, closer I don't know who he is what he wants but he won't let me be I can't breathe it's so hot so cold closer he's getting closer...

He could feel a surge in the air as he gripped the handset, finally noticing the persistent drumming in his head that now sounded like continuous thunder. Bullets suddenly pelted the ground around their position in a steady, nagging storm and he saw Fuente lean up against the berm and return fire, but he heard none of it; the atmosphere was assuming a frightening bend as he stared at the dead around him, friend and foe. His attention focused on the enemy soldier lying over Rangonni's stiffening body. "Hey, Top," he said, and he felt an odd hollowness to his voice. "Look at that gook over by Rangonni. You ever see one that big before?"

Fuente stared at the still form for a moment and shrugged his good left shoulder. "Chi-Com," he said indifferently. "Has to be. Sure as hell ain't your average-lookin' gook."

"Goddamn, another one," Joe said, closing his eyes and leaning his head against the tree, picking up the handset. "Sweet Angel, this is Swifter 1-2."

"Swifter 1-2, Sweet Angel here. Been waitin for ya, good

buddy. What we got down there?"

"Sweet Angel, things've gone from bad to shit down here. Stand by for fire in the battle area. Make preparations and wait for my command." There was a brief silence.

"Swifter 1-2, I hear ya li'l brother. Wait one."

...she tossed on the bed, her skin covered with a thin, gleaming film of sweat; her nightgown clung to her legs as she began to thrash, fighting now, fighting her way to the surface of the dream, knowing she was asleep but knowing she was being pursued and trying subconsciously to grasp reality while still facing the unrealness of the faceless figure of the dream. She struggled to breathe in the thick, hot pillow of air in the room...closer, he's so close I can feel him, but I can't see him and I don't know who he is or why he wants to destroy me, closer, he's so close...

His shoulder throbbed, his body ached. Voices rushed at him from the soupy swirl in his head: *"Do it now!...Kill him now!...Faster! Run faster! Give me your hand...!"*

"Swifter 1-2, this is Silver Eagle." Joe blinked in surprise at the sound of Hansen's voice, finally noticing the sound of the chopper from somewhere above. "Swifter, talk to me, son."

"Silver Eagle, I've instructed Sweet Angel to prepare for fire in the battle area. At my command, I want you to drop everything America has in her arsenal on my position. I'll wait for the gooks to make their move. You WILL fire on my command."

"...run faster!...don't let go!..."

"I can't do that, son." The heaviness in Hansen's voice was undisguised. "I just can't do that."

The siren's song rose around him, his shoulder throbbed, the voices warred within him. *"Kill him now...kill him!..."*

"You sonofabitch," Joe said, his voice ragged and intense with grief and pain. "I—am—in—command. Get off my fuckin' horn!"

The silence that followed was his only answer, the only answer there could have been. The order, when Joe gave it, had to be obeyed; it was his judgment call as the man standing in the heat. Joe dropped the handset and looked at Fuente, who had stopped firing long enough to reload and glance up.

He smiled at Joe, and winked. "What say, Cap? Let's see how many of these sheethaids we can take out with us."

...in the dream she reached a dead-end, a blank wall beyond which she could no longer run from the faceless, hairless being behind her. "It's not fair, this isn't fair, all I want is to be happy, I can't let this happen." In frustration and fear she saw her fists pound the wall in slow motion, and with a dim awakening of something conscious in her mind, the fear began to dissipate, and she realized as she whirled to face her pursuer that now she was getting angry...

The wailing inside him terraced upward in rising anguish as he watched Fuente's placid face. He saw him turn and begin firing again, saw him through the crazed warp in the atmosphere that slowed everything, made it all too clear, too close. He saw the tall soldier by Rangonni turn slowly, bringing his weapon around, firing as he turned. "No!" Joe roared inside as he saw the bullets thump into Fuente's back, saw his hands fly up, his head snap back, saw him fall forwards with his face slamming onto his gun, sightless eyes staring down at the naked hillside.

Joe's voice broke sluggishly through the air— *"NOOO!"* he heard as he raised his own weapon.

"...if you don't get up, I'm leaving you!..."

"NOOOOO, it won't WORRRRK!"

He saw the soldier's eyes, heard the voice, felt the cyclone reach its center. And he pulled the trigger.

All sound vanished, sucked away into the fracture at the core of the universe. All firing stopped from below, from above and around him. There was only the shy drone of the FAC circling overhead, a ridiculous, diminished sound when set against the emptiness of the silence below. There was no pain, no feeling. Only a reverberating echo of the final blasts...

He forced himself to move, pulled himself away from the tree where seeping blood from his back had dried. The soldier lay on his back, his arms thrown wide, eyes closed, his chest torn and bleeding. Dried blood on the side of his head caked over the wound that had flung him into the foxhole; his face was quiet, peaceful, simply asleep like Mat's. The body was lean and as tall as his own...something about his sleeping face, his strong features...

And then he noticed the ear. His left ear lobe was missing.

Without realizing he was doing it, Joe found his fingers working frantically with the buttons on the man's shirt, finally tearing it open and pushing it off the shoulder of his left arm. The welt was there, a heavy matting of scar tissue running from his elbow almost to his armpit. He heard a groan, a strained, agonized sound, and realized it was his own. His one good hand flew through the dead man's pockets looking for a document, a tag, a piece of paper, anything that would identify him. When he found the bundle of envelopes tied together with string, their edges curled and dirty from constant handling, he jerked the string away and leafed through them, staring at the meaningless Chinese characters. Something dropped from the bundle onto the man's chest and he reached for it, his hand freezing just inches from the photograph—an old, well-worn photo of three people: two small, unsmiling boys standing beside a young woman in a long Korean gown.

"...*forgive me*," the siren whispered, "*forgive me*..."

It began from somewhere deep in the backwaters of original life, a sound so twisted and pain-filled, piercing centuries of hate and war and loss, sent on the jungle wind as he stared at the photo—the twin to the one he had carried with him through the years...

"...*you will know...on the day he dies, you will know*..."

"NOOOO!" he screamed, throwing his head back, "no, you couldn't have known—you're dead, you're all dead!"

All dead—his father, his mother, Father Scully, Charlie, Mat, Fuente, his men—and now Yoon Chang Bok. A brother finally found.

The search was over. The dream was gone.

...she heard herself groan as the figure continued to move toward her. He moved out of the mist in slow motion and she saw him in a dim light, still faceless, still hairless, still undefined and nameless, simply—there. She knew he meant to crush her, to merely walk into her, through her, disintegrating her into nothingness, and

suddenly her anger was stronger than the fear, and she moved forward with clenched fists. "You—are—dead—" she said with the thick, tongue-tied mumble of all dreams. "You—are—dead—and—he—is—alive—and—it—is—over...over...over..."

He stared around him, gasping for air as he fought for control, battled for a retreating grasp on sanity. Nothing was the same, nothing felt the same, his body, his skin, the air around him, it was all different; he was still alive and yet he could feel the death inside and everything on the outside responded to it. He saw the stripped, clawed knoll all around him, saw the bodies and blood and bits of flesh and brains, saw the wind tugging at tattered, bloody clothing...the concentration camp after the massacre. Another knoll in another lifetime—the same death, the same waste. Burial, he thought. The refugees buried their dead that day. He looked around him anxiously; the massacre was over, the guards were gone and he had to bury his brother...

Dragging Andros and Erskine from their foxhole, barely feeling the scalding pain in his left shoulder, Joe reached beneath the body of his brother, sliding his arm around and grasping him beneath the scarred left arm. He dragged him slowly to the hole and, as carefully as he could, rolled him in. He knelt by the grave and tried to think, tried to know what he should do now, how he could condone simply pushing dirt in over his sleeping face. His hands trembled, his breathing was difficult and he searched the blazing sky, finding it as empty as his soul. "All of the years," he thought, "all the wasted years when you never knew I was alive, never knew where I was, never knew my name..."

He reached inside his own bloody shirt and felt the dog tags, squeezed his hand around them and pulled, snapping the chain. He stared at the tags in his hand, silver and red, smeared with his blood. As though it were a gift he had been meaning to give him all his life, Joe reached into the grave and closed his brother's fist around the tags, placing the fist over the shattered chest.

He heard the keening from across the years, the high-pitched song of finished life, of joy known and pain endured, of happiness sought and suffering found. With every scoop of dirt he pushed into the grave, he heard the wailing, felt its power and its sorrow. "More dirt," he thought as he clawed at the wet earth. "Not deep enough...the wolves can't have him..."

When the burial was done, when he sat against the tree, dimly realizing that the bleeding from his shoulder had begun again, he stared at the foxhole grave and quietly, uncontrollably began to shiver. *Cold...the snow is so cold...all I want to do is sleep...just for a little while...*

When he opened his eyes the heat had returned, the bullets had returned and the keening he heard was a fresh barrage of artillery from behind Hill 936. He saw the rolling mass of NVA soldiers at the bottom of the torn jungle, all moving toward him, and he wanted deeply to believe the end had arrived. He knew there was no way he could survive the onslaught, knew it was hopeless, wanted it to be hopeless. It was time...

He picked up the handset with a vast inward calm, and squeezed. "Sweet Angel," he said almost inaudibly, "this is Swifter 1-2."

"Swifter, this is Sweet Angel. Goddamn boy, where you been? I been tryin to reach you for over an hour."

"Sweet Angel, is everything in place?"

"That's affirmative, good buddy."

"Sweet Angel, wait for my command."

He lowered the handset and stared at the pile of weaponry taken from his brother's body, the final symbols of life and death and lost years: an AK-47, its bayonet drawn; two bandoleers of banana clips for the AK; a 9 mm pistol with a bandoleer of clips; and six of the odd Communist grenades—the same wooden-handled explosives carried by the drunken soldiers in his house when he blew it up...

He held one of the grenades in his useless left hand, turning it over and over, examining it with a cold, remote interest as he heard the tide of NVA coming closer. He waited until he could hear the sound of their footsteps, the rattle of their weaponry, almost the sound of their breathing. Then he raised the handset and screamed: "FIRE! FIRE!"

...she bolted upright in bed, a scream caught in her throat because she believed the room had suddenly burst into flame; her heart pounded with fear, her own dream-like voice still filling her senses as she had stood and faced the thing in her mind. But now the fear had returned and was new, stronger, more powerful than ever before, and she knew this time it was not a dream; this time the battle was real...

In the hours that followed, the jungle knew what it meant to die. It began with the napalm dropped by Navy fighters, exploding, spraying, splattering the soldiers with burning jelly. They fell to the ground and writhed until they died and for the first time Joe heard them scream, blood-chilling, gut-wrenching screams as they burned and died. The earth knew the agony of being pounded apart, shredded by mortal men as the artillery fire from Eagle's Nest raged and clawed at the mountain. Acre by acre the earth wretched and heaved and erupted with fire, dirt and blood, the savage explosions gouging out earth only a few feet from where he sat, throwing it over his body, in his face, smashing his radio.

The jungle knew stab wounds, sharp and deep, as the C-130's returned to knife her continually with their precise, blood-thirsty pattern of rounds that stopped only a meter from where he sat. He waited patiently for the inevitable round to blast away his head, but the giants disappeared over the horizon, leaving him to stare quietly up at the B-52's that replaced them, and the carnage continued.

So this is what it's like, he thought, to be a the focal point of all the negative energies of the world. Through the colorless lens of indifference, he watched the destruction of the mountain and knew he would feel the same bland distraction if he were witnessing the creation of a work of art; there was no distinction any longer between the vastly wrong and the ultimately right; there was no need to continue a life-long balancing act on the fine line between good and evil, between mercy and cruelty. It all came down to this waste, and none of it ever truly mattered.

As he watched a final wave of Navy fighters suffocate the

mountain with layers of napalm, he smiled wryly and thought of Father Scully. "This proves it, padre," he said through the smoke and stench of death, "this proves there is no god, no loving, caring being that believes in justice. If there was a god he would have let me die a long time ago and my brother would still be alive. Only a random, stupid universe would have left me here untouched after all this. A loving god would have let me die. There!" he said and began to chuckle in maniacal, twisted bursts. "That proves it! I'm alive, so God is dead! The argument is over, padre. We both lose."

The fighters finished their work, the macabre painters of the regurgitated canvas of war covering the living and dead remains of anything left in the aftermath of the B-52's. And as if repelled by the odor rising from the hillside, the jets dropped their last bomb and streaked away to less repugnant fields, leaving one man sitting against a splintered tree, following their retreat with cold, accusing eyes. "You didn't finish, motherfuckers," he said numbly to himself, to the jungle, to the Forces. "You left the wrong man alive."

...she was a small huddle on the edge of the bed, curled into herself and gripped as though she had been shot; her hair clung to her face in damp coils and she clenched her teeth with the heat and cold. Sam knew nothing of a man's war, of bloodshed and fire and death; but she knew of loss and waste and love and she knew that this thing, this darkness that surrounded Joe and his brother was a power that would destroy them both, if she allowed it, and she felt everything strong within her take up arms and shout in defiance; she felt the distance, could sense Joe moving away from her, away from himself, away from living, and she sat stone still, marshalling the forces she knew she was going to need...

There was no measurement of time, no way to know how long he had slumped in the silence; two hours, four hours, a lifetime, he didn't know. He didn't care. Though he understood he was still alive, he realized that Hansen and everyone else would be convinced he was dead. He smiled and coughed weakly, the sound falling strangely flat in the muted silence. Everyone else still believes in logic and in God, he thought, in right and wrong, in cause and effect. Of course they believe I'm dead. Even when he heard the heavy, air-thumping roar of a chopper circling overhead, knowing it would be Hansen, he didn't lift his head; he had no strength left to even raise his hand. It didn't matter. None of it mattered anymore.

When the first unit arrived sometime later, moving cautiously over the knoll, the company commander saw Joe's eyes open slowly, and he froze. At first, the Oriental features aroused an instant response to raise his weapon, but the torn, bloody American uniform made him hesitate and he finally stared in disbelief. The commander rushed to him and dropped to his knees.

"I'm Swifter 1-2," Joe barely whispered.

"How—how in the name of God...!" the commander stammered, reaching for his radio. "He's alive! He's alive!" he shouted into the handset. "Swifter 1-2 is alive!"

"...*alive...alive*," echoing down tunnels of ice as he slipped into the oblivion of blood loss and exhaustion... "*alive, your brother is alive...you will know the day he dies...*"

When he opened his eyes again, he stared at the lined, anxious face of Colonel Hansen and heard his voice from a great distance as he saw his head shake in disbelief.

"...incredible, unbelievable..."

He felt hands on him, heard voices calling to each other, heard a clutter of footsteps and movement and sound as the units scoured the slaughtering ground below and around him. A medic was tearing away his shirt and he heard the moist, ripping sound of the fabric as it pulled away from the seeping wound. He felt someone trying to pry open the fingers of his left hand, still paralyzed and rigid around the grenade. "Leave it," Hansen said, seeing the faint rebellion in the frozen fist. "Get him outa here quick. Use my chopper. Stay with him 'til he gets to a hospital."

The wind stroked his dirty, blood-spattered face as he felt the weightlessness of being carried to the chopper in a poncho litter. It touched his matted hair and caressed his eyes, whispering frantically to him like a departing lover, trying to make him hear, make him understand. But the breeze was laden with smoke and fire and wet wretched earth, and he turned his face away, closing his senses to the pleading voice of the jungle. *"Leave me alone,"* he groaned inside, *"it's over. I have nothing left. You took it all. You win, goddamn it, you WIN!"*

But the whispering persisted, and when he wouldn't listen, it began to rain—a steady, driving wall of water that began with a distant clap of thunder. Aboard the chopper he refused the medic's efforts to make him lie down, moving painfully to the doorway to stare one last time at the grave.

"...Please!" the siren whispered, *"please forgive..."*

"...let him go," she whispered to the searing darkness in the bedroom, throwing her head back and gasping, he's mine...let him go..."

"LET ME GOOO!" he shouted, as the chopper slowly lifted off the muddy ground. He never felt the grip of the medic's hand on his arm as he leaned forward and stared wildly at the receding, rain-soaked grave. *"You got what you wanted!"* he screamed with his mind. *"I'm the orphan I always was. You stripped me of all I ever had. I'm naked—I have nothing!"*

As the chopper lifted away, the powerful rotors pushed a current of rain and mist in rolling clouds beneath the blades. When Joe saw a cloud engulf the diminishing grave, saw the mist of the nightmare gather around it and turn skyward, he heard a strangled cry in his throat and felt the wild panic of the child in the back of the truck—only this time, though wounded and heartsick, he was no longer helpless; this time, he had a weapon! He reached for the pull-string on the grenade...

"I have you now," the beast roared from the cloud. *"He's finally dead...you did it yourself...and now you're alone—Captain Joseph Rutledge!"*

"...don't listen, don't look!" she whispered, knowing that he heard*"...fight it Joe, fight it for me...you're not alone, don't listen..."*

"Hey, Cap'n," the medic said, moving closer to him, "are you okay? Who you yellin' at?"

He saw the yellow eyes, heard his name hissed over and over, smelled the foul breath of the beast as the cloud began to swallow the chopper...

"LET ME GOOOO!" he screamed, and pulled the string...

...she sprang to her feet, head thrown back, eyes wide and furious as she filled the room with her screams...

She whirled into his vision in the face of the cloud, her hair flying in the wind and rain, her green eyes fear-stricken and full of love, her face streaked with rain and tears, her mouth open in a terrorized scream... *"NOOOO, NOT LIKE THIS!...you're not alone...you've never been alone...no one has ever loved you the way I do—not even your brother!...Joe, it's me, the love you've looked for, it's ME, it's HERE, it's ME!..."*

Time spun to a halt. He could hear nothing and see nothing except her eyes placed firmly between him and the hungry cloud; he was on his knees, gasping and trembling, suddenly realizing that he was facing either the last second of his life, or the beginning of—of what? He didn't know, he didn't know anything except that this was it, this was the fraction in time that his entire life had roared down to, and he would either die right now, or destroy the sick and angry thing that had kept him only half alive since the day he saw his brother fall away from the back of the truck.

He saw her eyes, felt her reaching for him, knowing that he wanted her, needed her, and was terrified of what the future would hold, knowing at the same instant that there would be no future for either of them unless the fear stopped here, now, with no looking back ; somewhere, somehow, there was a life worth living without the search, without the anger, without the guilt. Glaring at the beast held at bay by the love he felt from a woman ten thousand miles away, Joe drew his arm back and with a cry torn from the wrenched and screaming lighthouse man within his soul, threw the grenade with the last of his strength into the snarling cloud.

The men on the hillside below looked up through the rain to where they heard the blast, and saw a small, impacted cloud disintegrating just below the chopper, swirling and vanishing as though it were being pulled down some huge, invisible drain. The medic, who had lunged for the grenade when Joe pulled the string, sat back with a thud, his eyes wide with bewilderment and fear. Poor bastard's shell-shocked, he thought—howlin at nothin, prob'ly didn't even know he'd popped the goddamn grenade. Shell-shocked bigger'n hell—plumb damn crazy. He exchanged glances with the door gunner, both of them letting their breath out slowly in relief, shaking their heads. It had been the most nerve-wrenching four seconds of their lives.

"Sam," Joe called, slumping against the door frame, his useless left arm hanging limp and soaked with fresh blood. He saw her face framed against the tiny mound of dirt on the knoll below, felt the nearness of her, the overwhelming warmth of her existence as he watched the hungry cloud of his youth simply vanish from his mind. The death was still there—all the spent youth and dreams on the hillside below, all the loves of a shattered childhood, all the crushing hurt. But the longing was finished just as surely as if it too had been destroyed by the grenade, and in the instant that he felt it—the absence of the search—a sweet hunger, new and huge, rushed into the void with a pain as tender as anything he could remember. "Samantha..." he whispered, almost whimpering. And for the first time since the massacre of his family, he lowered his head and wept.

EPILOGUE

A gentle, laughing rain had coaxed the earth into renewal, chuckling against summer leaves in the village and skipping along the surface of waves against the shore. Here and there along the docks fishermen readied their boats while the market came to slow, chattering life with the voices of women doing their morning shopping. A dog barked in the distance and somewhere a child's laughter rose. Sam stared up at the strands of powerlines crisscrossing through the awakening village, and smiled.

"Look at all the birds!" she said. He put his arm around her as they walked toward the rocks, felt her warmth and child-like wonder as he glanced up at the swallows sitting in tight, lengthy bunches along the powerlines, ruffling their feathers and gurgling softly as they dried and preened themselves in the rising sun.

"That means much good fortune," he heard himself say, and she looked up at him, searching his face.

"Do you believe that's true?" she asked.

He took her hand and stepped up onto the rocks by the sea, staring out over the water spread with the glowing honey of sunrise. He breathed deeply in the fresh, rain-scrubbed air as the sea greeted him with a welcoming kiss of salt spray. "Yes," he replied to the ocean. "I believe that's true."

Sok-Cho lay quietly glistening along the shore behind them, humming softly to herself as she watched the young couple on the rocks. She whispered a children's song into the morning breeze that touched their faces, floated up and down the streets of neatly-constructed homes that knew nothing of war. Sok-Cho sighed to herself in the light from the ocean, feeling an odd, bitter-sweet pain in her breast as the breeze touched the moist soil of three fresh graves behind the old mission. She brushed the dried petals of the single Charleston gardenia placed on two of the mounds, and felt the tender, muted sorrow of the sun searching the rusted dog tags on the third.

The lullaby drifted around the rocks by the sea, surrounding and embracing him as the memories tumbled over themselves like the waves below, peaceful and persistent. He heard the voices of a young family on the shore in years gone by, heard the happy, rumbling laughter of his father and saw his mother's smile. He heard the squeals of children on the sand and in the snow, felt the warmth and childish serenity of a house that no longer existed.

Sam stood beside him and waited, her hand in his, working her way through memories that weren't hers, through a life she hadn't been able to share until it was almost too late. She felt him stir beside her. He stood gazing at the two worn photos in his hand, faded reminders of three lives that had been swept from the earth by irresistible forces, a generation snuffed out and buried behind the deserted mission.

He felt her fingers on his cheek, reminding him of the existence of greater forces, of infinitely stronger powers, of life-giving tides of strength against which the furies could rage and thrash and pound to no avail. In that one touch, that tender brush of a butterfly wing, he felt the unconquerable might of love.

"It's over, Joe," she said softly. "From the time you were separated from him there was no more life for the two of you. You never knew where he was, were never able to share any part of yourself with him. Your life together wasn't buried yesterday behind the mission; it was buried the day you lost him as a child. It's over now, Joe, please let it be over. Let go of the war—you're alive, so you won. Make peace with this angry thing in you once and for all. Call a truce between yourself and this god you keep pretending is dead. Forgive him, forgive yourself, and move on." She looked at the photos, the gleaming fringes of tears forming in her eyes. "For over twenty years you've been searching for a dead man," she whispered. "It's time now for the living."

Special Thanks

To Twila Small…for encouraging me to write. ("Heal!")
To Wayne Magwood and Alva Carullo Magwood for their
warm hospitality and help upon my return to Charleston.